IMAGES
of America

CLOVERDALE

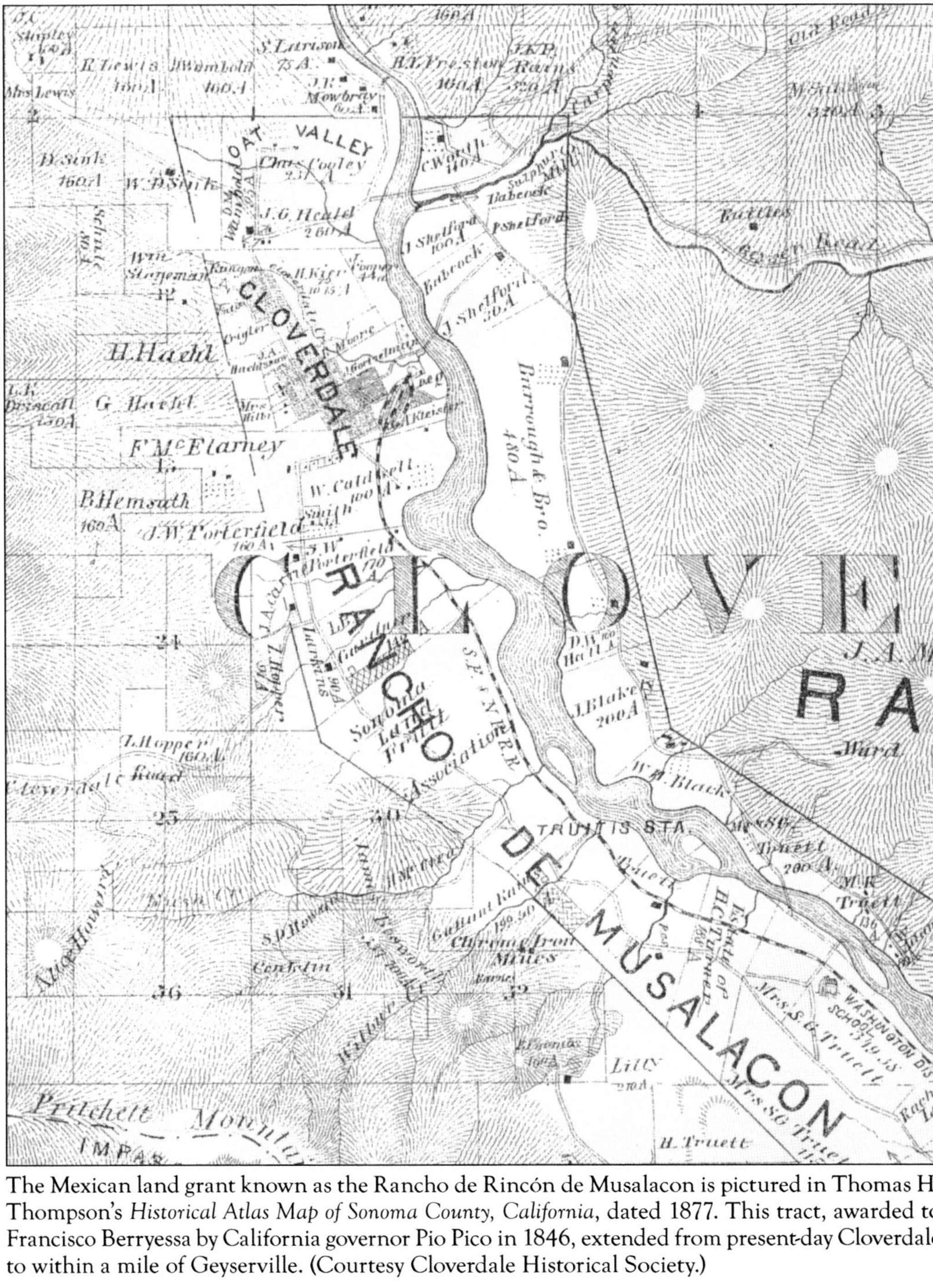

The Mexican land grant known as the Rancho de Rincón de Musalacon is pictured in Thomas H. Thompson's *Historical Atlas Map of Sonoma County, California*, dated 1877. This tract, awarded to Francisco Berryessa by California governor Pio Pico in 1846, extended from present-day Cloverdale to within a mile of Geyserville. (Courtesy Cloverdale Historical Society.)

ON THE COVER: On April 7, 1899, a group of hikers were exploring the geothermal wonders at The Geysers, the most famous of Cloverdale's turn-of-the-20th-century resorts. (Courtesy Cloverdale Historical Society.)

IMAGES
of America

CLOVERDALE

Joan Wagele, Marge Gray,
and the Cloverdale Historical Society

ARCADIA
PUBLISHING

ISBN 978-0-7385-5914-8

Published by Arcadia Publishing
Charleston, South Carolina

Printed in the United States of America

Library of Congress Catalog Card Number: 2008926296

For all general information contact Arcadia Publishing at:
Telephone 843-853-2070
Fax 843-853-0044
E-mail sales@arcadiapublishing.com

Visit us on the Internet at www.arcadiapublishing.com

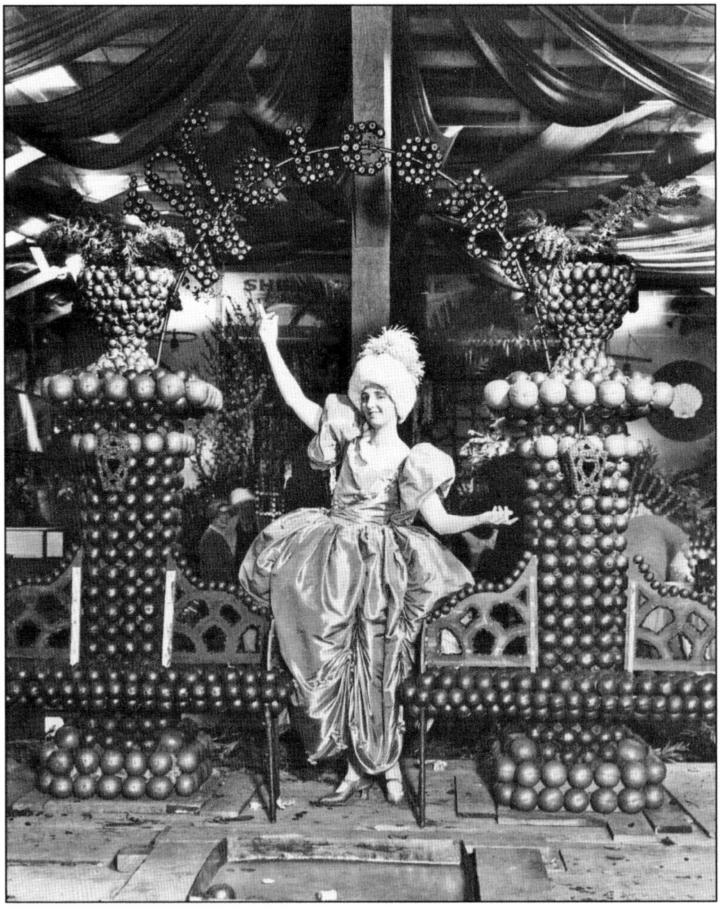

Edna Cobb Gorden welcomes visitors to the 1927 Citrus Fair. The fair, held annually in Cloverdale since 1893, celebrates the citrus industry with elaborate exhibits constructed out of oranges and other citrus. (Courtesy Cloverdale Historical Society.)

Contents

ACKNOWLEDGMENTS

The Cloverdale Historical Society has for some time wanted to tell the history of Cloverdale while showcasing images from its extensive collection. The encouragement and support of many society members have helped make this dream a reality, but the authors want to single out those who made critical contributions—Mike and Norma Trump for their wizardry with the technical aspects of publication; Jim Wagele, Sally Belford, and Dave Negus for never saying "no" when asked to research, write, or review text; and the incomparable Marie Hill for sharing with us her incredible knowledge of Cloverdale's past. Friends throughout the community, including our supporters at city hall, the chamber of commerce, and the *Cloverdale Reveille*, also readily responded to our requests for images, information, or feedback.

Others in the larger community who supported this effort include Tony Hoskins and Katherine Reinhart at the Sonoma County Library; Carl Bogner at Asti Winery; John Shubert and other members of the Heritage Network; and Dan Murley and Holly Hoods from the Healdsburg Historical Society. We are especially indebted to Holly for helping us bring the story of Madame Preston to life. Finally, we want to thank our Arcadia editor, Kelly Reed, for helping to carry the project across the finish line.

Several books proved helpful in our research: *Cloverdale: A History of the Area* by William Brush Wilson and *Cloverdale Then and Now* (both previously published by the Cloverdale Historical Society), *Cloverdale Memories* by Marie Vadon Hill, and *Legacy of a Village* by Jack Florence.

Almost all images in the text are from Cloverdale Historical Society archives. The few from personal or institutional collections are acknowledged individually throughout the text.

INTRODUCTION

The great Santa Rosa plain that dominates the geography of Sonoma County stretches northward into the Alexander Valley, famed for its vineyards and wineries. At the far north end, where the Mayacamas Mountains converge with the coastal hills, the Russian River emerges from a twisting gorge and spills onto the valley floor. Here, just west of the river, James Abram Kleiser in 1859 laid out the town of Cloverdale.

Kleiser, having traveled the state seeking the most advantageous place to settle, recognized the potential for successful agricultural ventures at the top of the Alexander Valley. Cloverdale's location, with its rich soil and favorable climate—suitable even for the cultivation of frost-sensitive citrus—gave rise to the town's most enduring image, "Cloverdale, the Orange City," the promotional slogan used in the 1898 *Illustrated Atlas of Sonoma County*.

Although the Pomo Indians were the first inhabitants to take advantage of the area's assets, the recorded history of the land begins with the Mexican land grant Rancho de Rincón de Musalacon, awarded to Francisco Berryessa by California governor Pio Pico in 1846. This tract, measuring up to 2 miles wide and a little over 8 miles long, extended from present-day Cloverdale to within a mile of Geyserville.

The town itself began as a trading post with a store and tavern erected by Richard B. Markle and W. J. Miller, who had bought 757 acres of the former rancho in 1858. Markle and Miller sold their interest in 1859 to Kleiser, who is considered Cloverdale's founder. Americans from the East and European immigrants, mostly from Ireland and Germany, formed the majority of Cloverdale's earliest settlers. Later they were joined by Italians, who were drawn to the area by the wine industry flourishing to the south of town at Asti.

Cloverdale's history includes the fascinating stories of three unique communities formed toward the end of the 19th century: Preston, organized around the healing and religious principles of Emily Preston; Icaria-Speranza, a utopian community of French immigrants; and the Italian Swiss Agricultural Colony, a winemaking enterprise that became one of the most successful premium wineries in the world.

In 1872, the city was incorporated. In that same year, the San Francisco and North Pacific Railroad reached Cloverdale, establishing it as the transportation hub for the entire region, a role it continued to play for more than 60 years. Passengers, crops, and local products were transported by rail from Cloverdale to the rest of the nation. The railroad also brought to town trainloads of visitors en route to local resorts and to Cloverdale's signature event, the annual Citrus Fair.

After construction of the Redwood Highway, which eventually stretched from San Francisco into Oregon, cars and trucks began to replace trains as the primary movers of people and freight. The highway reached Cloverdale in 1926, and for 70 years, it ran down its main thoroughfare, causing Cloverdale's role as a transportation hub to wane and a new role to emerge—that of providing food, fuel, and lodging to the motorists and truckers passing through.

Despite being located at the junction of important transportation routes, Cloverdale remained a small rural community, with a population that hovered between 700 and 800 well into the 1940s.

After World War II, California's housing boom increased the demand for lumber, and Cloverdale, located on a highway near vast forests of redwood and fir, was able to capitalize on its strategic location. Large mills were built in and around town, while logging operations expanded into the surrounding region. These developments created jobs and attracted residents, many from out of state. Cloverdale's population reached 1,300 by 1950 and more than doubled in the following decade.

Cloverdale's first subdivisions were built in the late 1940s and early 1950s to house its growing population—the Haehl Tract and Las Colinas on the west side of town and the Tarman Tract and other neighborhoods to the south. When Cloverdale's population continued to grow, reaching just under 4,000 by 1980, new subdivisions stretched the town farther to the south. As growth continued, fueled largely by retirees and those commuting to jobs outside Cloverdale, undeveloped land and well-tended vineyards gave way to residential neighborhoods: Clover Springs, Vintage Meadows, Jefferson Springs, the Cottages, and the Bungalows, among others. With a population of 8,500 and an easy freeway ride to shopping centers and "big box" stores north and south, today's Cloverdale is no longer the small, self-sufficient rural town of its earlier days.

In some respects, however, Cloverdale has not changed much at all. Grape growing, winemaking, and lumber products remain important enterprises. Residents and visitors appreciate, as they always have, the area's warm summers, mild winters, and mostly fog-free climate. They still cherish Cloverdale's largely unaltered vistas of wooded hills and colorful "patchwork-quilt" vineyards. Residents still come out en force to support the 115-year-old Citrus Fair and other community events.

At its heart, Cloverdale is still a small town, a "hometown," just as it was in 1937, when a guide to California highways described Cloverdale as having a residential area with wide tree-shaded streets and neat frame houses fronted by picket fences and well-tended lawns. This portrayal evokes an image of the quintessential American small town, the essence of which is still valid today. One important characteristic remains as constant now as in the past—an impressive community spirit. Here friendly and generous residents—lifelong and recent, young and old, working families and retired seniors—invariably come together in support of one another, suggesting that Cloverdale's greatest asset is not its fertile soil, its balmy climate, or its strategic location. Cloverdale's greatest asset has been and remains its people.

One

The Early Years

Long before the town of Cloverdale existed, the land was home to native people known as the Makahmo Pomos. According to oral tradition, they originated here from the earth thousands of years ago and will be here for generations to come. In the 1850s, however, increasing pressure from white settlers resulted in a roundup of local Pomos by the U.S. Army and a forced removal to reservations in Mendocino and Round Valley—what Pomos remember as their "Death March." Over time, many escaped and returned to their home areas, only to find themselves landless and largely unwelcome. The federal government finally recognized the plight of the Cloverdale Pomos in 1921, providing them with 27 acres south of town for home sites. The Pomos have long been recognized for their exquisite baskets, which utilize sage root, bulrushes, bark, and other local vegetation. When the last significant sources of these and other traditional materials were threatened by the building of Warm Springs Dam in the 1970s, the U.S. Army Corps of Engineers and Sonoma State University collaborated with Pomo elders to organize a successful relocation of plants. Today the Cloverdale Rancheria of Pomo Indians maintains an active presence in Cloverdale.

Settlement of Cloverdale by white people began in the 1850s. By 1857, the Cloverdale Post Office was operating, and by 1858, Richard B. Markle had bought the property where his Cloverdale House hotel and saloon were located. In 1859, James Kleiser purchased Markle's interest for $16,000 and had the first city plat laid out. Thus the town of Cloverdale was born. Cloverdale's importance grew after 1872, when the San Francisco and North Pacific Railroad made Cloverdale its northern terminus. Agricultural products from the north, west, and east were shipped south from Cloverdale, and stagecoaches ran in all directions as connectors from the train. As the 19th century drew to a close, the city promoted itself as a place endowed with an ideal climate, fertile soil, resorts, and natural wonders.

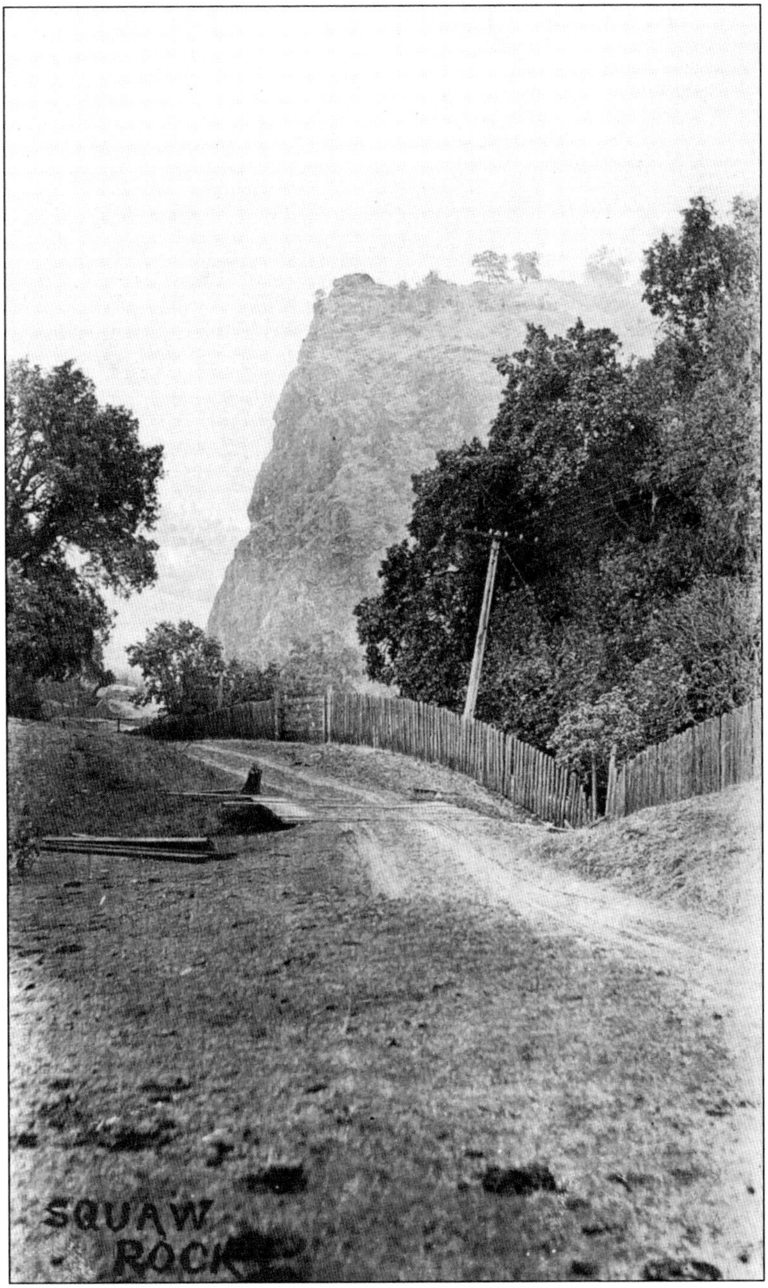

Along the Russian River 10 miles north of Cloverdale stands the imposing "Squaw Rock," the site of ancient American Indian petroglyphs and the subject of several American Indian legends. According to Pomo tradition, the rock was so named because a group of women staged a protest there to prevent warring factions from going to battle. According to a more romantic tale, a 19th-century Sanel maiden lost her lover, a chief from the village of Cloverdale, to another woman. When she saw the faithless lover and his new bride asleep at the foot of the giant rock, "she clasped in her arms a stone as large as she could lift and sprang off the fearful height upon her sleeping victims." Regardless of which story is the most authentic, the site has popularly been known as "Lovers' Leap."

The Pomos of Northern California spoke seven distinct but linguistically related languages. The Cloverdale Pomos, along with their neighbors of the Dry Creek tribelet, spoke dialects of Southern Pomo. Cloverdale Pomo territory, with six villages on both sides of the river, extended from the valley of the Russian River to the mountainous Mayacamas region. Cloverdale is one of only two dialects that survived long enough to be recorded by linguists. (Based on a map in *Mihilakawna and Makahmo Pomo: The People of Lake Sonoma*, U.S. Army Corps of Engineers, 1984.)

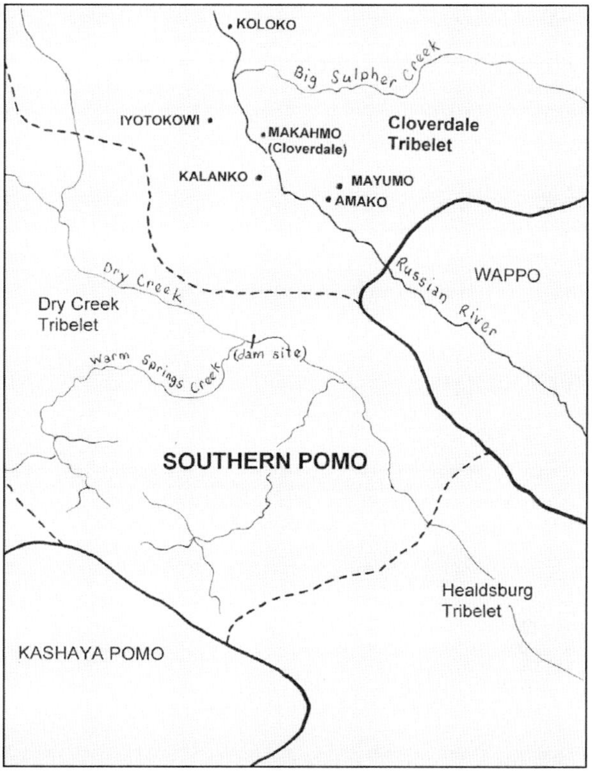

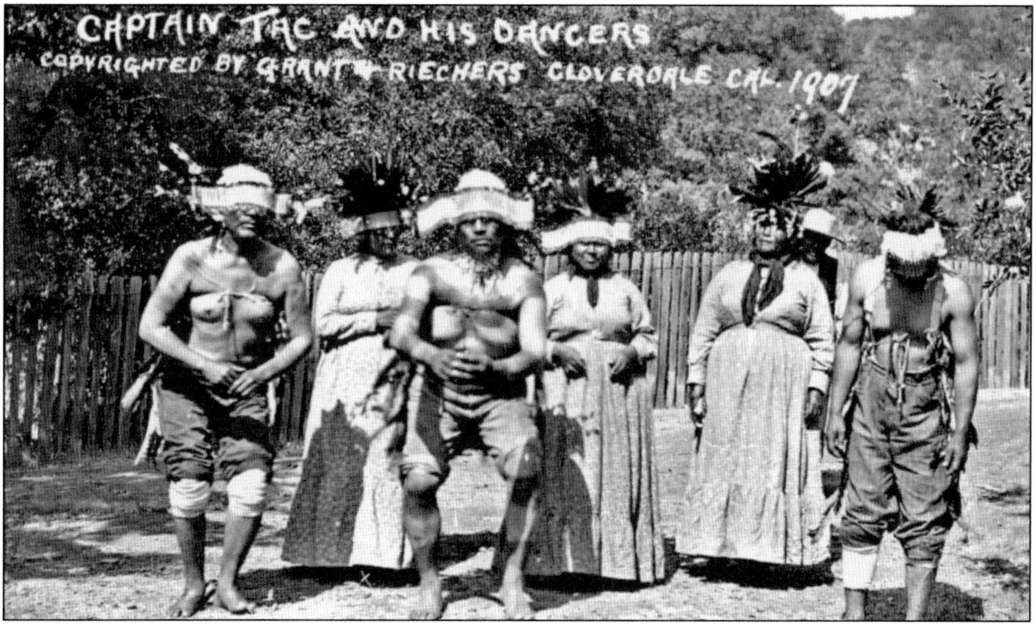

Traditional Pomos were peaceful hunter-gatherers, using regional plants and game for food, but their primary food source was acorns. In addition to basket weaving, jewelry making was an important part of their culture. Using abalone, clamshells, and other natural resources, Pomo artists created intricate necklaces that were worn by both men and women during dances and ritual celebrations.

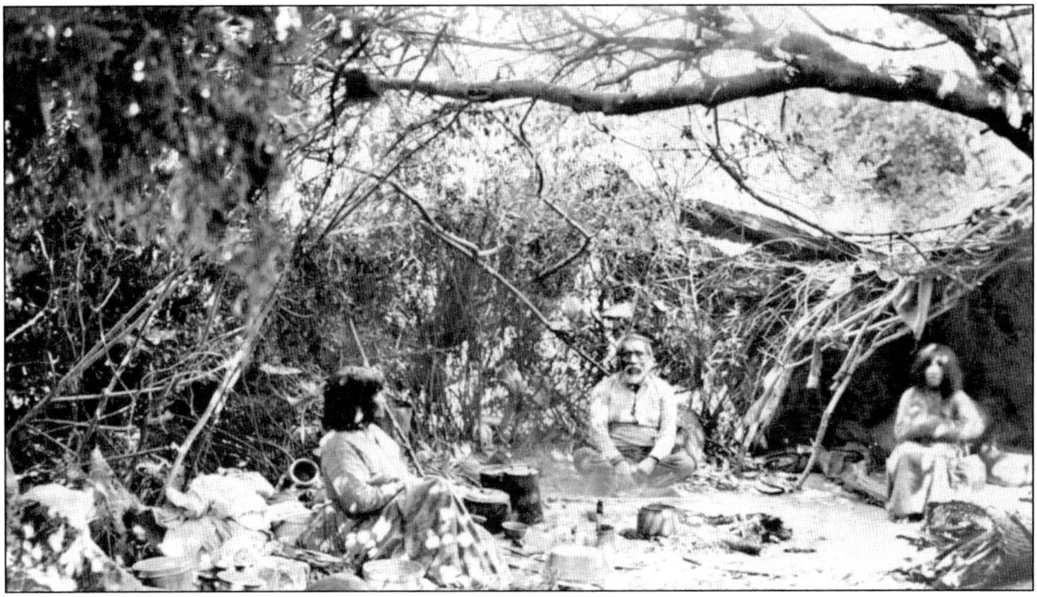

A family identified as Kyman, wife, Mary (right), and daughter, Susie (left), camped around 1875 along the Russian River near where the Pomo village of Makahmo had been located. When Pomos returned from the forced relocations of the 1850s, they found themselves landless and homeless, and unable to fully practice their traditional way of life.

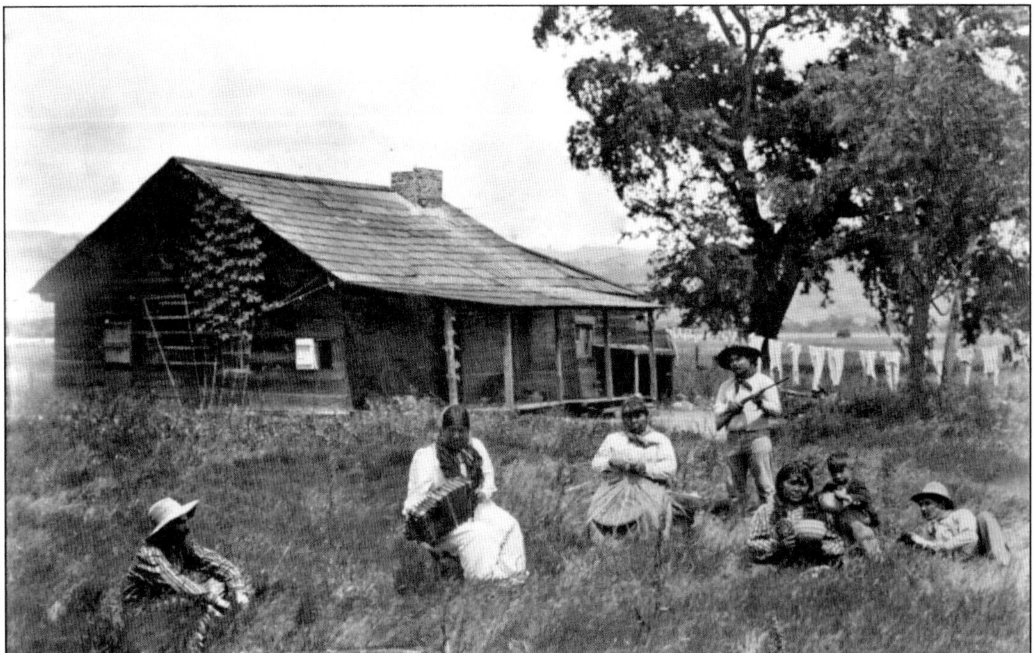

In this undated photograph, one Pomo is seen weaving a basket. Baskets were used in all facets of life—for cooking, food gathering, storage, rituals, family memorials, and healing. Fine art basket weaving, more lucrative than manual labor jobs, was first recognized as a significant means of livelihood in the late 1880s. In the opinion of many experts, Pomo baskets are considered the most beautiful in the world.

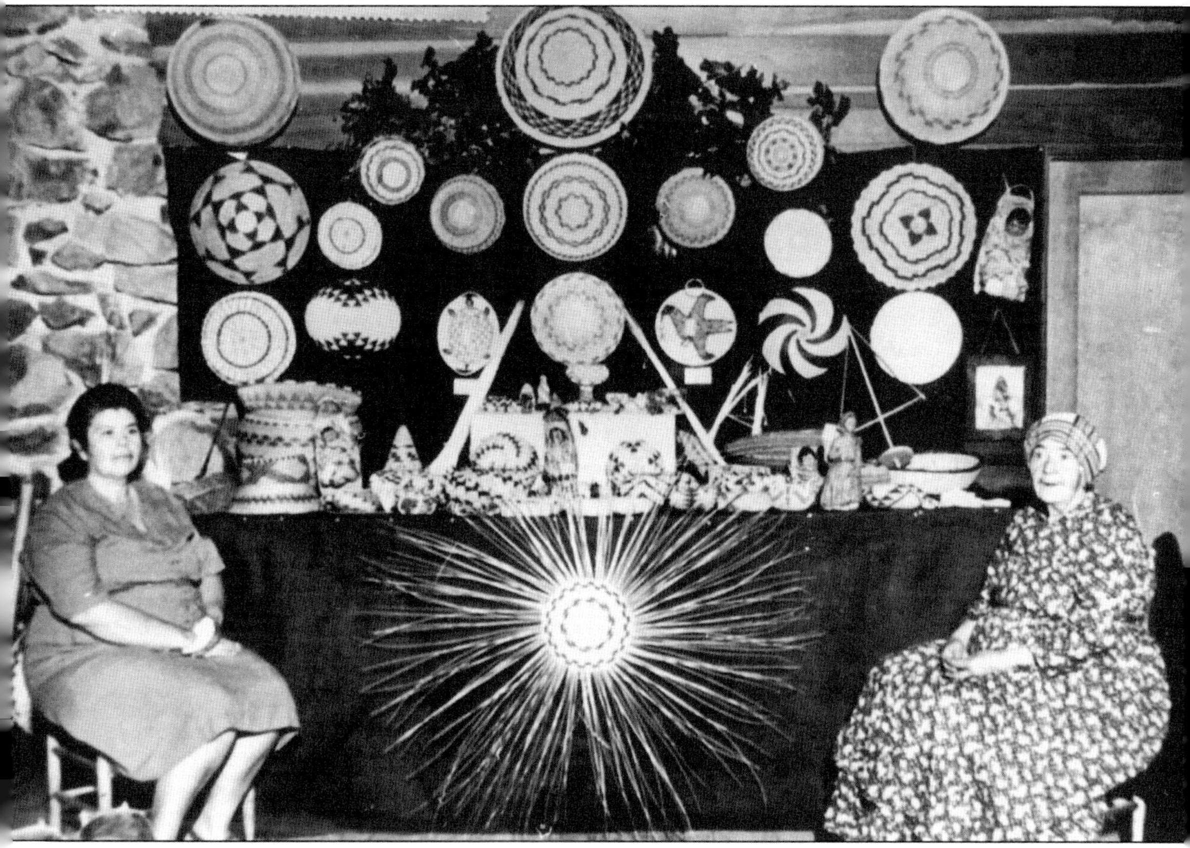

Famed basket weaver Elsie Allen (left) and her mother, Annie Burke, pose in 1949 in front of a small portion of the family's extensive basket collection. Elsie was born in 1899 near Santa Rosa, but as a young child she lived with her grandmother Nellie Burke near Cloverdale. Elsie did not learn to speak English until the age of 13 while attending an American Indian boarding school. She moved to the Pinoleville reservation near Ukiah in 1919 and lived there for almost 70 years. Most of her life, she worked as a farm laborer to help support her family. Elsie learned the art of basket making by watching her mother and grandmother, but not until she was 62 did she start to devote significant time to basket making and to teaching the art form to the next generation. By the time of her death at age 91, Elsie was recognized for her efforts to preserve the Pomo language and culture. Her creations are in public and private collections throughout the world. (Courtesy Sonoma County Public Library.)

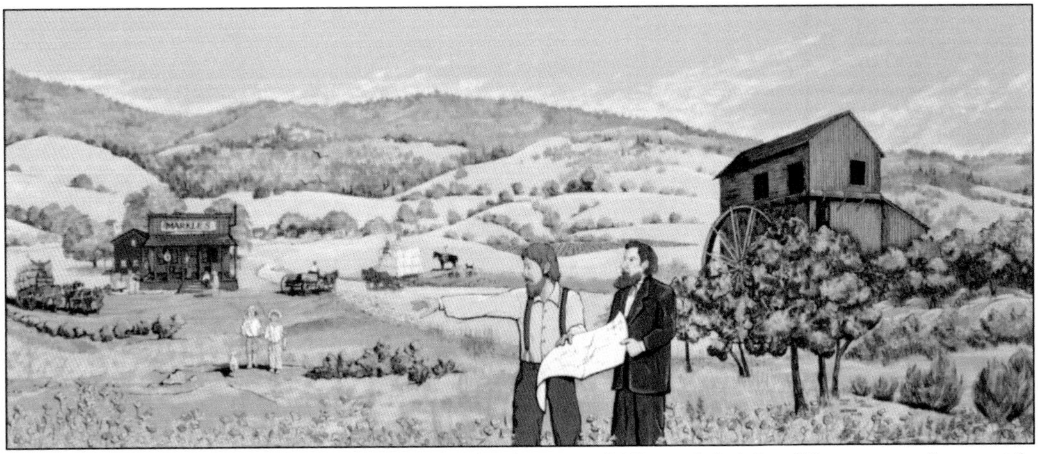

This painting by Cloverdale artists is part of the four-panel Cloverdale Mural Project on the outside wall of the Sciaini Building, located at 124 South Cloverdale Boulevard, which was unveiled in 1995 after two years of planning and execution. James Kleiser is seen purchasing 757 acres in 1859 from Richard Markle, who had acquired the property a year earlier. The settlement, later referred to as Markle's Place, had a hotel known as Cloverdale House and a saloon.

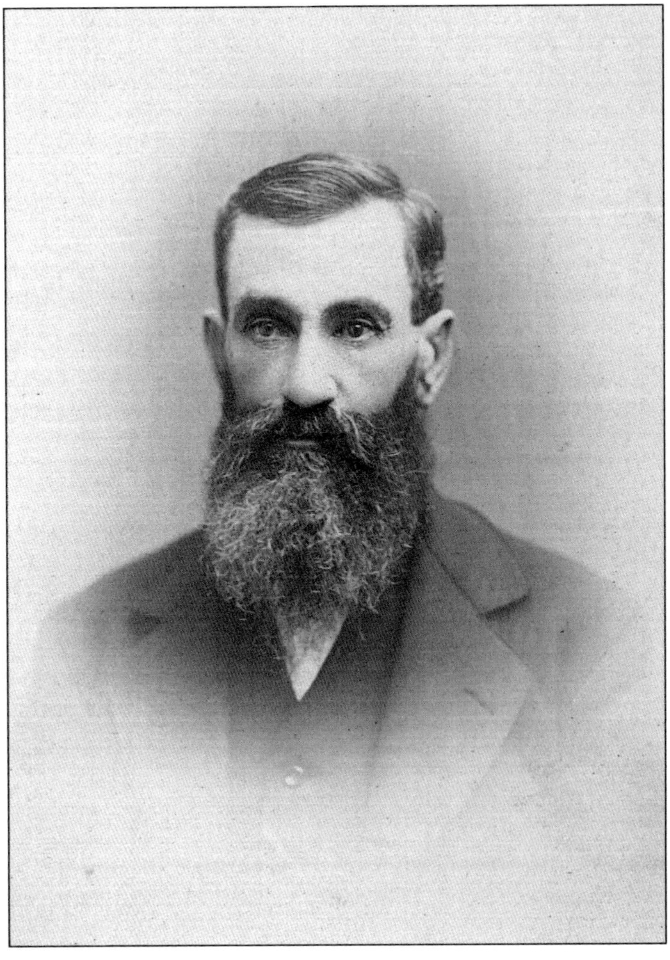

James Abram Kleiser (1818–1906), Cloverdale's founder, purchased the land and hired the surveyor who laid out the city's first streets. Among Kleiser's many accomplishments was superintending the construction of snowsheds for the railroad's crossing of the Sierra Nevada. He also built depots, bridges, roads, and railroads throughout Sonoma, Lake, and Mendocino Counties, including the first toll road to The Geysers. Kleiser's holdings in Cloverdale included olive and peach orchards south of town.

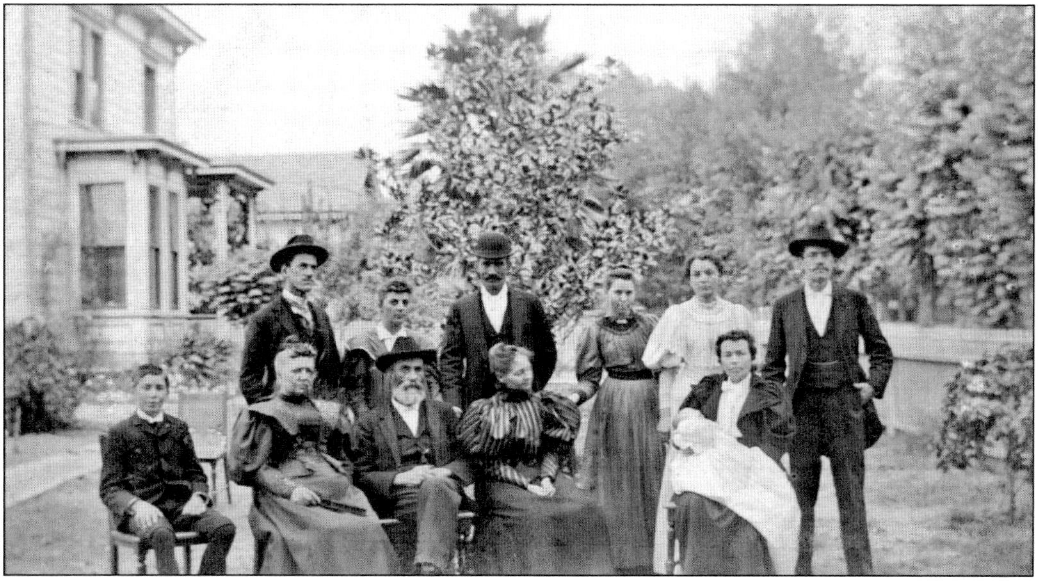

James Kleiser's home, constructed in 1882, is the backdrop for this 1890s family portrait. Kleiser is seated in the center with his second wife, Elizabeth, on his left. The house was razed in the 1960s, and today Cloverdale's public library occupies this site.

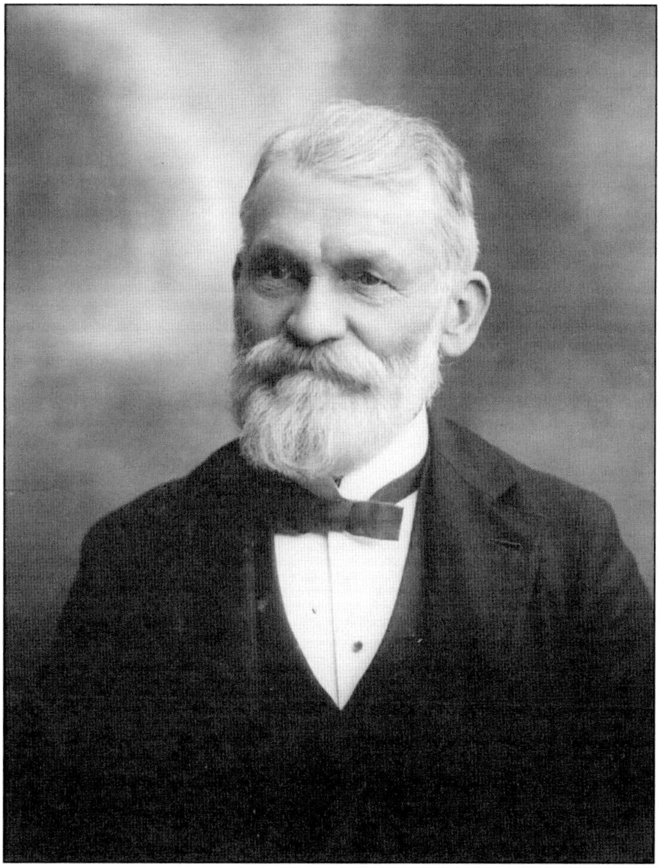

Isaac E. Shaw (1829–1905) was "one of the pioneers of the Pacific Coast . . . a unique figure in California life," according to his obituary. Originally from New York, Shaw came to Cloverdale in 1872. He formed a partnership in a mercantile company with J. R. Bowman and erected one of the first major buildings in town. He was the first president of the Cloverdale Banking and Commercial Company and assisted in starting the Citrus Fair in 1892.

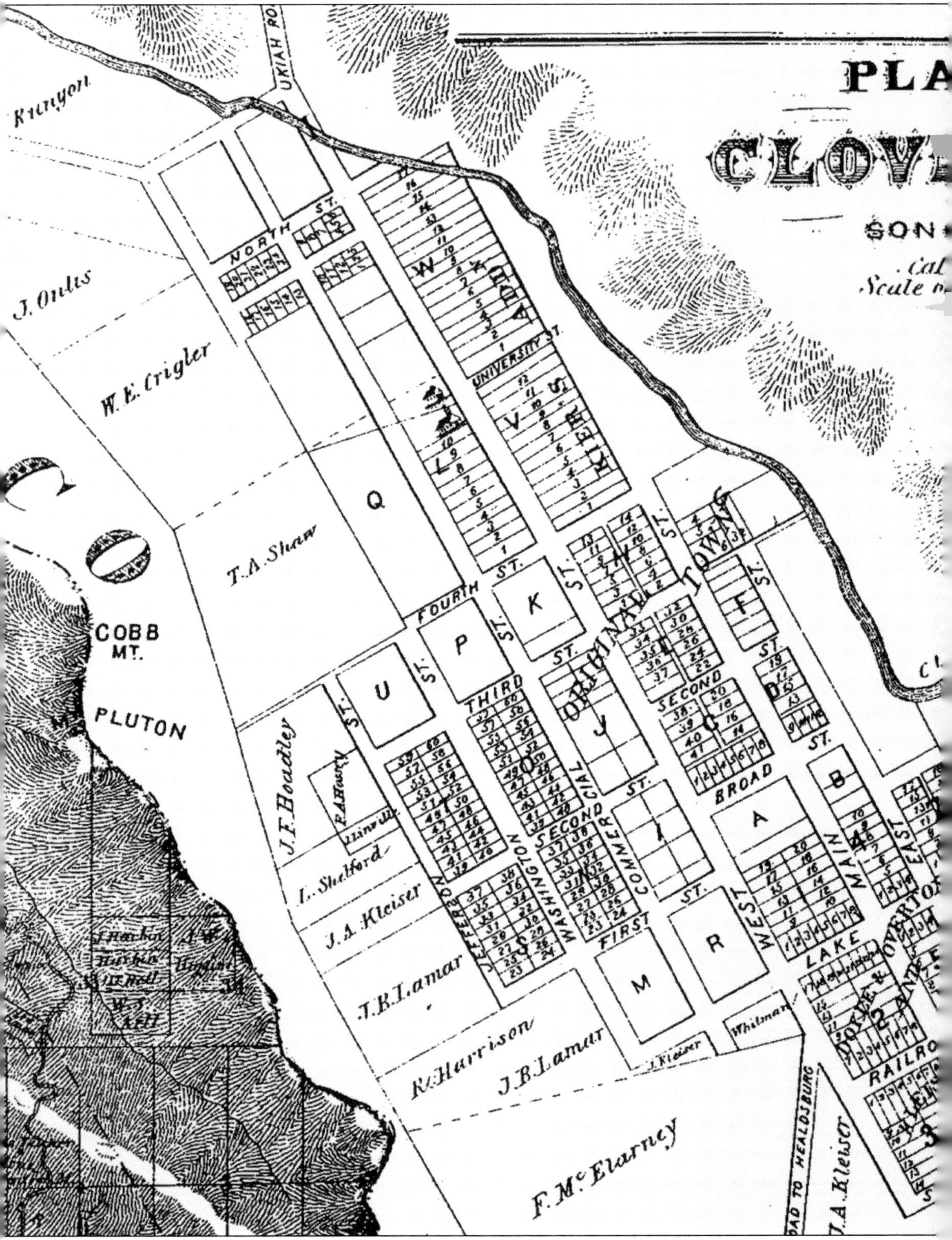
Runyon
UKIAH RO
J. Oults
W. E. Crigler
T. A. Shaw
COBB MT.
PLUTON
J. F. Hoadley
L. Shelford
J. A. Kleiser
J. B. Lamar
R. Harrison
J. B. Lamar
F. Mc Elarney
J. A. Kleiser
Whitman
NORTH ST.
UNIVERSITY ST.
FOURTH ST.
THIRD
SECOND
FIRST
BROAD
WEST
MAIN
EAST
LAKE
JEFFERSON
WASHINGTON
COMMERCIAL
ORIGINAL TOWN
KIER'S
ADD
OAD TO HEALDSBURG

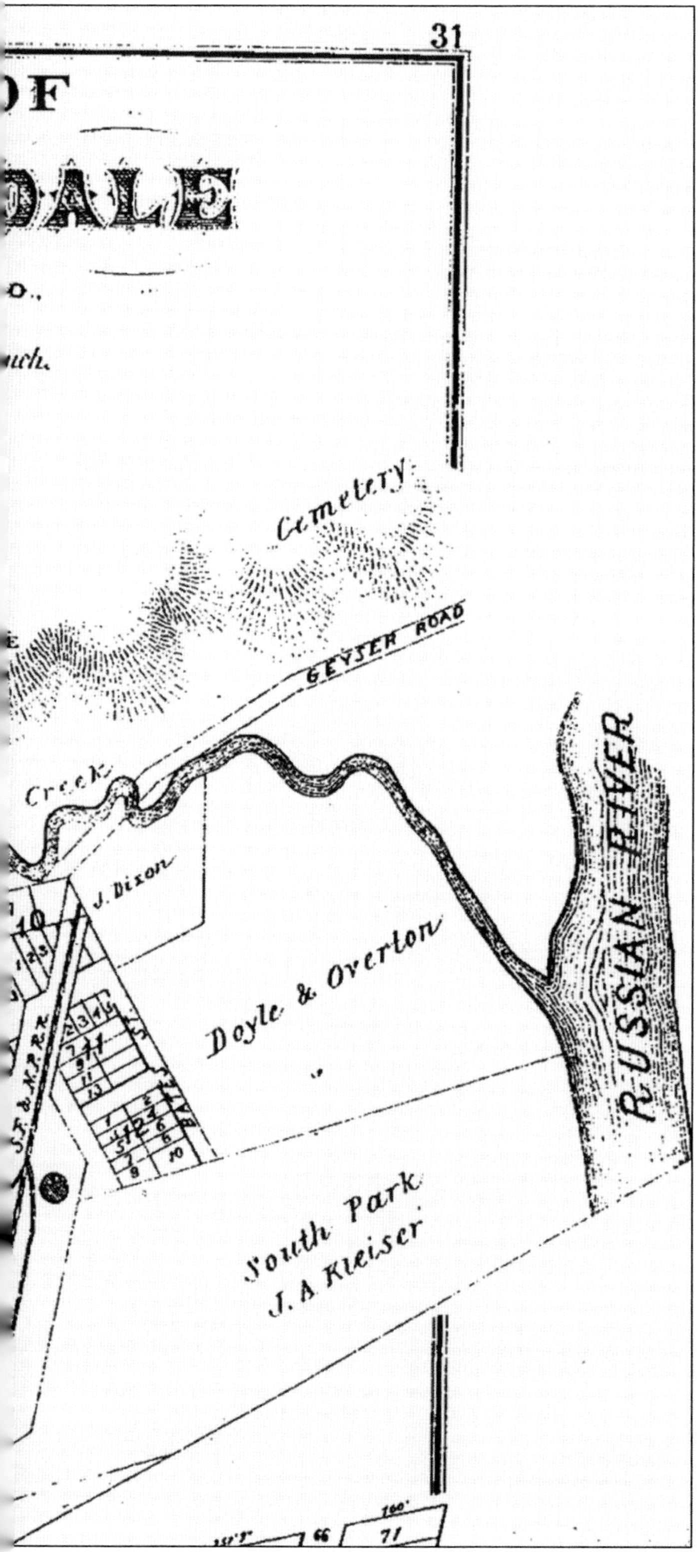

The initial plat of Cloverdale was completed in 1859 by J. B. Brown for James Kleiser. This updated version appeared in the 1877 Sonoma County atlas published by Thomas H. Thompson and Company. West Street (today's Cloverdale Boulevard), which points to the upper left, was the town's most important business and transportation artery. Main Street, one block to the east, seems to have never served the purpose that its name denotes. While West Street connected on the south with the road to Healdsburg and on the north to Ukiah, the route east was an extension of First Street labeled Geyser Road. Near the bottom right, at the east end of Railroad Avenue, are the train depot and tracks of the San Francisco and North Pacific Railroad. The tract of land just to the right of the tracks labeled "South Park–J. A. Kleiser" was the location of the founder's olive and peach orchards.

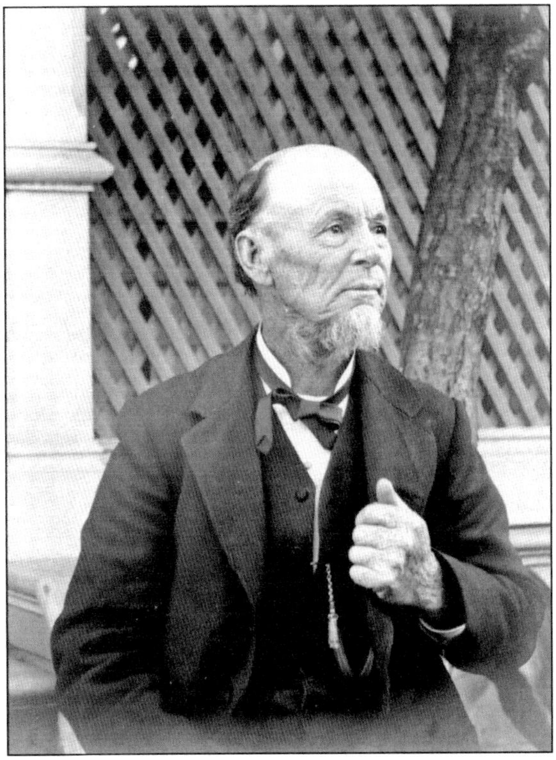

John Chalfant (1825–1905), a carpenter by trade, came to California in 1849. He worked in San Francisco and Mendocino before settling in 1880 in Cloverdale, where he married Susan Hayes and had two children, Nellie Louise and Mattie. Mattie married William Porterfield (Kate Porterfield's brother), a livery stable proprietor and son of Tennessee native John W. Porterfield. They had two daughters, Alice and Helen.

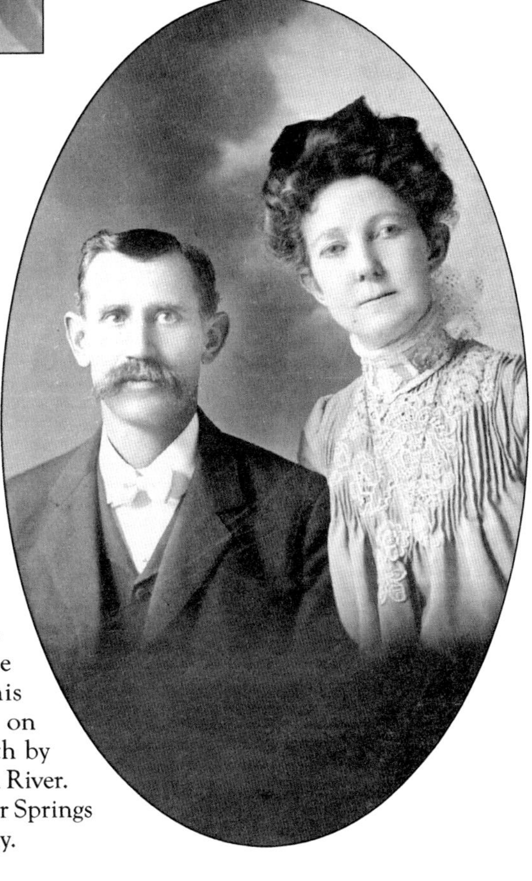

In 1904, William Leist, the owner of a Cloverdale bakery, married Kate Porterfield. Kate was the daughter of John W. Porterfield, who had come to California in 1849. In 1868, John and his wife, Elizabeth, purchased property bounded on the north by Cherry Creek Road, on the south by Porterfield Creek, and on the east by the Russian River. Porterfield Creek, which runs through the Clover Springs development, was named for this pioneer family.

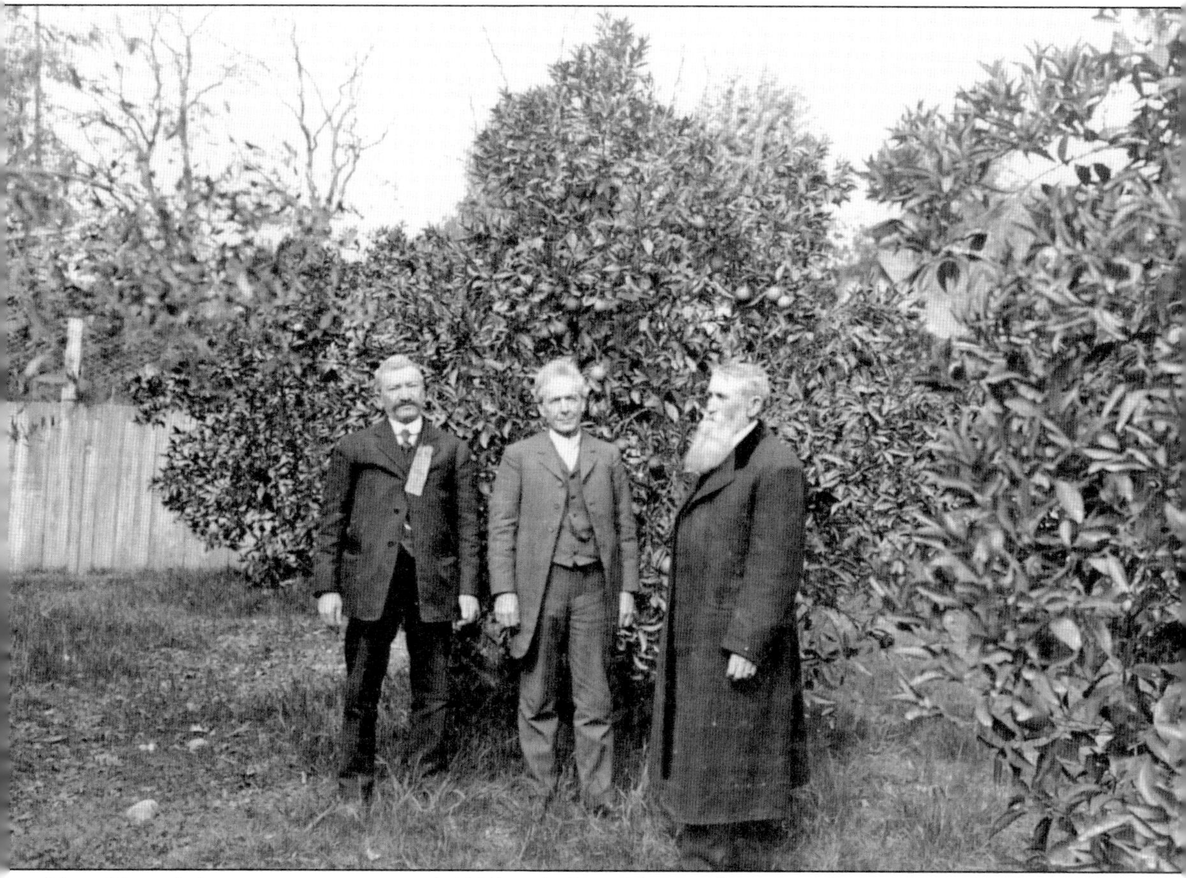

Two Cloverdale citizens pose around 1905 with famed horticulturist Luther Burbank (center) in front of one of Cloverdale's original orange trees. On the right is William T. Brush (1842–1910), the son of David Brush, who had come to Cloverdale some time before 1859 and purchased all the land on the east side of town. The elder Brush planted some of the first grapes in the area and built a winery on Lake Street. W. T. Brush, a prominent citizen in his own right, was engaged in the mercantile business for many years. In the 1870s, he had a grocery store on West Street. He was president of the Bank of Cloverdale, one of the leading organizers of the Cloverdale Citrus Fairs, and the city treasurer for more than two decades. On the left is Simon Pinschower. In the early 1870s, Pinschower's dry-goods emporium offered an "unparalleled array" of clothing, trimmings, millinery, toilet articles, and notions.

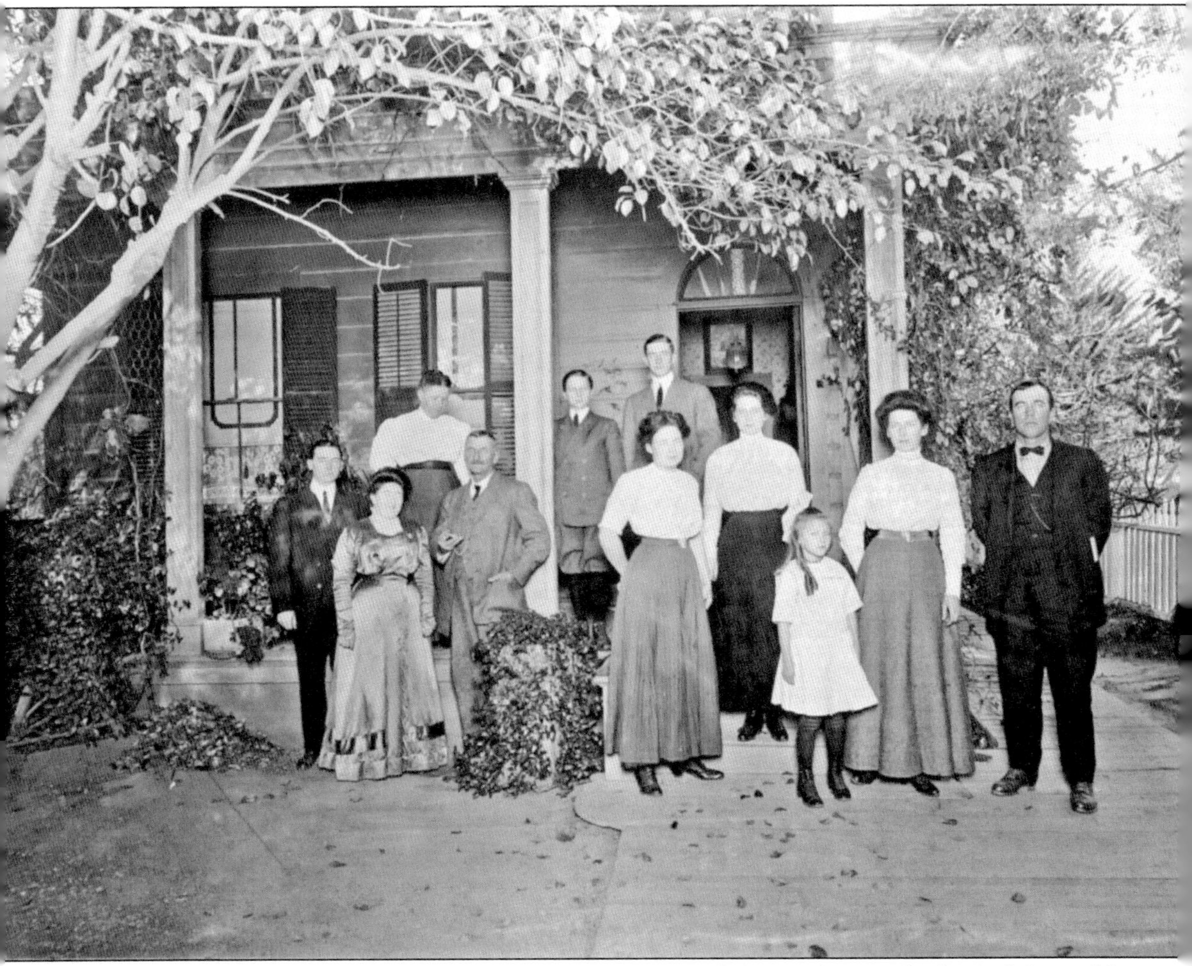

Three generations of Sedgleys pose for the camera. From left to right are Charles Sedgley and his wife, Florence; matriarch Caroline and patriarch Jotham Loring Sedgley; Jotham Palmer, Walter Frank, Nellie, and Emma Sedgley McClelland; and granddaughter Bernice with her parents, Carl and Mary Sedgley Haehl. Jotham L. Sedgley, who came to Cloverdale sometime before 1880, drove the Cloverdale-Ukiah stage for years. He married Caroline Yordi in 1879. Their son Charles L. Sedgley (1880–1946), a lifelong resident of Cloverdale, was the town's lamplighter at the age of 14 and an employee of the Cloverdale Post Office. In 1903, he took a position in the Cloverdale First National Bank, where he served as cashier until his death in 1946. Emma McClelland was a teacher in Cloverdale for many years. Carl Haehl was the son of Conrad, who had begun planting vineyards in Cloverdale in 1879 on land to the west of Jefferson Street between School and Third Streets. Haehl Street was named for this pioneer family.

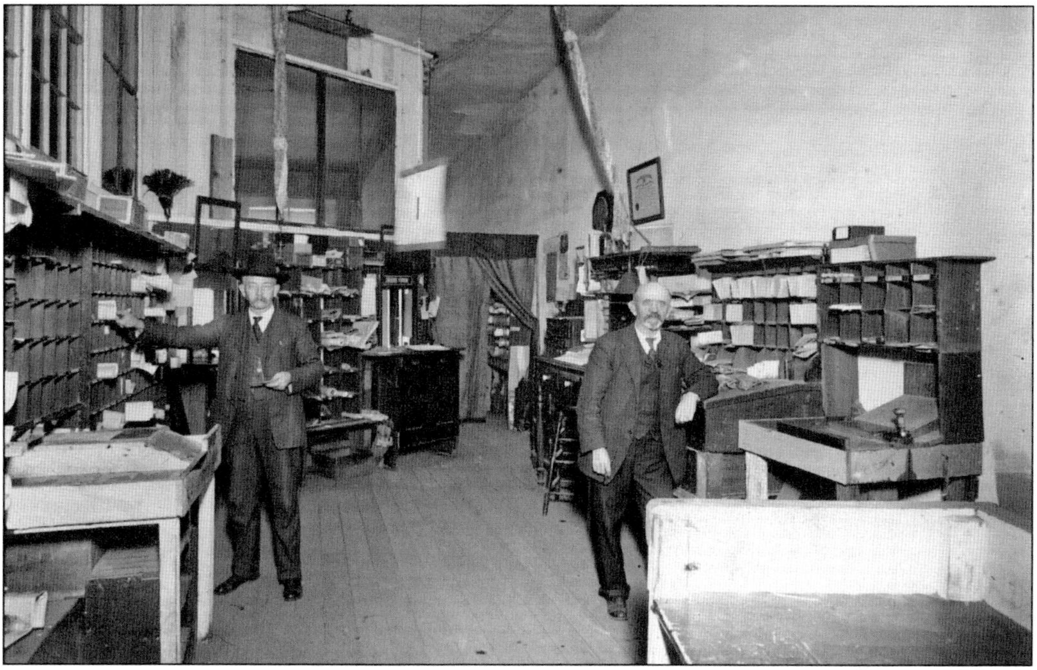

In the first post office in 1857, folks had to fish their own letters from the barrel of incoming mail. Thomas Beggs Wilson (right), seen here working in a more "modern" post office, was postmaster in the 1890s as well as the director of the Citrus Fair from 1894 to 1907. Wilson married Sarah Ann Brush, and their son, William Brush Wilson, published the first Cloverdale history book in 1972. The second man working in the post office is a Mr. Brown, a clerk.

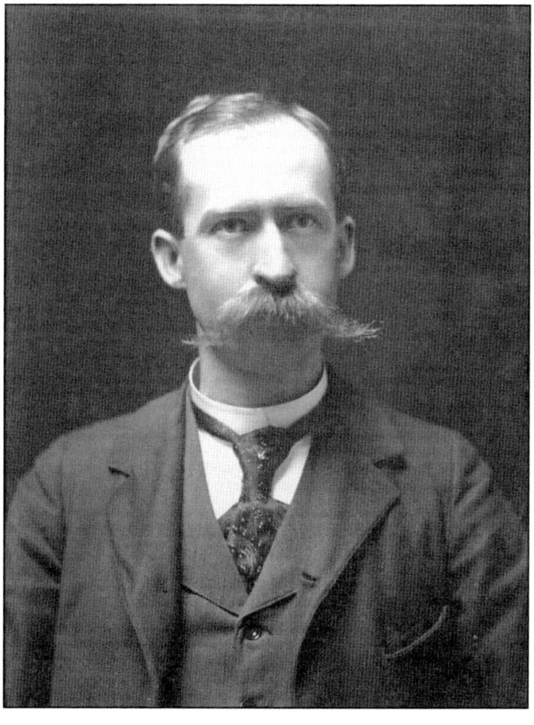

George Baer came to Cloverdale in 1885. He sold real estate and insurance, and was one of the early editors of the *Cloverdale Reveille*. A descriptive pamphlet printed in 1888 by Baer promoted the sale of property and attracted settlers to the "Orange District of Cloverdale." Baer was involved in the Culver-Baer Mining Company, which produced quicksilver—used during World War I in the manufacture of ammunition.

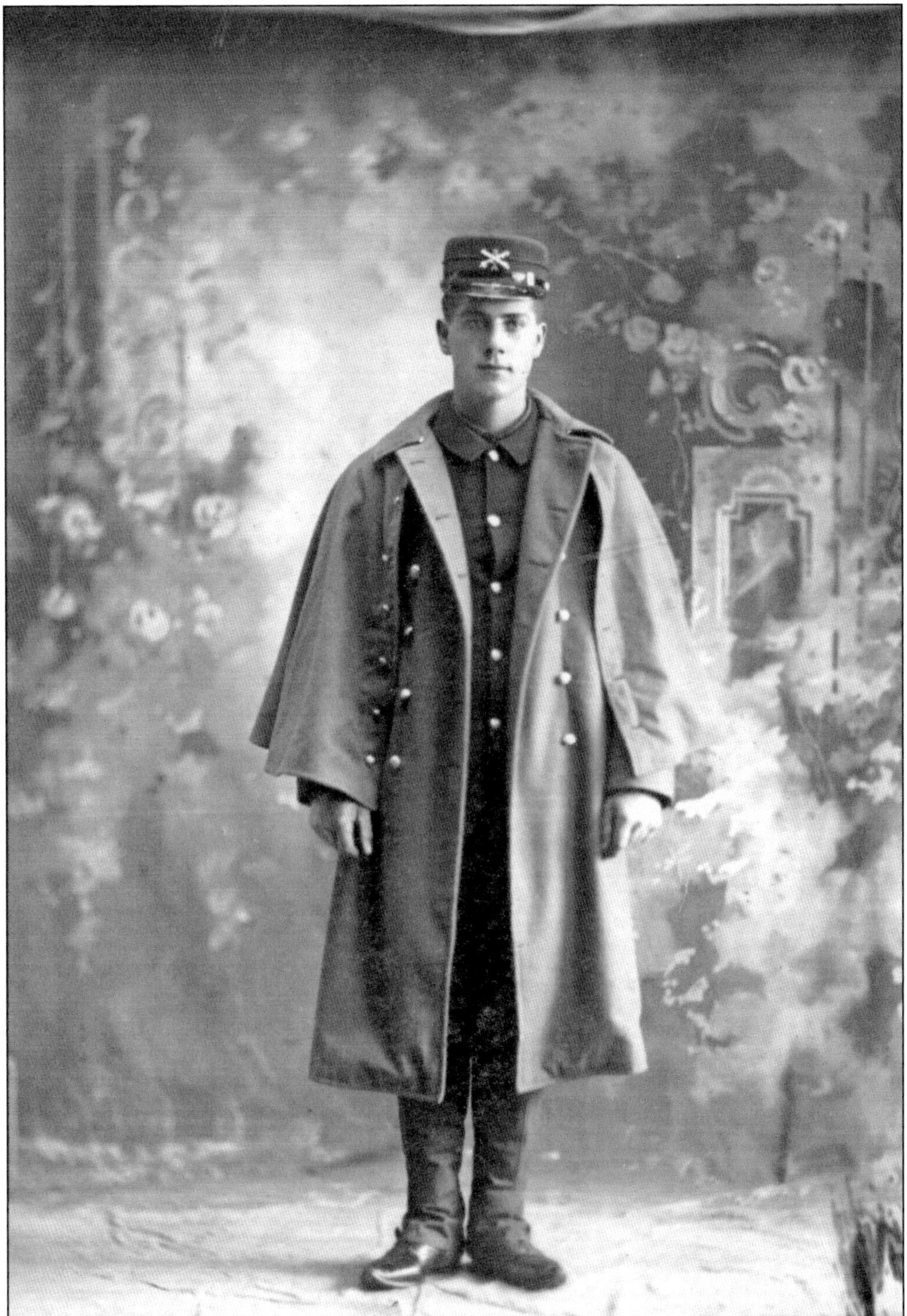

Joseph Lile, who came to Cloverdale as a young boy, was stationed in Alaska during the Spanish-American War. He is seen here in his military uniform in 1898. Joseph married Eliza Ingram, the daughter of another pioneer family, who had settled in Boonville in 1870. Their son, Bernard, was born in 1907 on his grandfather George Lile's farm east of the current terminus of Hot Springs Road, where the Liles operated a dairy in the 1930s and 1940s. Members of the Lile family still reside in Cloverdale.

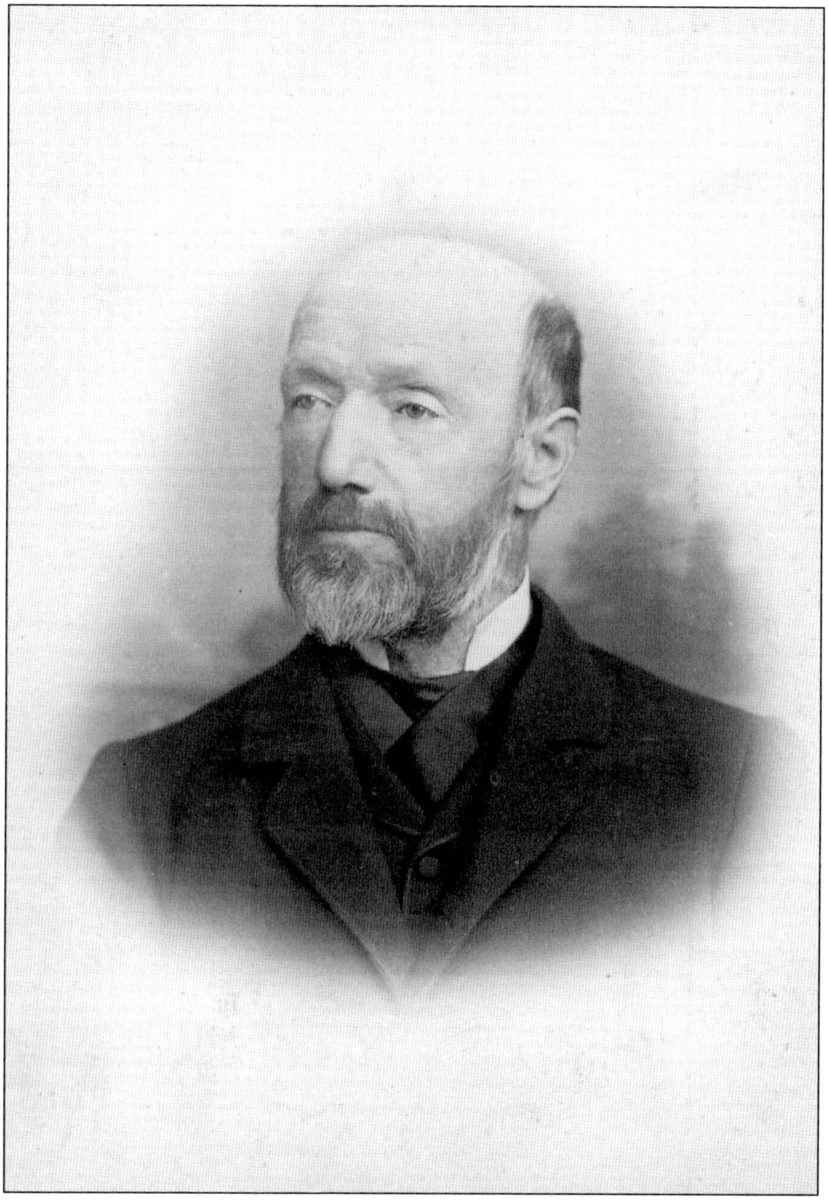

Charles Henry Cooley Sr. came west from Ohio in 1850 and bought a 200-acre parcel on the north side of Oat Valley. The home he built on the property still stands today. Cooley and fellow Oat Valley resident Daniel Sink operated a toll road that went north from Alder Glen to Mountain House. On this Sink and Cooley toll road ran the stage line to Boonville, Navarro Ridge, and Mendocino. Five children were born to Charles and his wife, Esther N. Fuller: John Buckingham, Edward Andrew, Milton Van Horn, Marietta, and Charles Henry Jr. When son John Buckingham married Nancy Elliott, two pioneer families were joined. William Bell Elliott, Nancy's grandfather, participated in the Bear Flag Revolt in 1846 and is credited with being the first white man to encounter the fumaroles at The Geysers. Son Ed Andrew was the owner of the furniture and undertaking business in Cloverdale from the early 1900s until his death in 1917. Daughter Marietta married William Sink, and their winery was named after her. (Courtesy Crawford Cooley.)

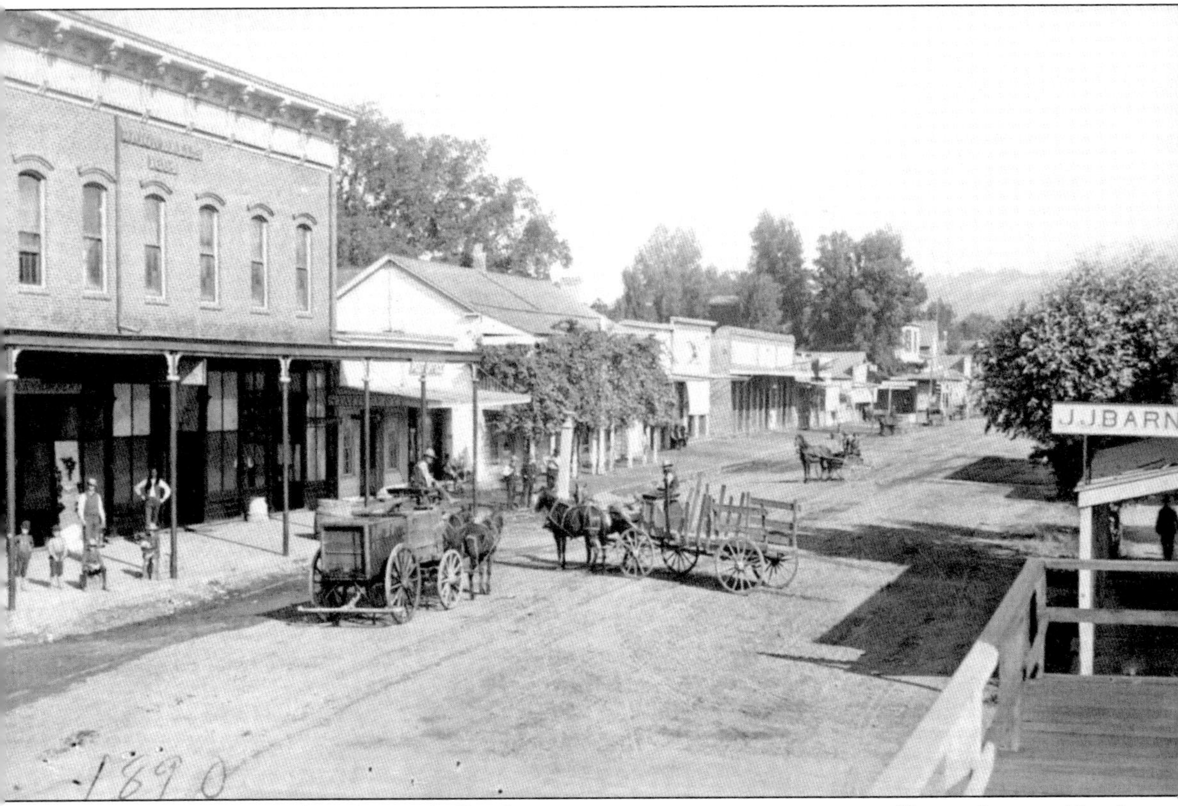

By 1890, Cloverdale had a city hall, a fire station, a water company, a post office, a chartered bank, a high school, a library, and a newspaper—the *Cloverdale Reveille*. There were telephone lines, coal oil streetlights, three hotels, five churches, and numerous saloons. Cloverdale did not yet have electricity or paved streets. This photograph, taken sometime after 1884, shows water trucks hosing down the streets to control the dust. The earliest sidewalks built on the commercial blocks were about 18 inches above the street. As the wood deteriorated, the sidewalks were brought to street level, leaving many store entrances two steps above the street. The two-story building in the foreground, on the corner of West and First Streets, was built in 1884 for James Hoadley's mercantile business. On the second floor was Charles Humbert's opera house. On the same block were a restaurant, a jewelry store, a market, the Cloverdale Hotel, a grocery store, a barbershop, and three saloons.

Two

Early Communities

During the last decades of the 19th century, when America saw the development of special communities based on religious, utopian, or other secular principles, three colonies formed in the Cloverdale area.

The roots of the Preston community go back to the 1870s, when San Francisco attorney Hartwell Preston began purchasing land east of the Russian River about 1.5 miles north of Cloverdale. In 1875, Hartwell moved to the ranch with his new wife, Emily, who had had a profound religious experience that she claimed enabled her to diagnose and treat the sick. The ranch evolved into a community when many of those who came to "Madam" Preston for treatment ended up staying, committed to Emily and her religious teachings. Her message was simple—"It's what's in your heart that matters." At its peak in 1895, Preston numbered about 150 people but declined sharply after Emily's death in 1909. In recent years, there have been efforts to preserve the heritage of this historic site.

Between 1881 and 1886, a group of French immigrants joined together in a communal living experiment called Icaria-Speranza based on the value of cooperation and the need for a harmonious society. In 1881, the group bought 885 acres about three miles south of Cloverdale. The industrious colony enjoyed a period of prosperity, but by 1886, a number of unfortunate circumstances converged to doom the enterprise. All that remains today is a historic landmark plaque to mark the spot of this fascinating experiment in utopian living.

To the immediate south of Icaria-Speranza and formed in the same year was the Italian Swiss Agricultural Colony, which included vineyards, a winery, and a community named Asti. It was the intention of Italian American businessman Andrea Sbarboro to provide work to San Francisco's unemployed Italian immigrants. With the entrepreneurial vision of Sbarboro and the genius of winemaker Pietro Carlo Rossi, the enterprise grew into the largest, most successful premium winery in the world. While the Italian Swiss brand is gone today, vineyards and winemaking still flourish at the site now known as Asti Winery.

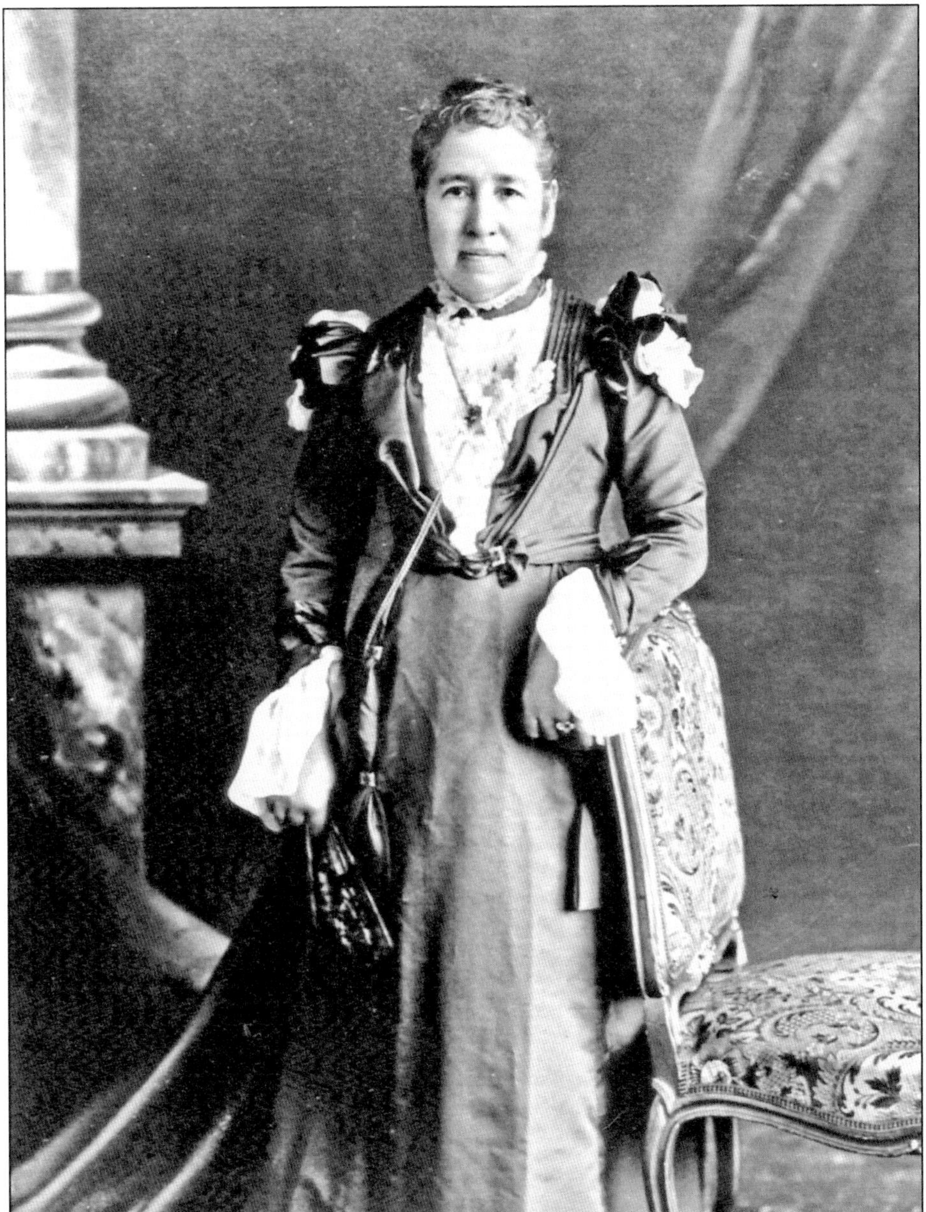

Emily Preston (1819–1909), one of the most intriguing women in Sonoma County history, was the charismatic healer and religious leader around which the small community of Preston developed. Claiming to have received special powers from God, Emily diagnosed and treated ailments that did not respond to traditional medical practices of the time. Many came to Preston seeking her help and advice; those too poor to pay were treated for free. Her prescriptions included fresh air and exercise, as well as herbal tonics and medicinal spirits, although alcohol per se was prohibited to colonists. While she had many devoted followers who attested to the effectiveness of her methods, she elicited skepticism and at times was under attack from traditional practitioners of medicine. She continued her practice, led the Preston community, and managed the 1,500-acre Preston Ranch until her death at the age of 90. Her passing was recognized by Sonoma County newspapers as the loss of an influential and respected leader. (Courtesy Holly Hoods.)

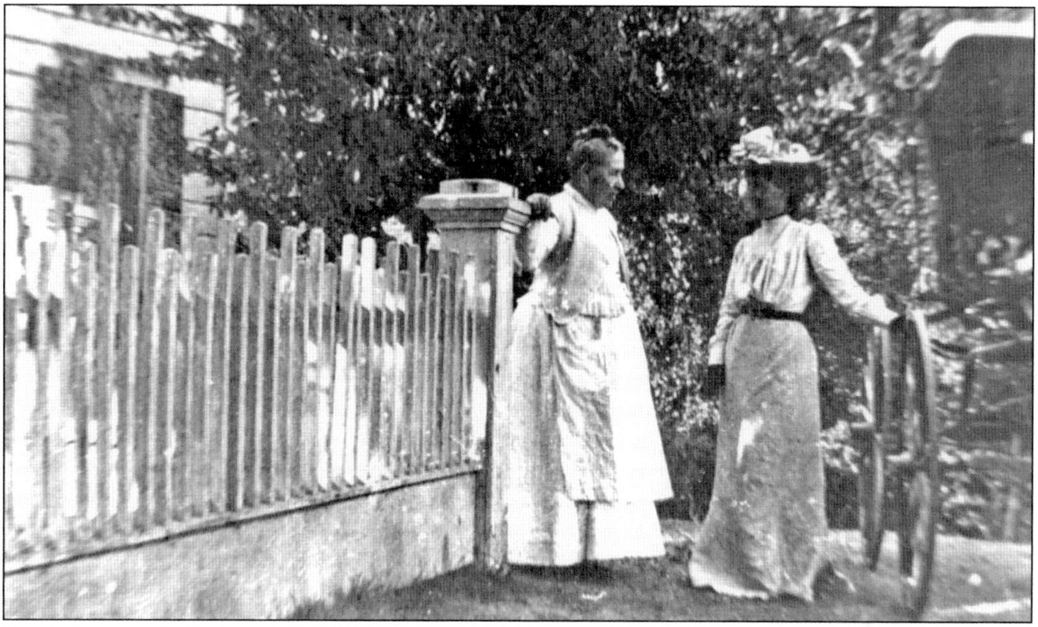

Emily Preston (left) converses with an unidentified woman in front of the Preston home. Although the Prestons had intended to retire when they moved to their ranch in 1875, Emily's followers continued to seek her out, and she felt she could not refuse to help them. People seeking medical and spiritual guidance continued to come to Preston for more than three decades.

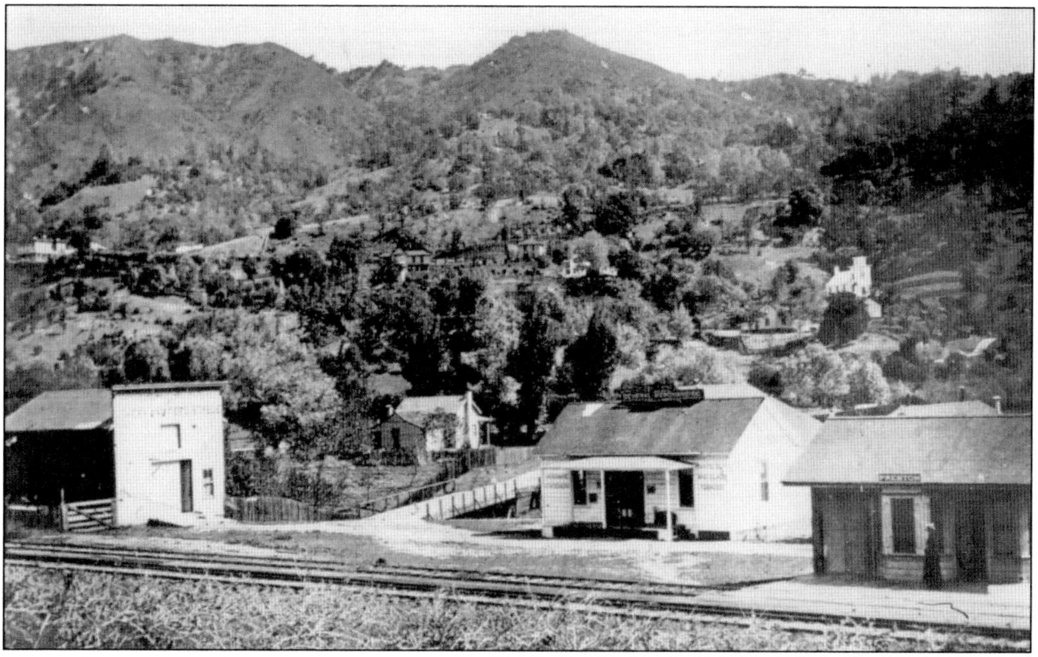

Preston's commercial district was near the Northwestern Pacific Railroad tracks just west of the Russian River. In this *c.* 1910 view are, from left to right, the livery stable, the general store/post office, and the train depot. Other businesses included a lumberyard, a planing mill, and the Kolling mineral water bottling works. Preston residences, the school, and the church are visible on the hill behind the depot.

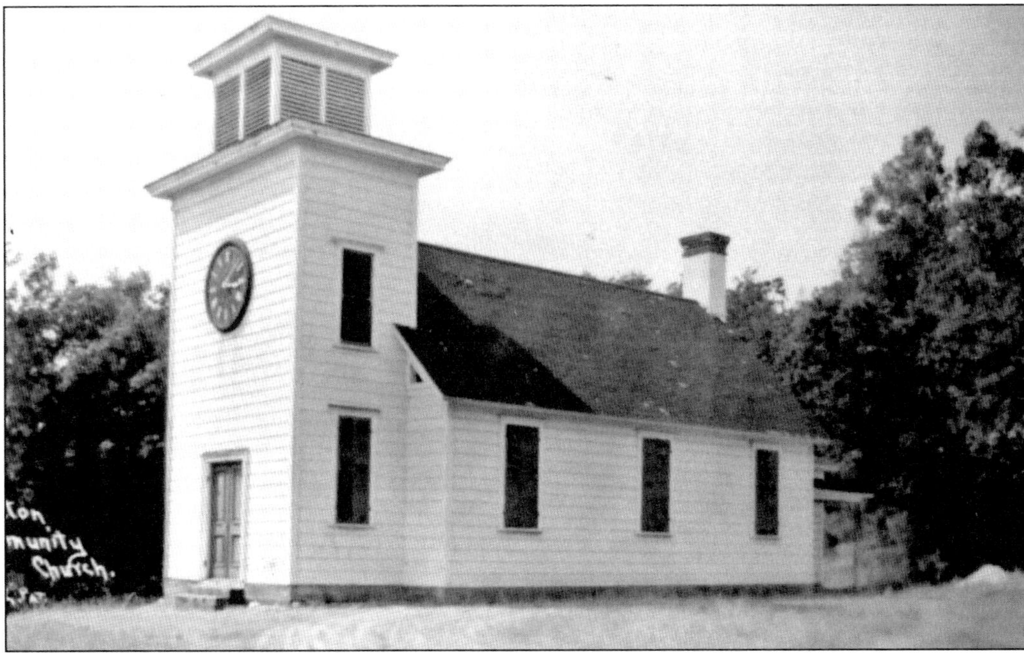

The Free Pilgrim's Covenant Church was one of the earliest buildings erected for the community. Built in 1886 by one of Madame Preston's wealthy followers, the church was the community's hub, serving also as a facility for meetings and musical performances. Spared by the fire of 1988, it stands today, its Seth Thomas clock still announcing the hours. (Courtesy Holly Hoods.)

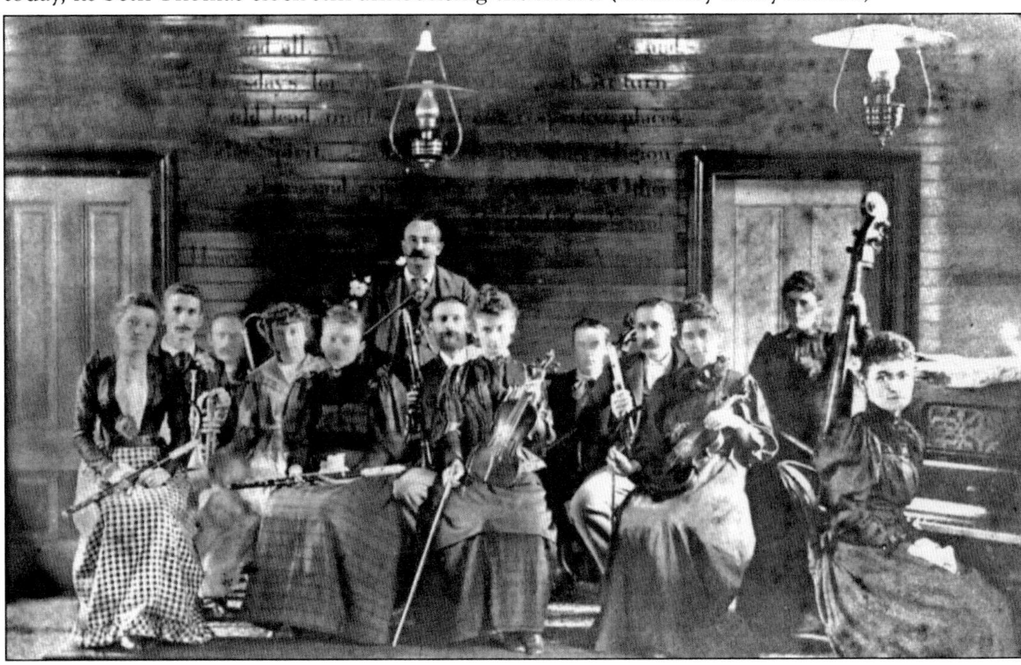

Music was encouraged and enjoyed throughout the community. Preston musicians played for church services and held regular concerts. These musicians posed around 1890 inside the Preston church, where inspirational words on the walls read in part, "Truth is our motto! Purity is our pass-word into Eternal Life." (Courtesy Holly Hoods.)

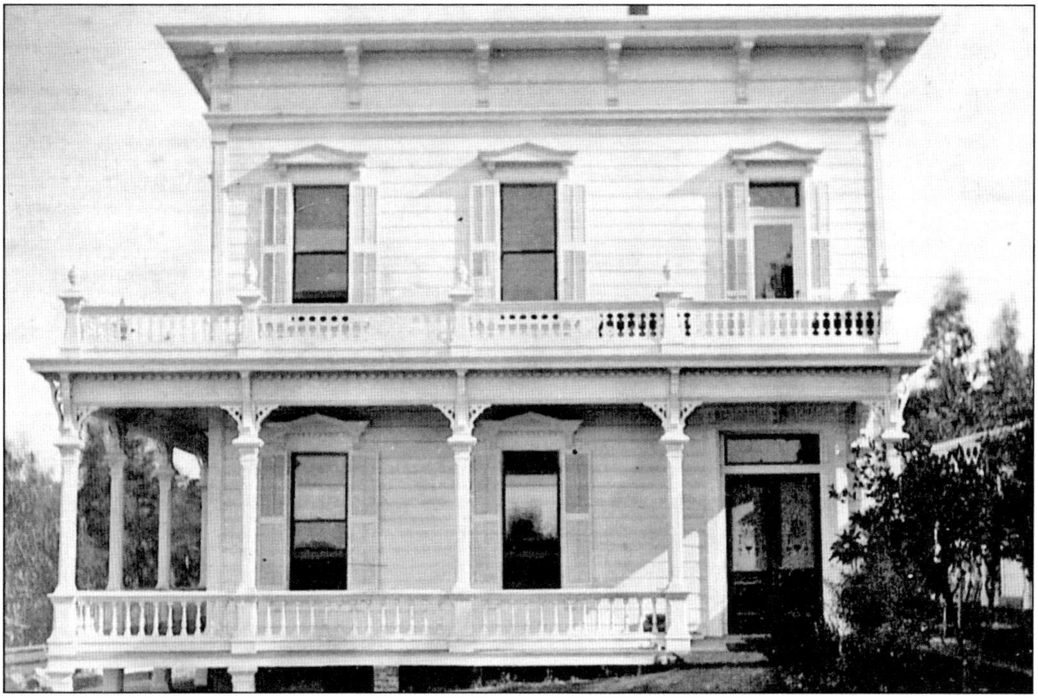

This two-story Italianate structure, photographed between 1886 and 1887, served as the Prestons' residence beginning in 1883. Around this 18-room home was a cluster of other buildings that included Emily's workshop, where she prepared medicines, and "Medicine House," where medicines were sold and packed for her thriving mail-order business. Nearby were the hospital/boardinghouse, a cottage, and three barns. Tragically, none of these structures survived the 1988 fire that swept the area. (Courtesy Holly Hoods.)

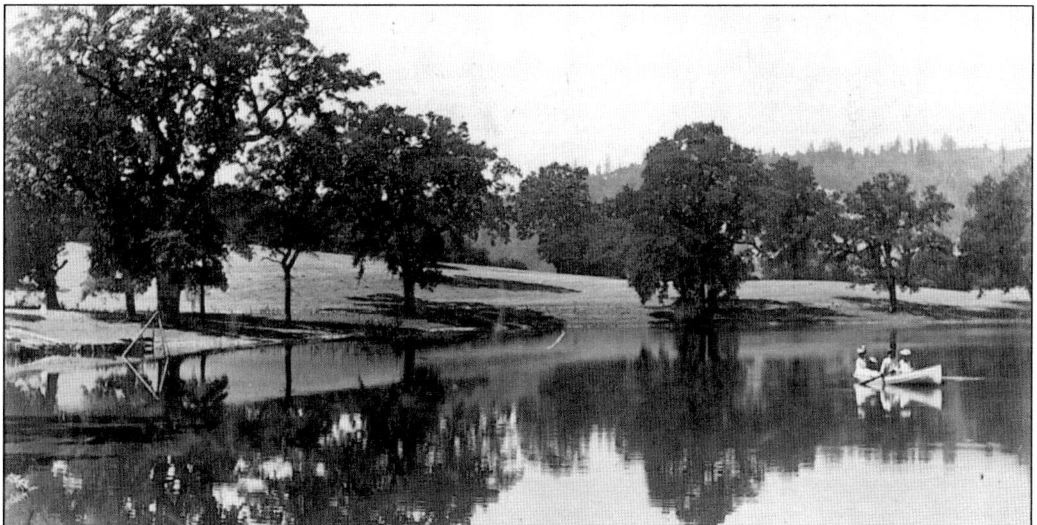

The 1,500-acre Preston Ranch included vineyards, orchards, open space, and various facilities used by colonists. Pictured here is the three-acre, spring-fed Preston Lake, the site of an annual Fourth of July celebration. Near the lake was Inland Camp, where colonists resided while participating in religious retreats each summer.

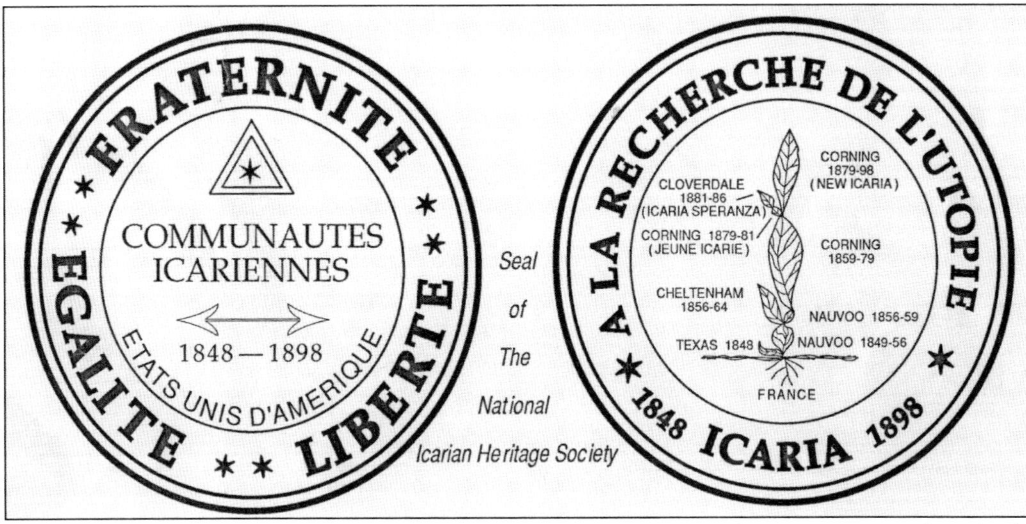

Icarians were followers of French dissident Etienne Cabet, whose novel *Voyage En Icarie* described a social organization proposed to bring about peace and equality. Icarians immigrated to America to organize utopian communities between 1848 and 1898. The seal of the National Icarian Heritage Society displays their central beliefs—fraternity, equality, and liberty—and their seven American colonies.

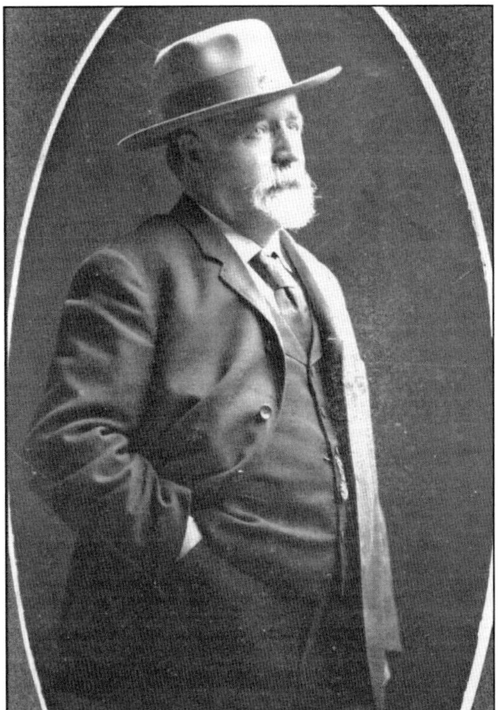

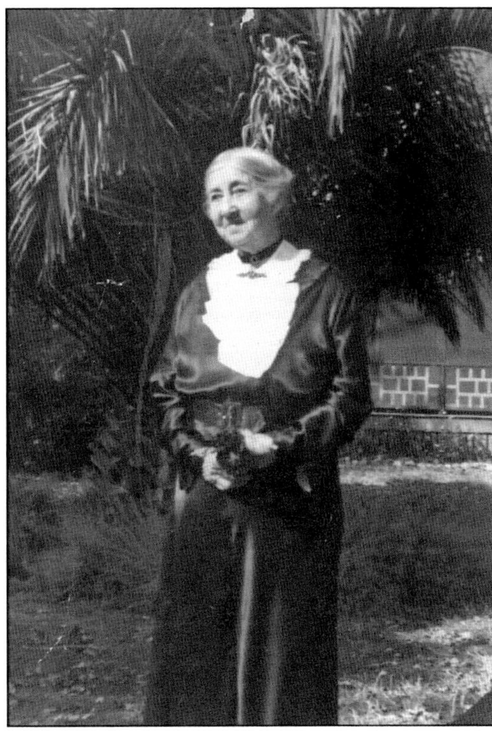

Armand Dehay (left), cofounder of the Icarian-Speranza colony in Cloverdale, came to California with his wife, Marie, in 1881 to organize their new utopian community. They were joined by Armand's father-in-law, social activist Jules Leroux, and Jules's sons Pierre and Paul. After the colony dissolved in 1886, Dehay and several former Icarians formed the French American Wine Company, which became the Dehay Winery in the early 1890s.

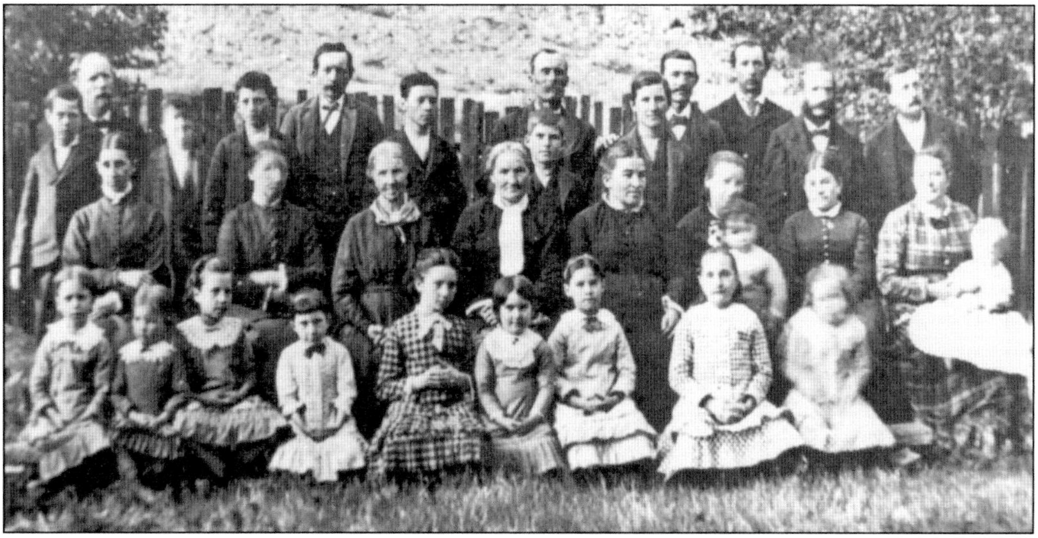

This picture shows colony members in 1885. Seated at far left in the second row, behind the unidentified children, is Marie Leroux Dehay. In the third row, from left to right, are Paul Dehay, Armand J. Dehay Sr., Emile Ben Dehay, Henri Zurcher, Amile Zurcher, Ulysses Zurcher, Eugene Mourot, Albert Mourot, Leon Bettanier Jr., Alexis Marchand, Paul Leroux, Pierre Leroux, and Gustave Provost.

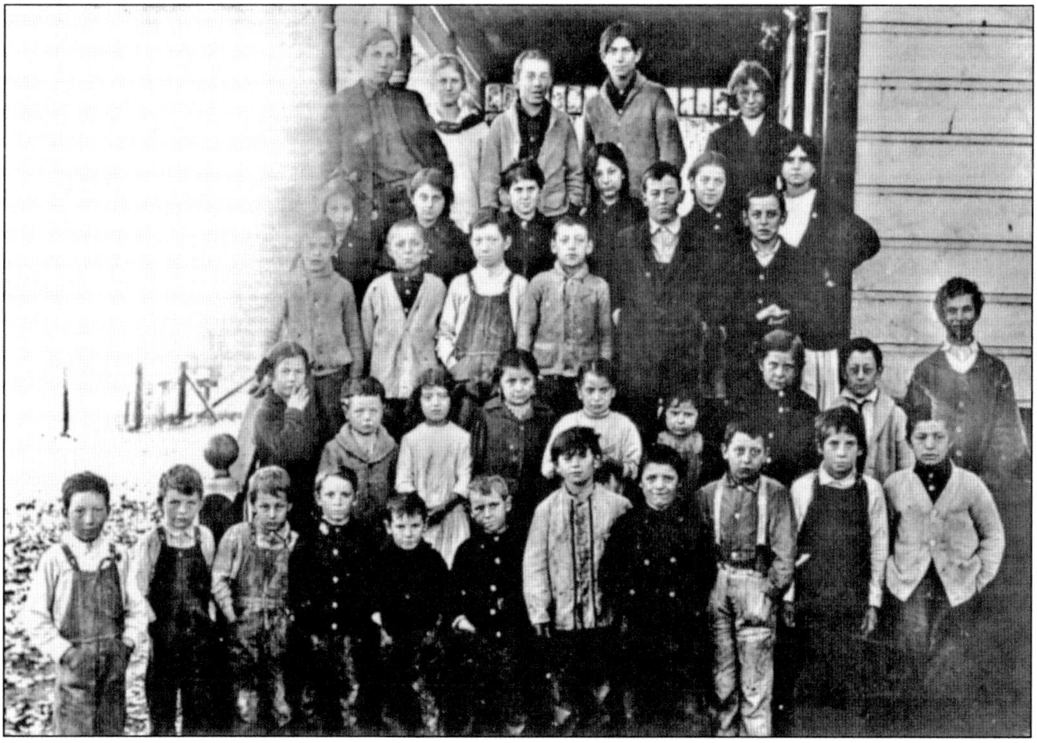

Education was one of the highest goals of the community. The one-room Icaria School, built in 1881, is pictured here in 1913, some 27 years after the dissolution of the colony. Historical Marker No. 981, located south of Cloverdale on the west side of Asti Road, marks the site where the schoolhouse once stood.

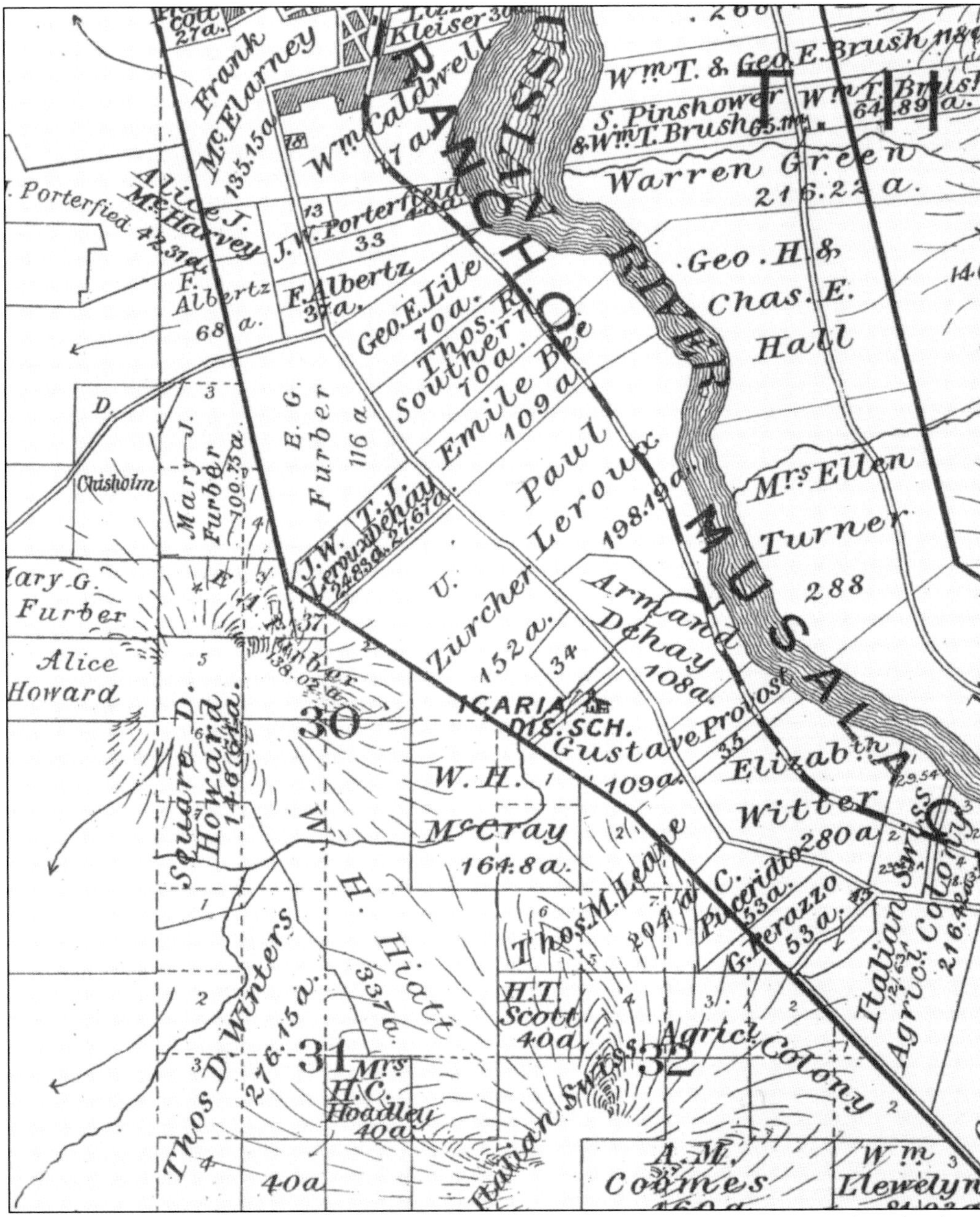

This map, from the 1898 *Illustrated Atlas of Sonoma County*, shows how Icarian Colony land was divided up among its members. Colony property starts at the south boundary of E. G. Furber and Thomas R. Southern. Colony members included J. W. Leroux, T. J. Dehay, U. Zurcher, Emile Bee, Paul Leroux, Armand Dehay, and Gustave Provost.

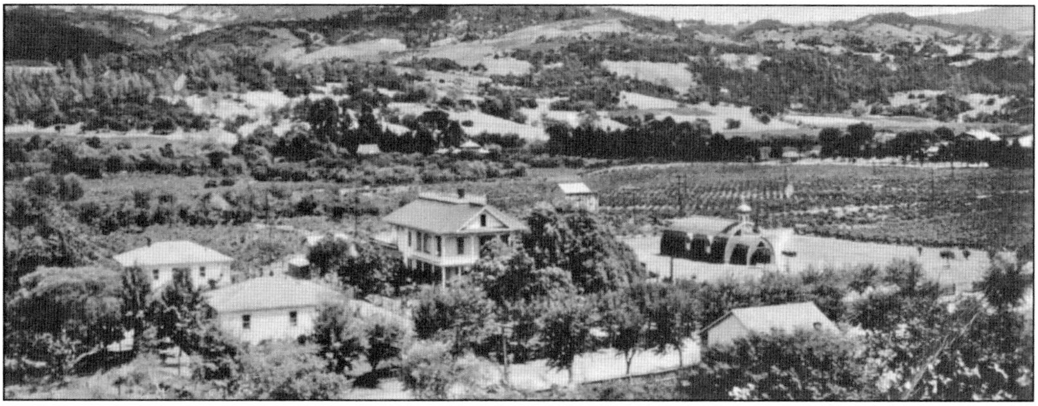

This *c.* 1910 view looks east over Italian Swiss Colony vineyards. The land was purchased in 1881, and planting began the following year. Andrea Sbarboro's idea was to set jobless Italian immigrants to work. The men earned $30 to $40 a month plus room, board, and a generous ration of wine. Some descendants of these Italian families are to this day still involved in the local wine business. (Courtesy Asti Winery.)

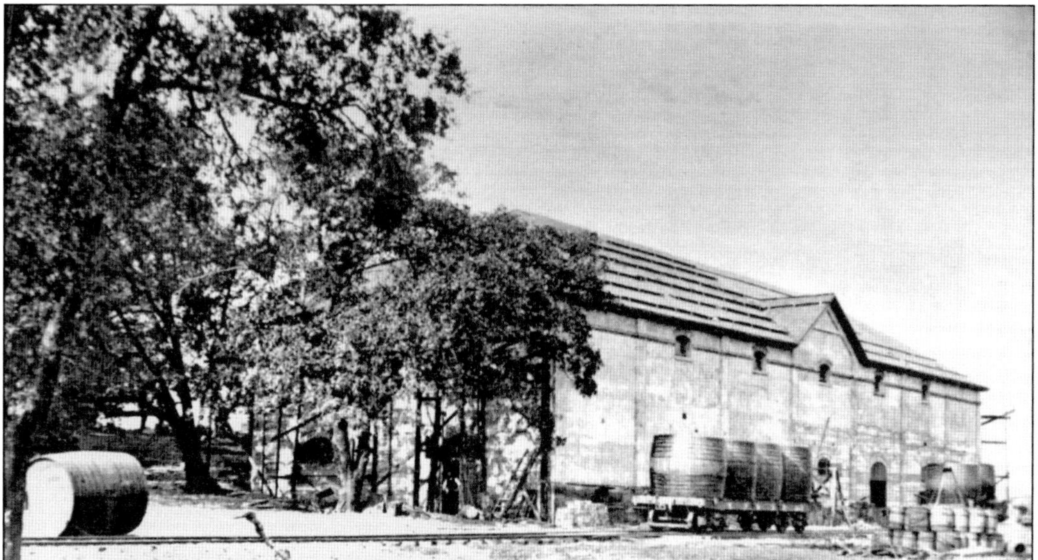

This two-story concrete building, the first winery at the Italian Swiss Colony (ISC), is still in use at Asti Winery. It was originally built to hold the 1887 crush. Just four years later, ISC won the first of what would be many gold medals in American as well as European competitions. By 1937, the Italian Swiss Colony was the largest producer of table wines in the United States.

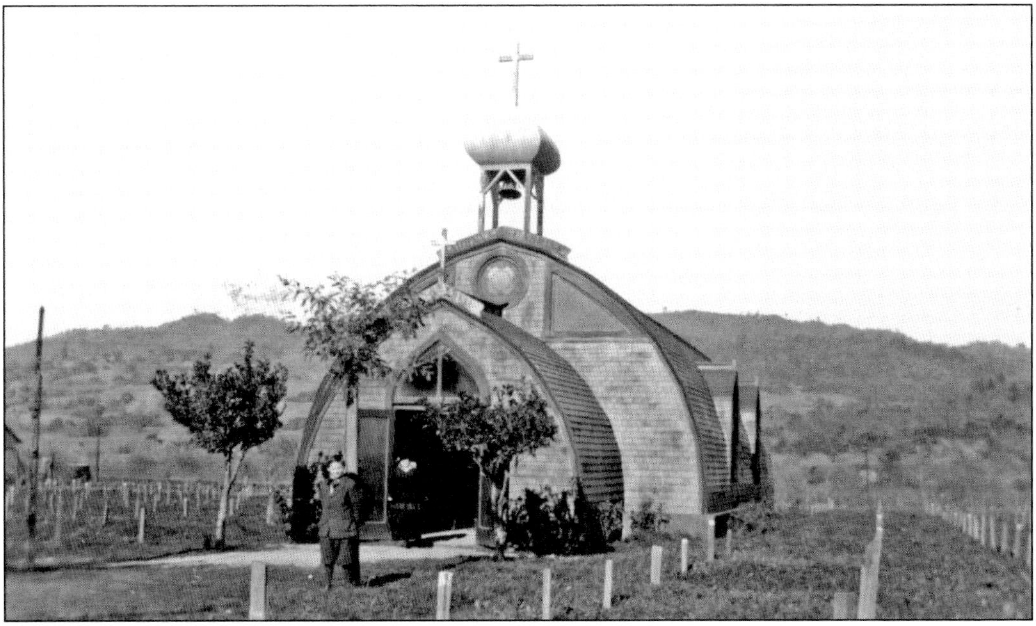

Madonna del Carmine, seen above around 1919, was dedicated in 1907 as a place of worship for Italian Swiss families. The tiny church, known as El Carmelo—the church built like a wine barrel—was actually built from a remodeled ISC greenhouse. It had millions of visitors over the years, and its image was used heavily in the company's advertising. It was replaced in 1960 with Our Lady of Mount Carmel (below, left), the ceiling of which was constructed of redwood from old wine tanks. Many had hoped to restore the beloved El Carmelo, and there were fund-raising efforts over the years, but not enough was raised to save the badly deteriorated chapel, remnants of which were finally removed in 2005.

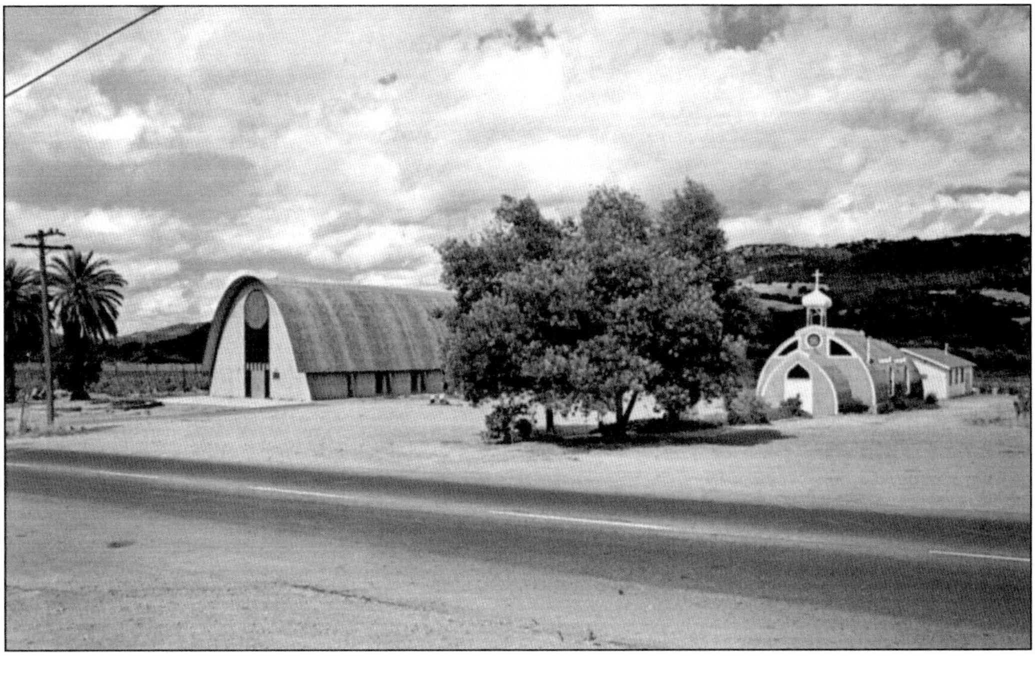

Villa Pompeii, which still stands on Asti Winery grounds, was the weekend and summer home of Italian Swiss Colony founder Andrea Sbarboro. The home was built in 1902 as an exact replica of Casa dei Vetti, an ancient Roman villa that had entranced Sbarboro while visiting Pompeii, Italy. Villa Pompeii was known for the festive parties Sbarboro hosted there for his guests. (Courtesy Asti Winery.)

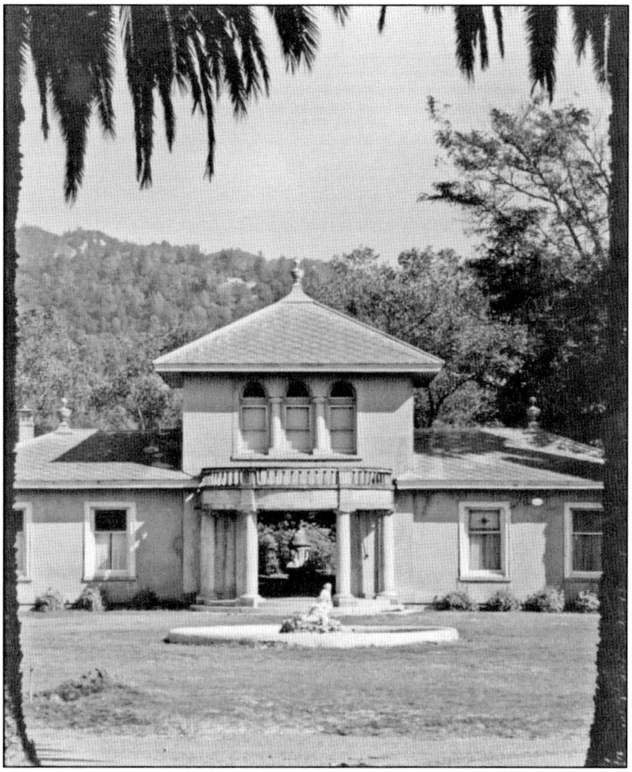

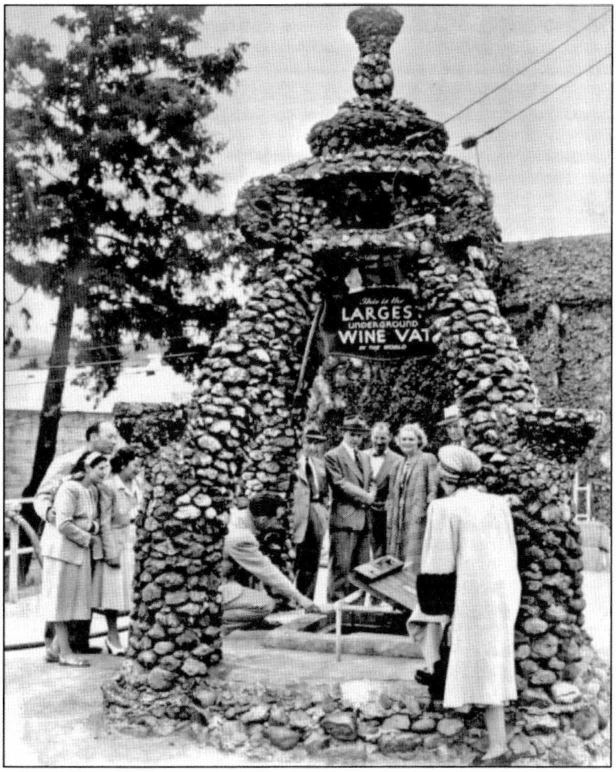

Visitors enjoy exploring the entrance to ISC's underground tank, called the "largest wine vat in the world." Twenty-four feet high, 80 feet long, and 34 feet wide, the tank could hold the equivalent of 200,000 cases of wine. Its most celebrated moment came when Sbarboro held a dance in the tank, complete with a 10-piece brass band and more than 200 guests. (Courtesy Asti Winery.)

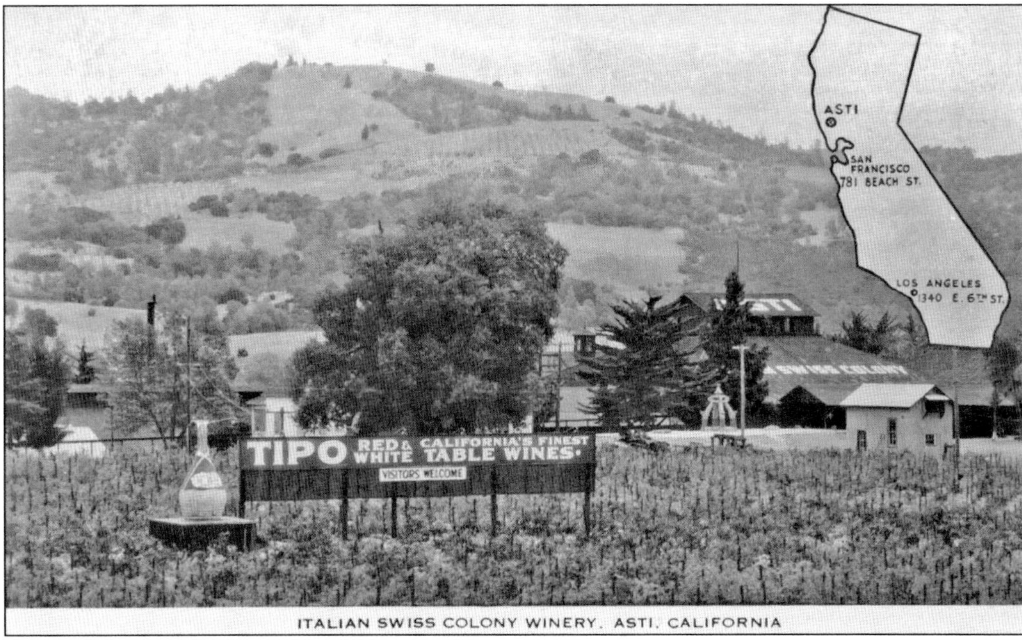

This sign and giant wine bottle welcomed countless visitors to Asti. At the start of the 20th century, the Italian Swiss Colony's premium table wine was Tipo ("type" in Italian) Chianti. Before Prohibition, Tipo was selling well in the New York and Chicago markets. By the late 1960s, however, after Heublein acquired ISC, the marketing budget for Tipo was eliminated, and the product was dropped.

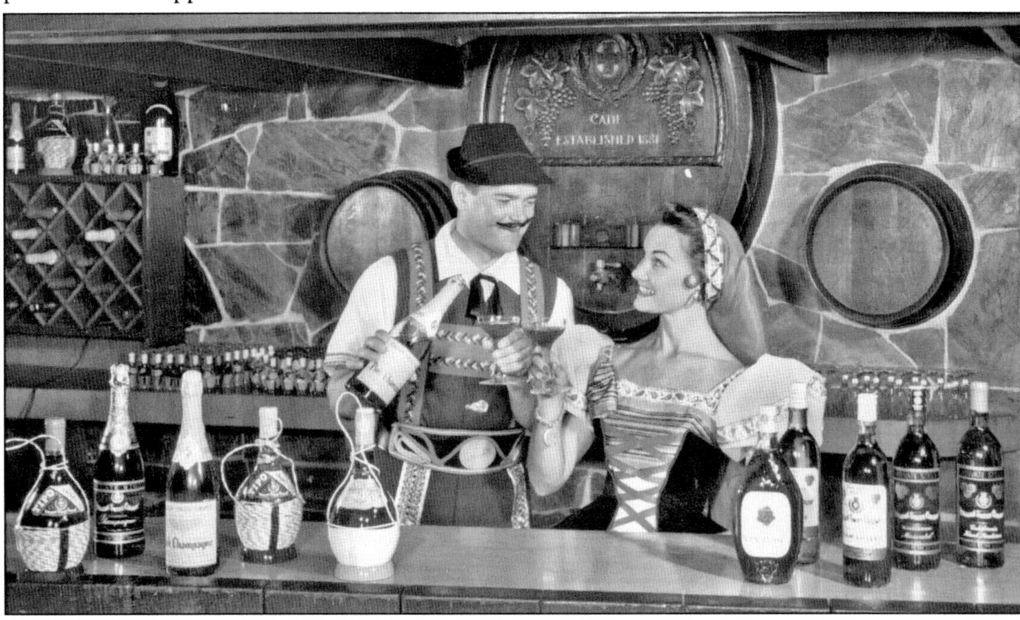

Costume-clad greeters in the tasting room were part of the Italian Swiss Colony's advertising campaign, which also included immensely popular television spots starring "The Little Old Winemaker." By 1960, ISC was the largest producer of table wines in the world, and its tasting room became one of California's most popular tourist destinations, welcoming approximately 400,000 visitors at its peak in 1962. (Courtesy Asti Winery.)

Three

Agricultural and Industrial Enterprises

Cloverdale's economic base has historically stemmed from the natural resources of the surrounding area—the fertile soil, forests, grasslands, and minerals.

Commercial agriculture in Cloverdale's early years included wine grapes, hops, citrus, olives, peaches, prunes, and, for a short time, tobacco. Although citrus is the theme of Cloverdale's historic Citrus Fair, commercially grown citrus never had the success enjoyed by wine grapes and prunes. Sheep ranching, tanbark, and mining were other notable commercial activities in the early decades.

In the early 1900s, several wineries were operating in Cloverdale and to the north, east, and south of town. Among the early winemakers were Mazzini, Sink, Berti, Hollis Black, Haehl, Ledger, Ghiotti, Furber, Moulton, DeHay, Vadon, Zanzi, Italian Swiss Colony, and Seghesio. When Prohibition took effect in 1919, it struck a major blow to local grape growers and wineries. Many vineyards were replanted with other crops, primarily prunes, and some wineries closed, never to reopen.

After Prohibition ended in 1933, grape growing and winemaking made a slow comeback. Over time, vineyards eventually replaced the prune orchards, and grapes became the area's dominant crop. Growing wine grapes is now Cloverdale's leading industry, with 4,050 acres of vines as of December 2005. Of the original wineries, however, only Seghesio and successors to the Italian Swiss Colony are still operating.

In the years after World War II, Cloverdale became known for its lumber mills. Sawmills, remanufacturing, and plywood mills became major sources of employment, while logging operations, mainly to the west and north, provided the timber. Early mills such as Triplett and Cloverdale Lumber were smaller, independent operations, but over time, larger corporate-owned mills predominated. Among the town's important mills were Barnes Lumber, Coastal Plywood, Malalla, and Rounds. As was the case for other North Coast lumber towns, Cloverdale's lumber-based economy began to decline in the 1970s as environmental activism and regulations curtailed logging.

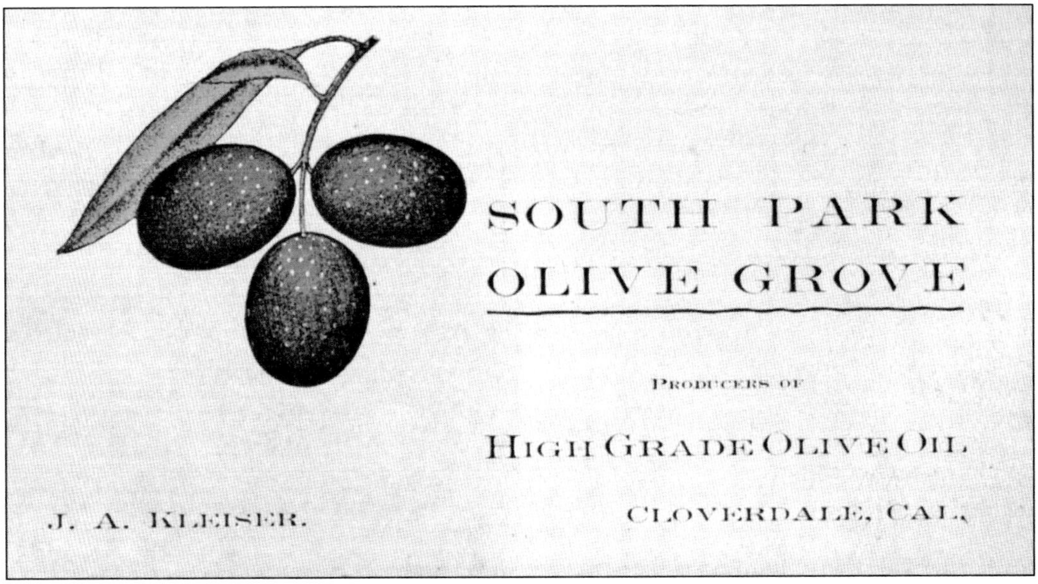

Town founder James Kleiser had a flourishing olive orchard south of town, from which he manufactured a "superior brand of olive oil and a fine grade of pickled olives."

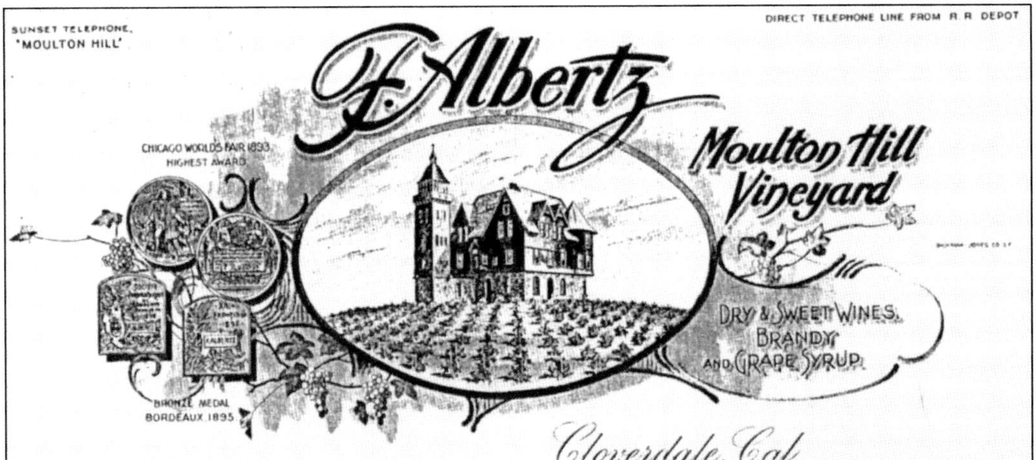

Josiah Moulton founded the Moulton Hill Winery in 1882 on land south of Cloverdale previously planted to vineyard with partner Joseph Carrie, a Cloverdale merchant. In 1890, Moulton's widow, Adeline, leased the winery and vineyard to an ambitious Danish immigrant, Hans Frederick Albertz, who added 200 acres of vines east of the Russian River and built the large four-story "castle" and winery seen on the label above. Albertz's quality wine won medals in Chicago (1893) and Bordeaux (1895). By 1896, the capacity of his winery had increased to 600,000 gallons a year. Albertz is also known for generating power for Cloverdale's first electric streetlights in 1897. During Prohibition, a large gin still housed in the castle's basement was destroyed by IRS agents. As the story goes, alcohol was poured into the creek running through the property and set on fire, producing a river of flames. Ruins of the winery buildings are preserved today in the Clover Springs development.

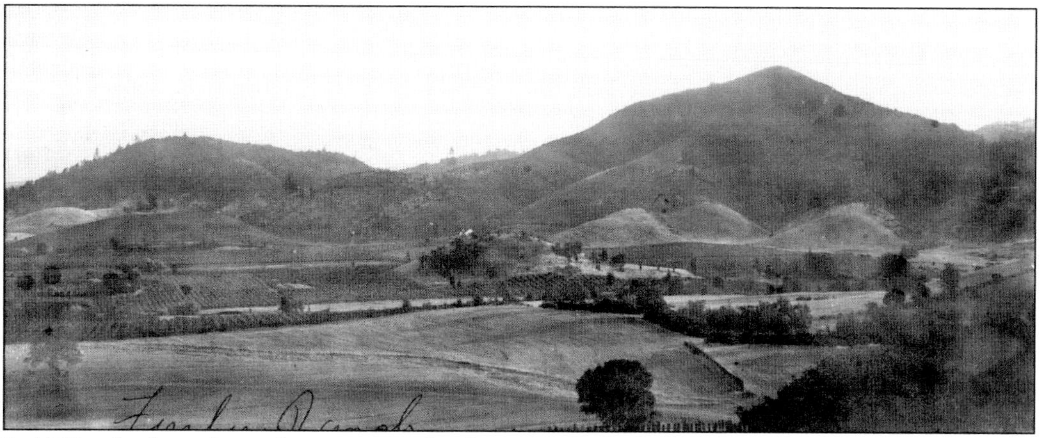

In 1880, a fair-haired man from Maine, Elbridge G. Furber, purchased 640 acres south of Cloverdale. He and his wife, Mary, cleared the land, planted more than 100 acres in grapes, and, in 1886, built a winery on Hot Springs Road. Their son William, who took over the ranch in 1915, had 200,000 gallons of wine in storage when Prohibition was passed. Their grandson Al Furber still lives on the property today. Furber Ranch, at the base of the hills on the right, is today the site of Furber Plaza, several residential neighborhoods, and Furber Park.

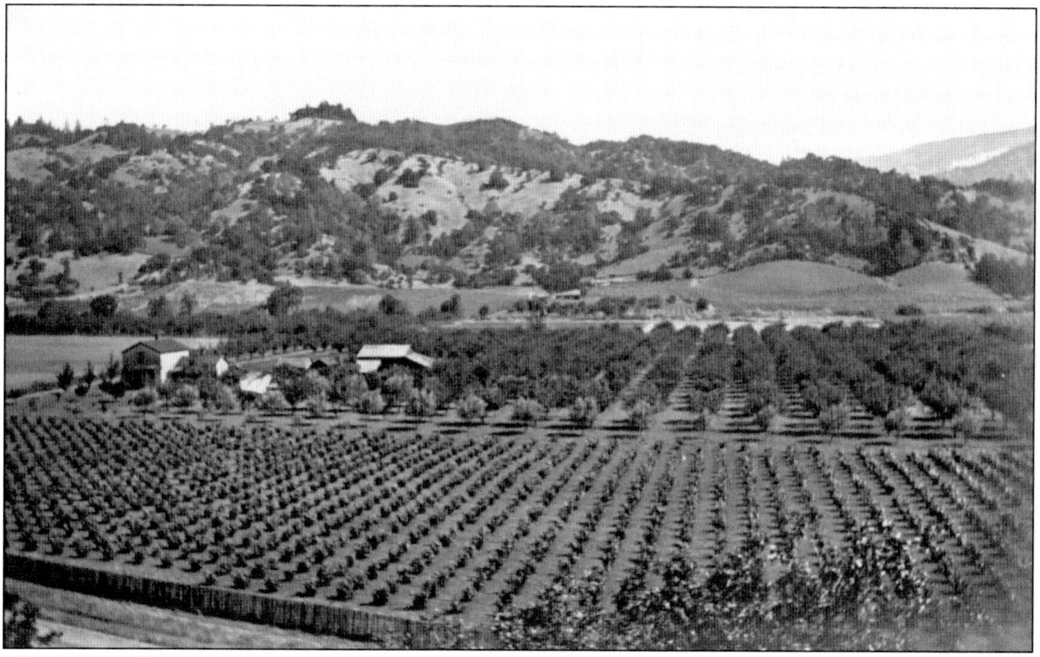

This Oat Valley vineyard, pictured in the late 1800s, was the property of William Daniel "Bill" Sink, whose father, Daniel, had come to Cloverdale in 1859. By 1896, Bill Sink was the sole owner of the 200,000-gallon Marietta Winery, named in honor of his wife. The winery was built with stone quarried on the Oat Valley ranch. Sink helped establish the Cloverdale Wine Company and was its guiding force until his death in 1912. The land remains in the Sink family today. (Courtesy Lucille Sink.)

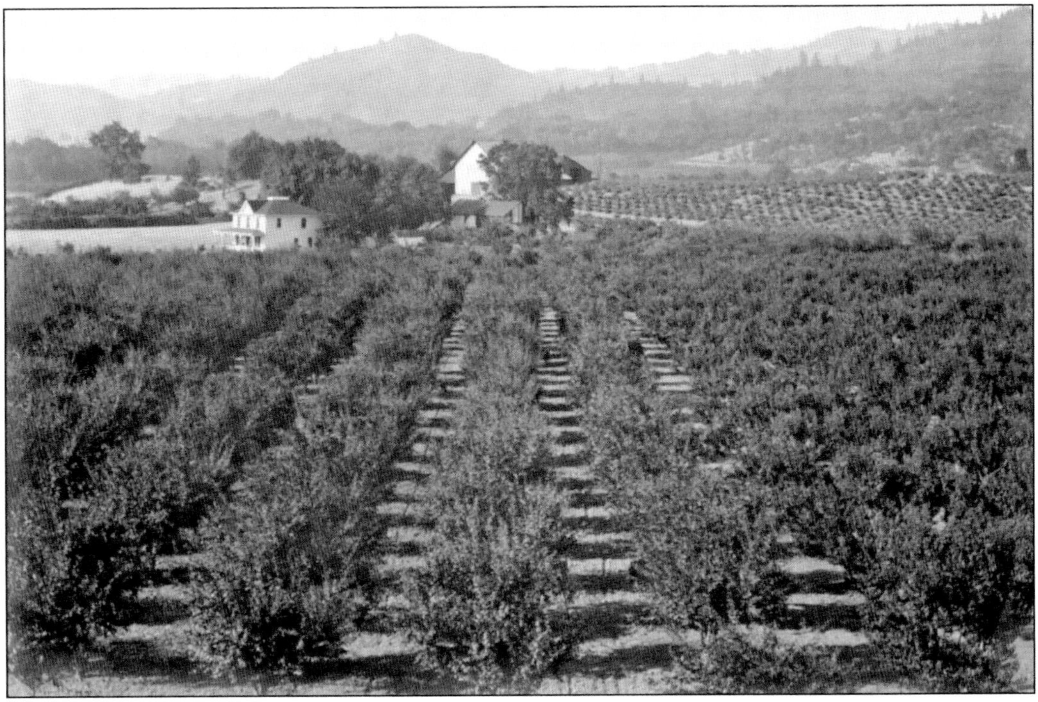

This vintage photograph was labeled, "Peach orchard and vineyard near Cloverdale." Many of Cloverdale's earliest settlers planted orchards—Hartwell Preston, James Kleiser, and Icarian colonists to name a few. The atlas of 1898 reported, "Extensive prune and peach orchards are found . . . growing in the most successful and prosperous manner."

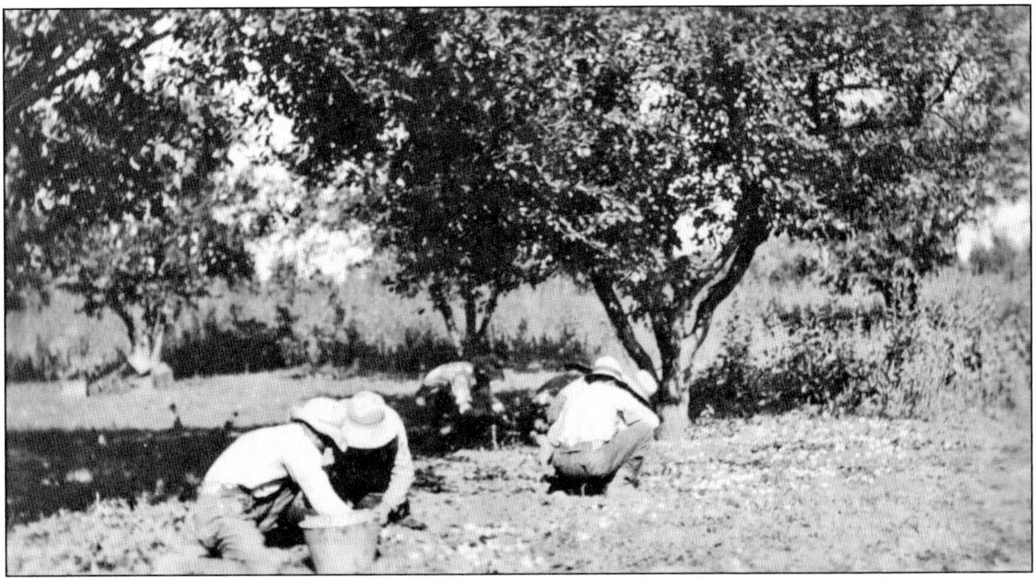

These individuals are picking prunes at the Coen Ranch on Cherry Creek Road. Prunes were harvested by shaking the tree and gathering the fallen fruit. The county's prune business, begun in 1881 when Luther Burbank helped a local grower plant 20,000 trees, grew in the 1920s when Prohibition reduced the demand for grapes and technology was developed to mechanically dehydrate prunes. By the 1970s, farmers were turning away from prunes and returning to grapes.

Sarah Ann "Annie" Brush Wilson (1866–1961) was reputedly the first white girl born in Cloverdale. Annie and her mother, Rachel Ann, brought the first oranges to Cloverdale from Panama in 1869. One of the trees planted from those first seeds eventually grew through the roof of a home on the Brush property. A few years before her death at the age of 96, Annie served as the grand marshal of the Citrus Fair parade, an event she helped create.

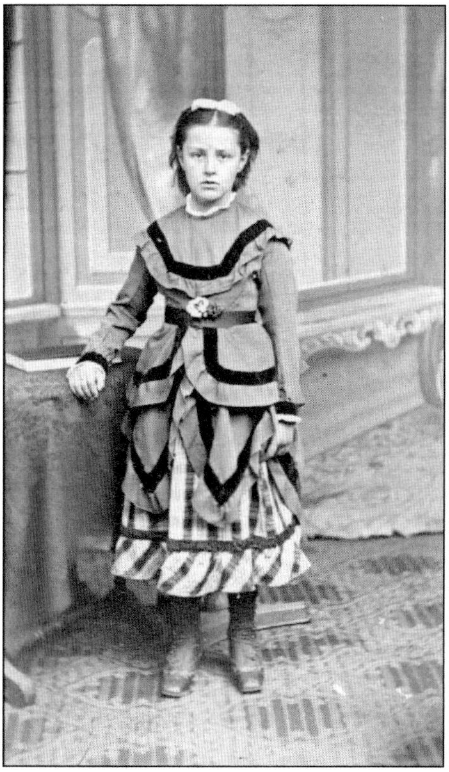

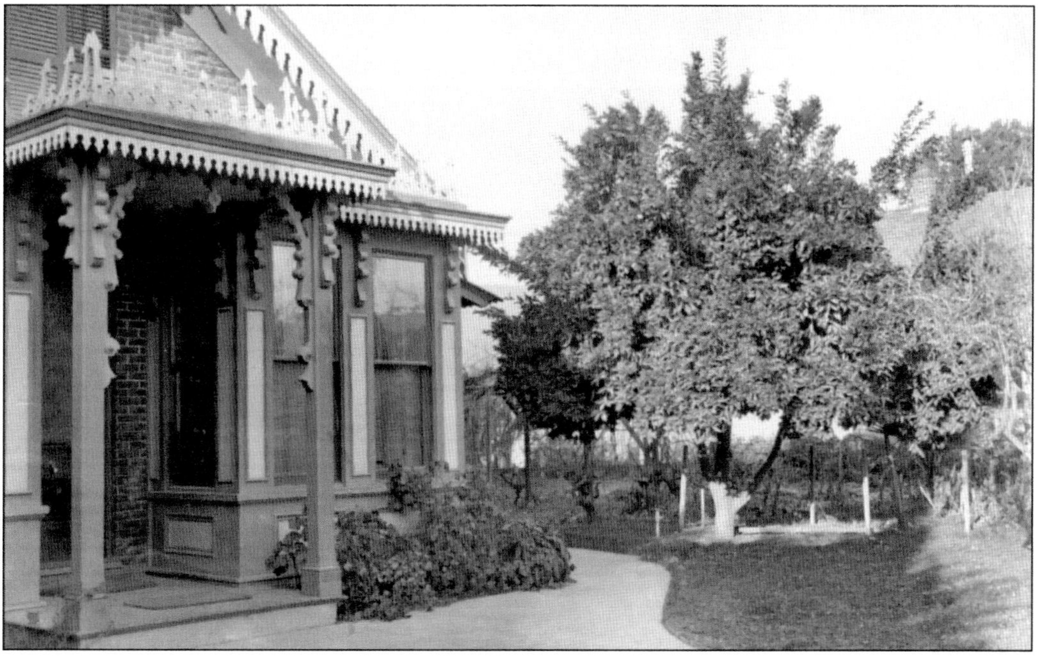

The Cloverdale citrus industry was promoted heavily in the 1890s. The many orange trees seen around town today give testimony to that bygone era when Cloverdale was known as the "Orange Belt of Sonoma County." This early specimen, still growing in front of the Gould-Shaw House Museum, is more than 100 years old.

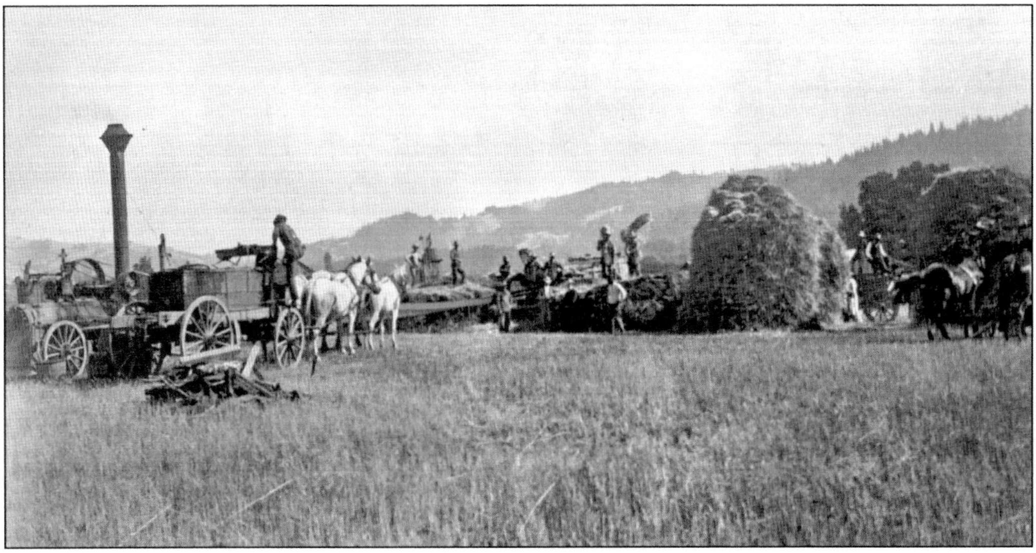

It is harvest time in the 1890s in Oat Valley, an area first settled by Americans around 1855. There is a steam thresher on the left and laborers baling hay in the background. In the 19th century, hay was a commercial crop, supplying livery stables and animal owners with feed. Steam-powered equipment began to appear in the 1880s.

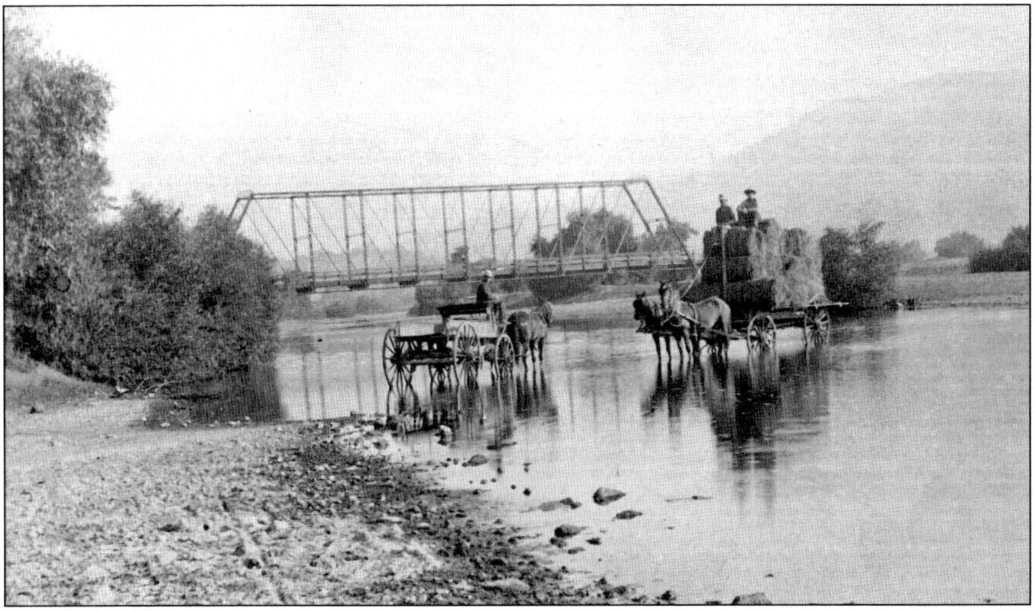

Drivers transporting crops into Cloverdale often stopped in the Russian River to soak the wagon's wooden wheels to keep them from drying out. The wagon on the right is hauling a load of hay into town. The original First Street Bridge is seen in the background.

The flour mill on Sulphur Creek, built about 1868, was acquired in 1880 by John Bowman, I. E. Shaw's mercantile partner. Wheat had been a commercial crop in Cloverdale, but when the international market declined and farmers stopped growing wheat for home consumption, the need for the mill vanished. Around 1900, the mill was torn down, and a power station was built on the site to supply electricity to the Italian Swiss Colony. In the 1960s, the powerhouse was remodeled as a residence for town banker Arthur Foster.

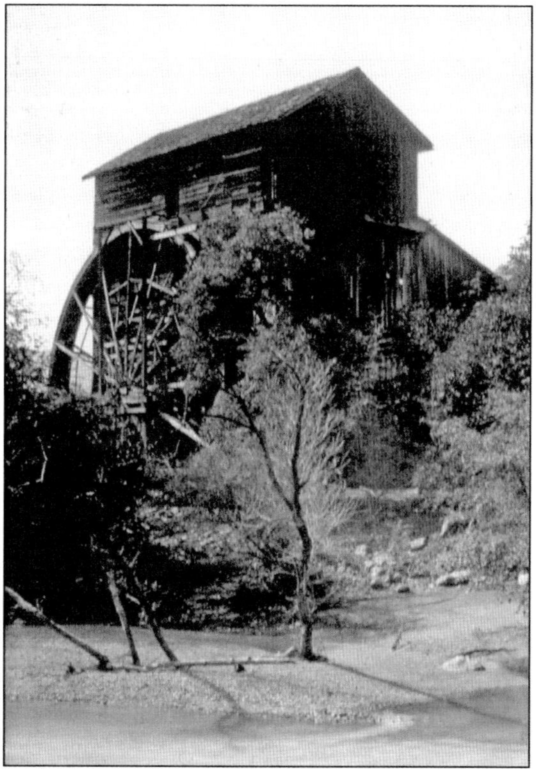

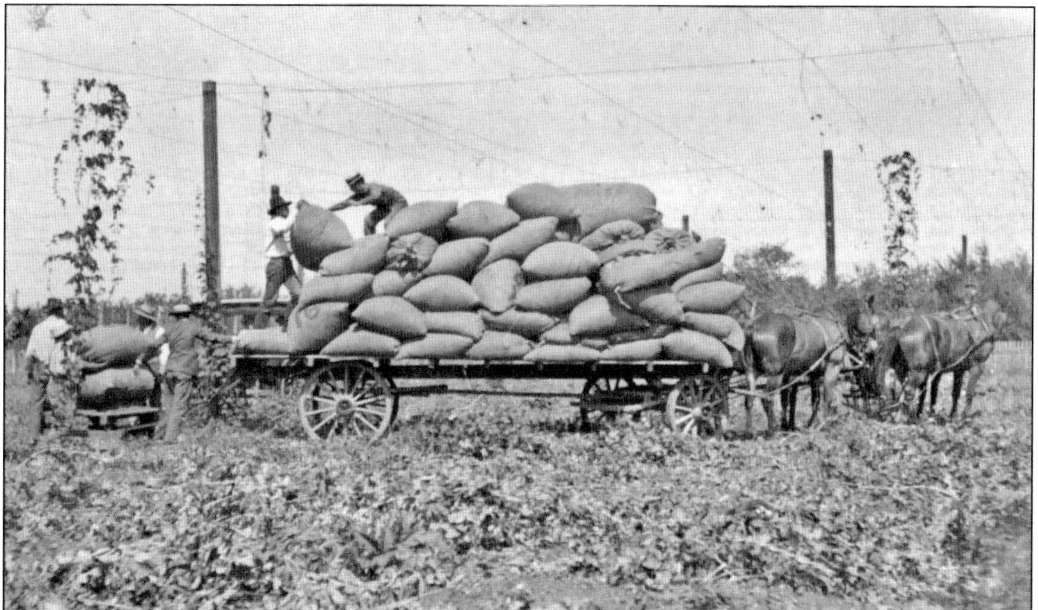

Hop picking was difficult, labor-intensive work. Growers advertised to recruit workers, touting the chance for camping outside and having a "festive" time. Pickers would get paid as little as 1¢ per pound, but a good picker could earn \$2 to \$3 in one day. Historical records report 1,630 bales of hops weighing 327,201 pounds were shipped from Cloverdale in 1876.

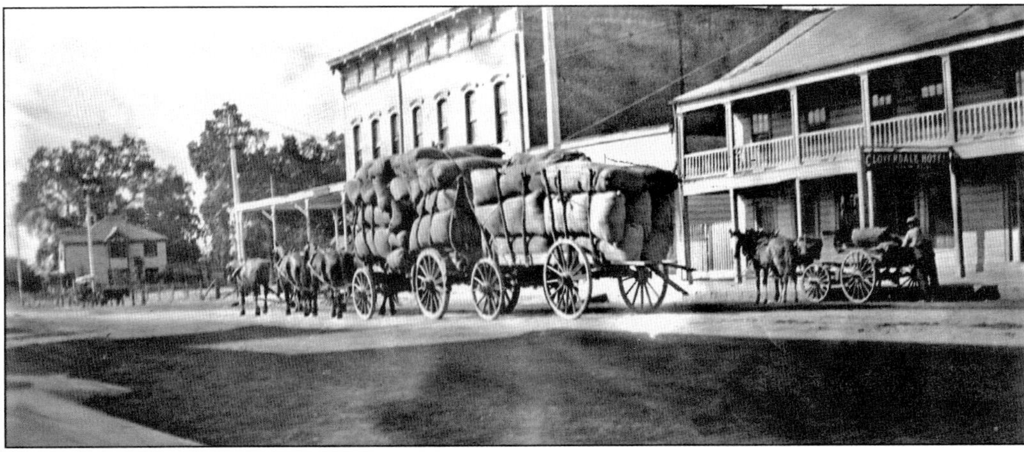

Wool was a prime crop in the hillside ranches around Cloverdale from the time of the earliest settlers. When the railroad arrived in 1872, brokers like James Hoadley, owner of the two-story building in the background, bought wool from surrounding counties as well. At one time, Walter Ink employed 12 American Indians to shear 2,300 sheep on his 3,000-acre ranch north of Sulphur Creek.

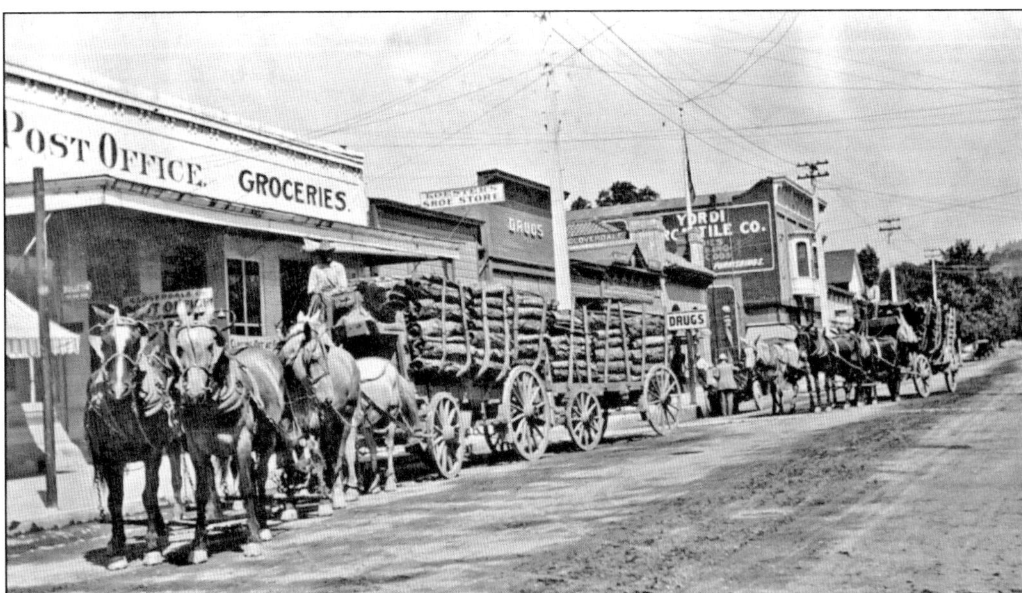

Around the dawn of the 20th century, harvesting and transporting of the bark of tan oak trees was important to the economy of Cloverdale. Crews would cut the trees and strip the bark in 4-foot lengths. After drying, the bark was loaded onto pack mules or mule-drawn carts, and transported out of the hills for shipment to tanneries. Wagons hauling tanbark were a common sight heading through town. The wagons pictured above are on West Street on the way to the rail line

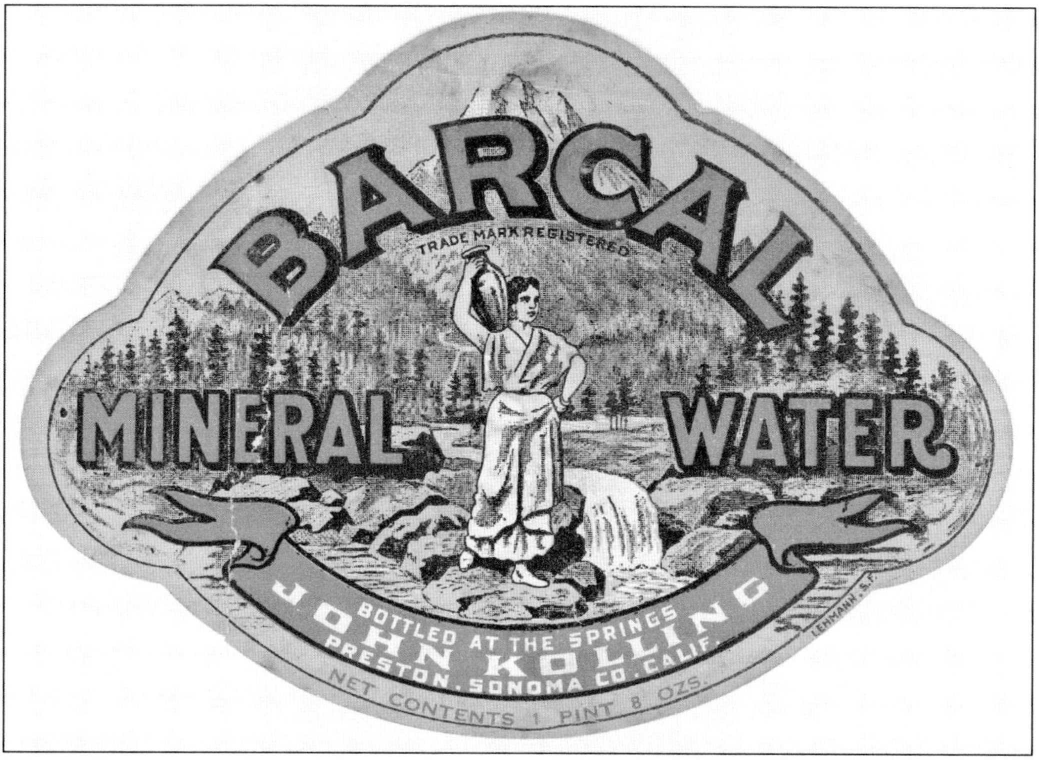

John Kolling came to Cloverdale around 1900. After discovering a natural spring on his Pine Mountain property, he built a bottling plant near the railroad in Preston. The company, incorporated as Pine Mountain Mineral Springs in 1907, later became Barcal Mineral Water. The Kollings also produced flavored soda water and a drink called "B&B" (Barcal and bourbon). Kolling's descendants still live in the area today.

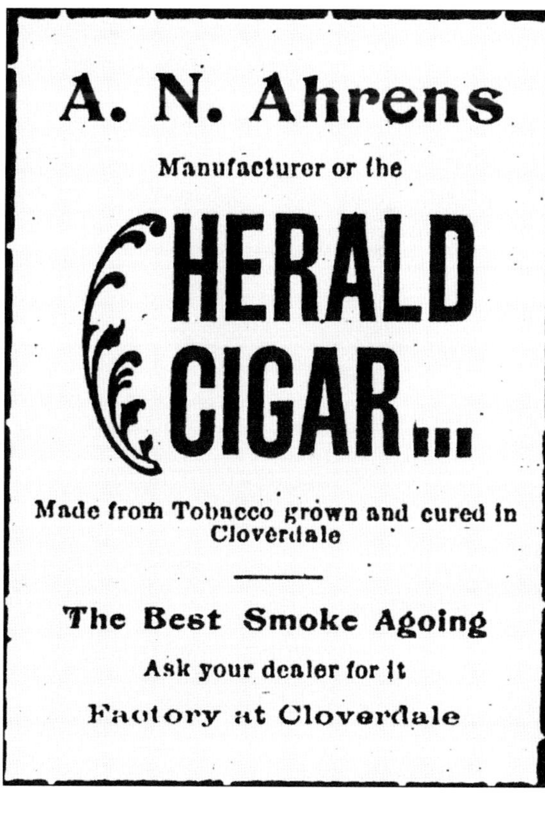

This 1905 *Cloverdale Reveille* advertisement promoted cigars made locally by the Hermitage Tobacco Company, incorporated in 1901. When its officers came to Cloverdale looking for a warehouse site, they were welcomed by a brass band and parade. The company, which had acres of tobacco planted southwest of Cloverdale and in Oat Valley, employed local labor at its factory. Although cigar sales were initially promising, later harvests disappointed, and the company failed by 1907.

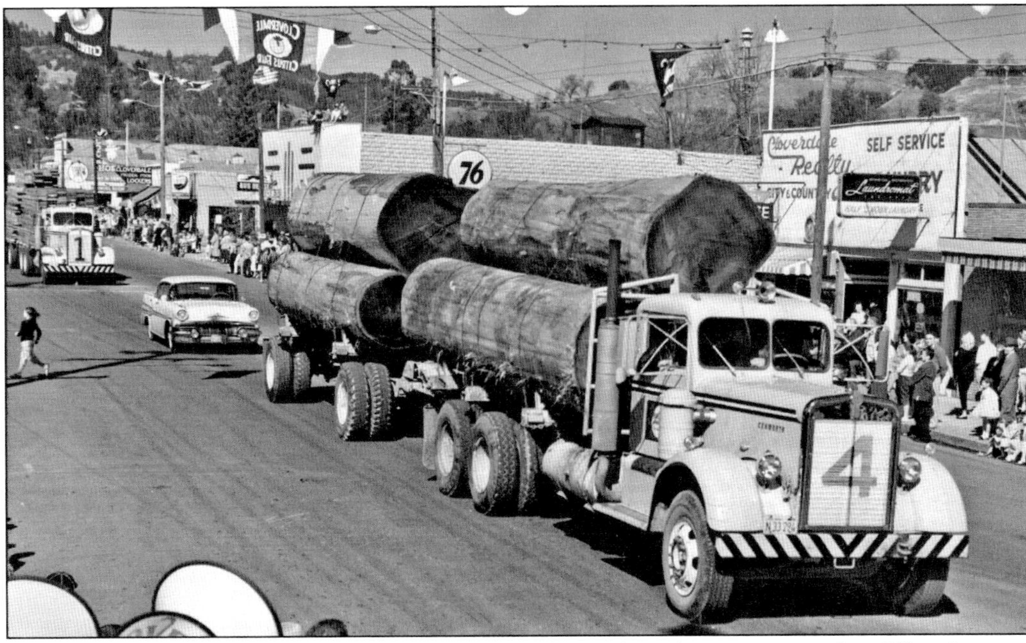

In the decades following World War II, logging trucks, such as this one pictured on West Street in 1960, were a common sight in and around Cloverdale as they headed to mills with redwood and other conifers. Equally common were the lumber trucks passing through Cloverdale at all times of day and night, transporting the finished product out of the local mills and mills farther north to the Bay Area and beyond.

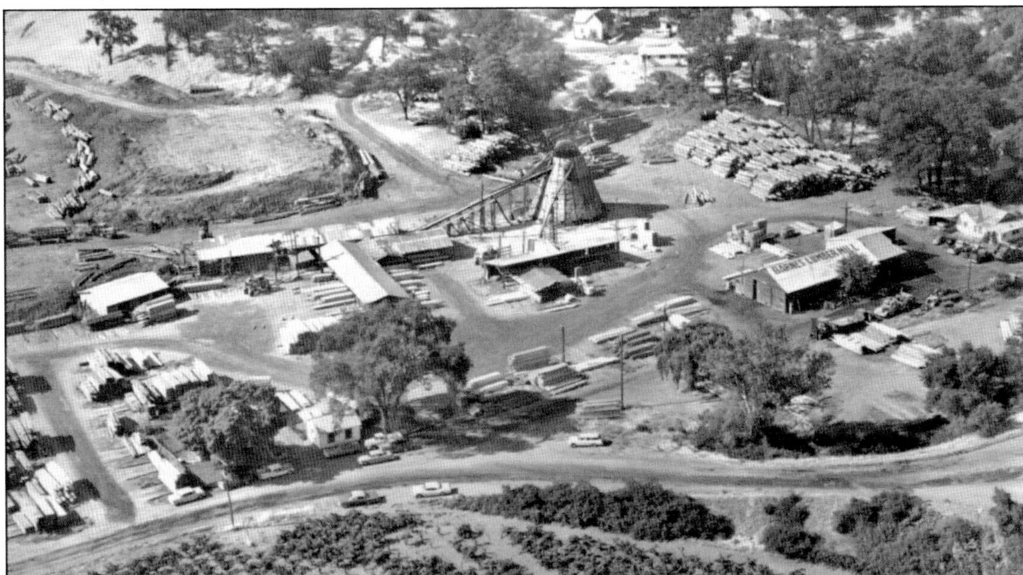

The sawmill on McCray Road, built in 1947 by Robert and Pauline Barnes, milled 100,000 board feet of douglas fir and redwood every day at its peak. This bird's-eye view of Barnes Lumber was taken in 1966, when Leonard, Lloyd, and Francis Mittelstadt, sons of Bob and Pauline, were running the mill. It became a retail yard in 1972 after the mill burned down and has been run by Karl Mittlelstadt and Lynmarie Hoyer since 1995. (Courtesy Barnes Lumber.)

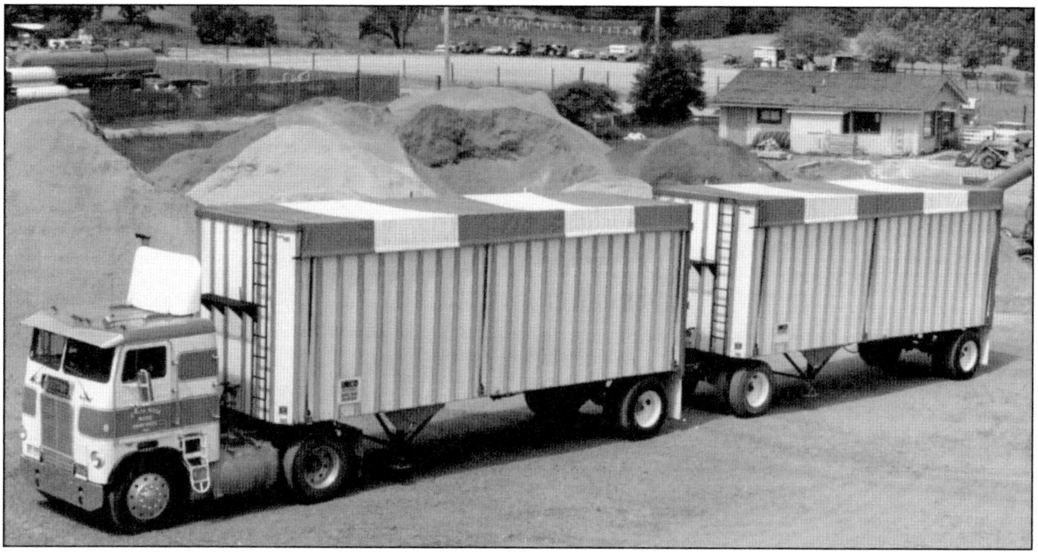

Ernest Reuser was one of Cloverdale's first lumbermen back in the 1940s, and his legacy lives on. Son Bruce has focused on mill waste management since "teepee burners" went out of use beginning in the 1960s. Reuser, Inc., operated by Bruce and his two sons, John and Merle, distributes landscaping materials throughout the Bay Area with a fleet of 14 trucks. In 1981, the business was using the two-trailer truck pictured here. (Courtesy Reuser, Inc.)

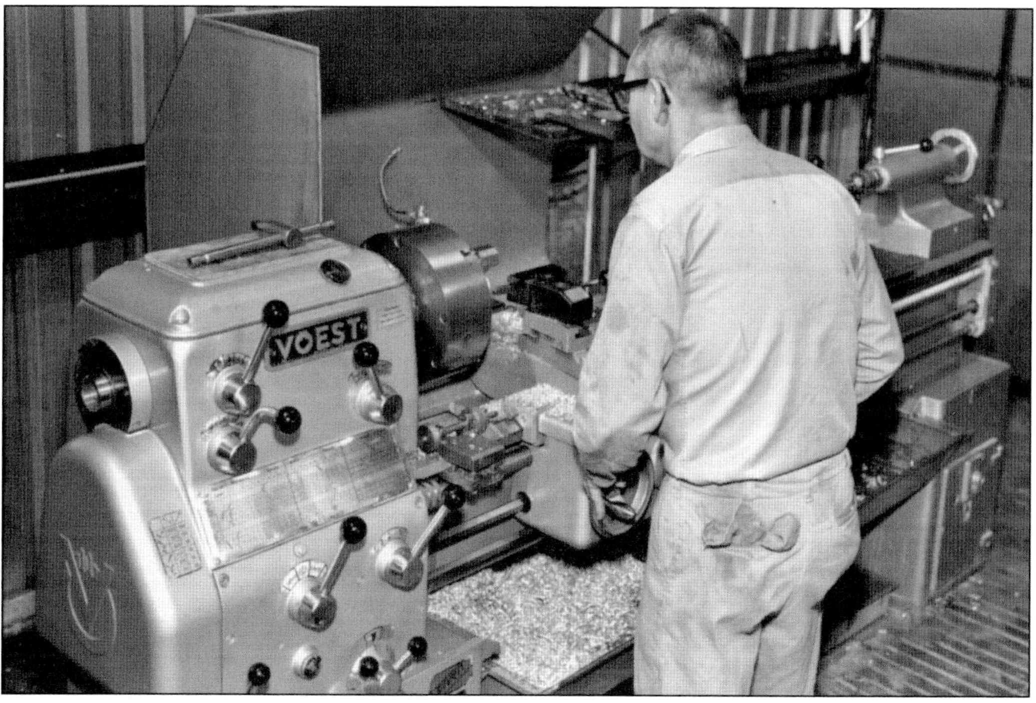

Another local business with roots in the timber industry is MGM Brakes, founded in 1956 by John L. Miller, Swen G. Gummer, and Joseph T. Meyers in response to safety challenges in the logging business. They invented and eventually became the worldwide supplier of spring brake actuators for large commercial vehicles. Pictured here in 1964 is Fuzz Foster operating a Voest engine lathe in the MGM Brake machine shop. (Courtesy MGM Brakes.)

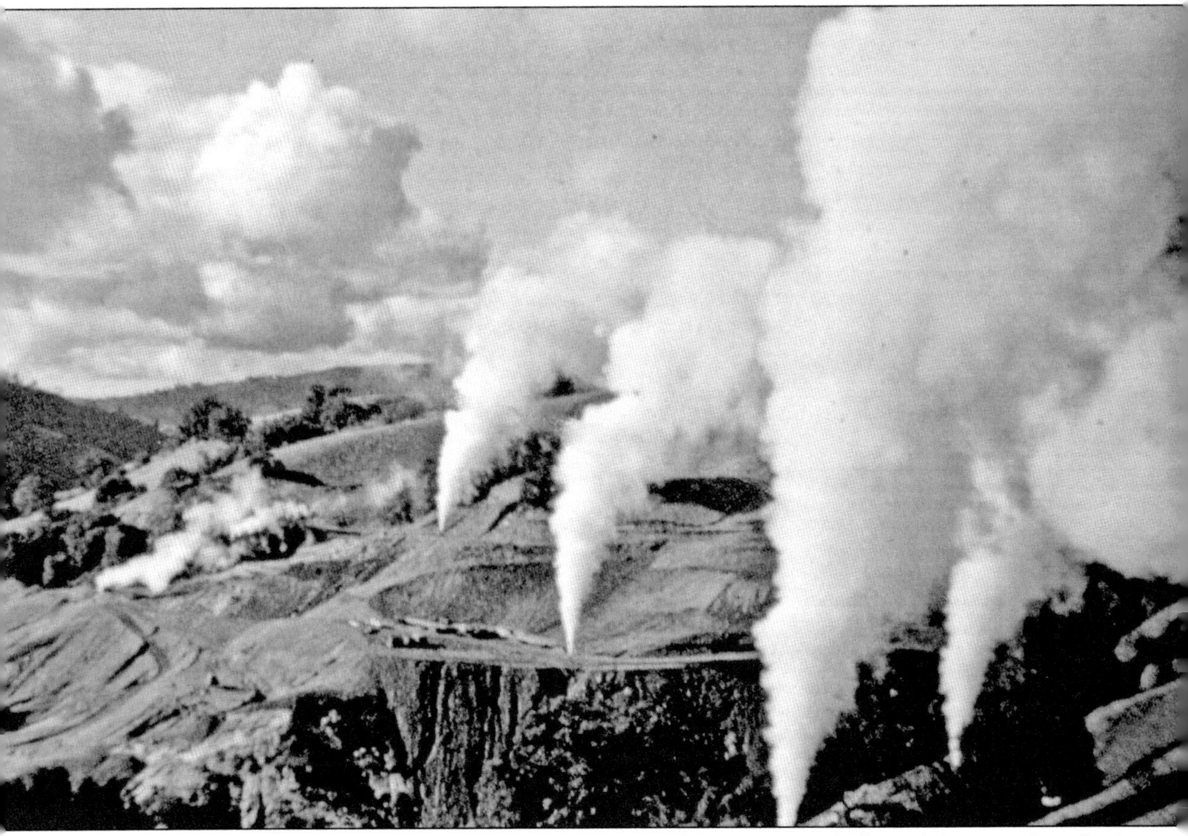

Some 12,000 years ago, American Indians came into this area east of Cloverdale to cook with the steam and bathe in the waters for pleasure and cures. William Bell Elliott, who discovered the thermal features while hunting a grizzly, named the area "The Geysers," a misnomer that persists today. During the first half of the 20th century, a new use of the steam fumaroles developed. The generation of electricity from geothermal steam, the first ever in the United States, took place here in the 1920s on an experimental basis. Some 40 years later, another more successful attempt was made. The Pacific Gas and Electric Company brought its first unit online in 1960. To prolong the life of the project, waste water is now being piped to The Geysers and injected back into the ground. Currently, there are 22 plants generating about 1,000 megawatts of electricity into the power grid for Santa Rosa and other North Bay cities. The Geysers is the world's largest geothermal energy facility.

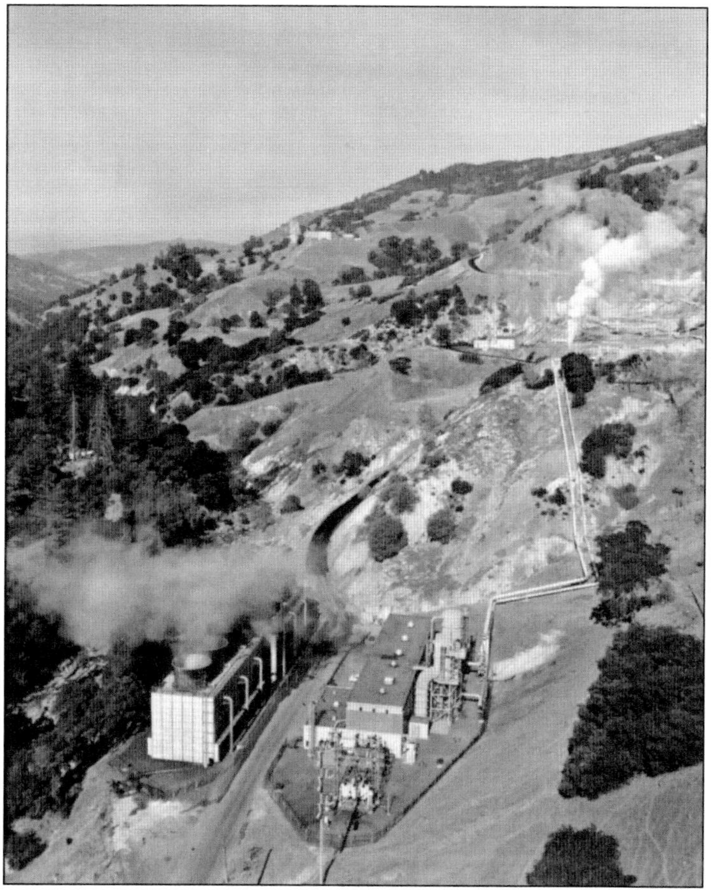

The first two units of the Pacific Gas and Electric (PG&E) Company's power facility at The Geysers came online in the 1960s—the 11,000-kilowatt Unit 1 in 1960 and the 13,000-kilowatt Unit 2 three years later. At its peak two decades ago, 27 plants produced about 1,900 megawatts at The Geysers.

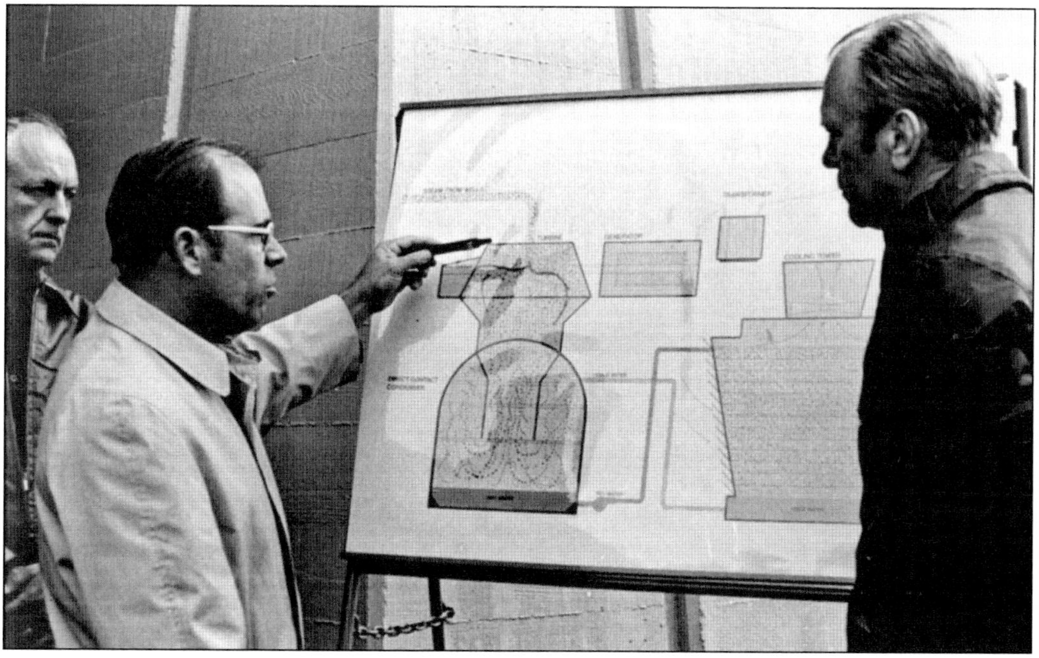

On April 4, 1975, Pres. Gerald Ford (right) made a 90-minute visit to the geothermal field at The Geysers. He is seen here speaking with two unidentified PG&E employees. Ford was in San Francisco to attend a meeting of Western governors on energy policy.

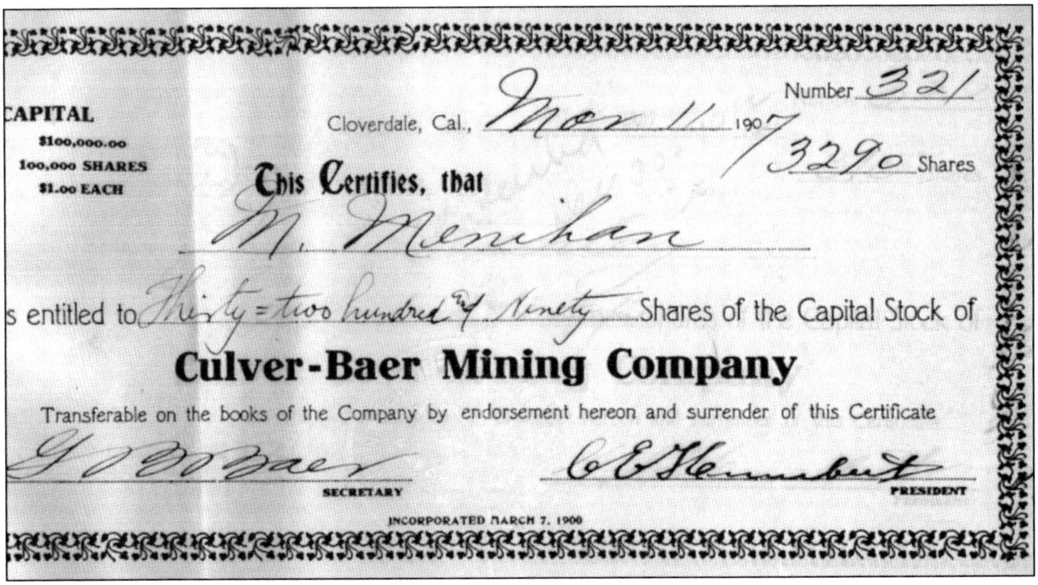
APITAL
$100,000.00
100,000 SHARES
$1.00 EACH

Number 321

Cloverdale, Cal., Nov 11 1907

3290 Shares

This Certifies, that M. Menihan

is entitled to Thirty-two hundred & Ninety Shares of the Capital Stock of

Culver-Baer Mining Company

Transferable on the books of the Company by endorsement hereon and surrender of this Certificate

G. W. Baer
SECRETARY

C. E. Humbert
PRESIDENT

INCORPORATED MARCH 7, 1900

Michael Menihan, proprietor of the U.S. Hotel, bought 3,290 shares in the Culver-Baer Mining Company in 1907, at which time Charles Humbert was company president and George Baer secretary. The company had extensive holdings near The Geysers, where abundant amounts of cinnabar had been discovered in 1859. Cinnabar is the mineral from which quicksilver (mercury) is extracted. Two years later, the enterprise was given up because of the low price of quicksilver and the scarcity of labor, but in 1872, interest was revived, a mining town sprang up, and at least 500 men were put to work. By 1889, there were two valuable claims—the Oakland Mine near Geyser Peak and the Cloverdale Mine on Sulphur Creek (pictured below). During World War I, the Cloverdale Mining Company was considered a million-dollar operation. Quicksilver mining, still active in the 1950s, was finally abandoned in the 1970s.

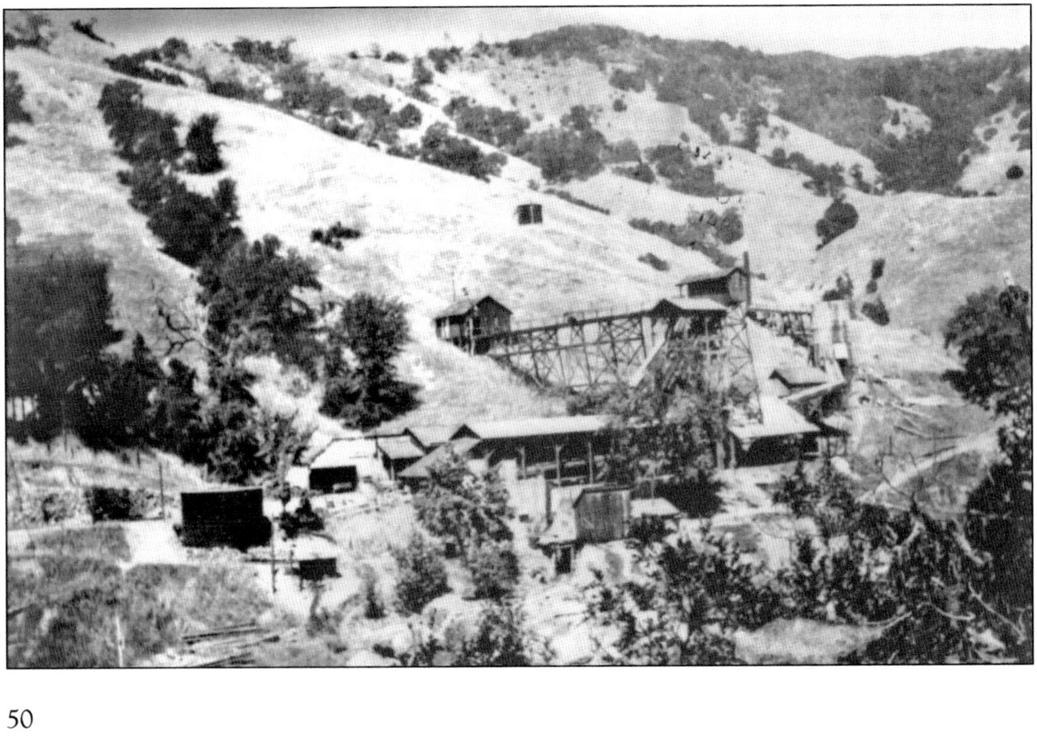

Four

Small Town Downtown

For much of Cloverdale's history, "Downtown" referred to a five-block stretch of West Street from Railroad Avenue to Third Street. Business activity flourished here, as well as near the train depot, where a feed and farm supply store and two hotels were located. After the Redwood Highway came to Cloverdale in the 1920s, businesses appeared to cater to local motorists and travelers passing through. By 1940, Cloverdale had eight service stations, four hotels, four auto dealers, and a drive-in restaurant. Bars and cafés on the outskirts provided three more gas pumps. At that time, the town had four grocery stores, a furniture store/mortuary, a variety store, two pharmacies, a department store, and other shops for hardware, shoe repair, paint, jewelry, baked goods, and pretty much anything else residents could possibly need. In the early 1950s, development on East First Street expanded the commercial area with additional businesses, including an appliance store and shops for men's and women's clothing. During the mid-20th century, as in its earliest days, Cloverdale was a self-sufficient town.

By the 1960s, portions of the Redwood Highway, by then known as Highway 101, had been converted to freeway status, with huge implications for the economy of Cloverdale. Traveling south for jobs and shopping became fast and easy. As larger retailers and shopping centers lured consumers, the vitality of downtown Cloverdale began to wane. When the freeway bypass was completed in 1994, businesses serving the traveling public lost customers, dealing the economy a further blow. Revitalization of the business district was undertaken, and residents were reminded to shop locally, an encouragement unnecessary during Cloverdale's first 100 years.

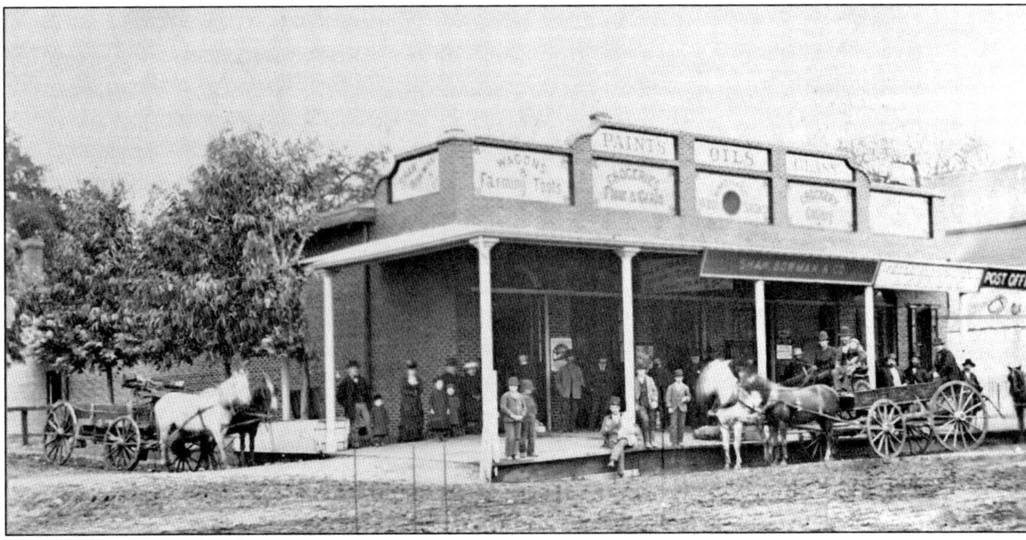

Isaac Ellis Shaw, who arrived in Cloverdale in 1872 at the age of 43, had by 1878 formed a partnership with John Bowman. The building erected on the corner of Second and West Streets to house their mercantile business is pictured here in 1881.

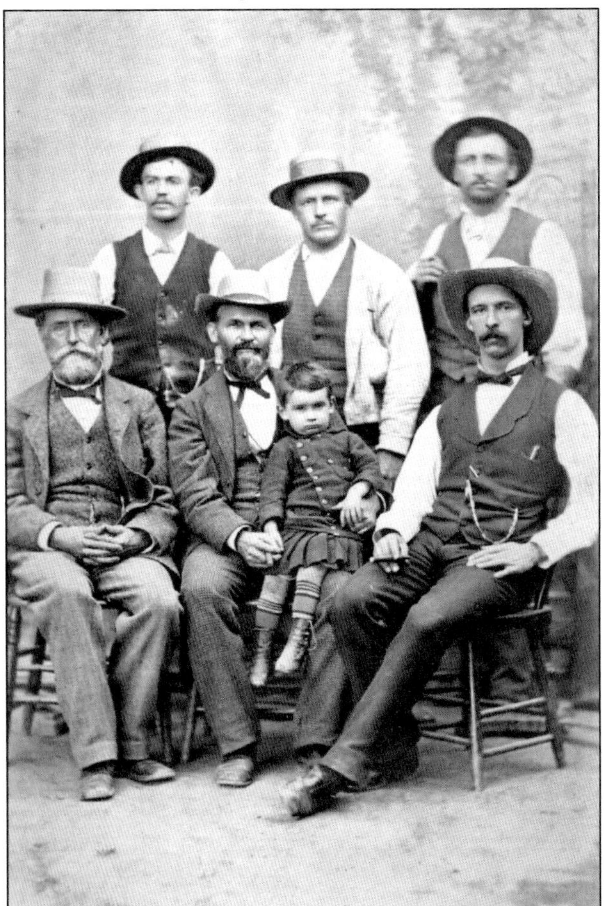

These early merchants posed for the photographer around 1880. From left to right are (seated) John Bowman, I. E. Shaw with son Frank on his lap, and John Harman; (standing) clerks Armand W. McCray, Peter Ludwig, and Jotham Sedgley. According to his obituary, Shaw was "one of the first men to operate trains of 'prairie schooners' across the continent to carry goods for his business and made a large fortune in that way."

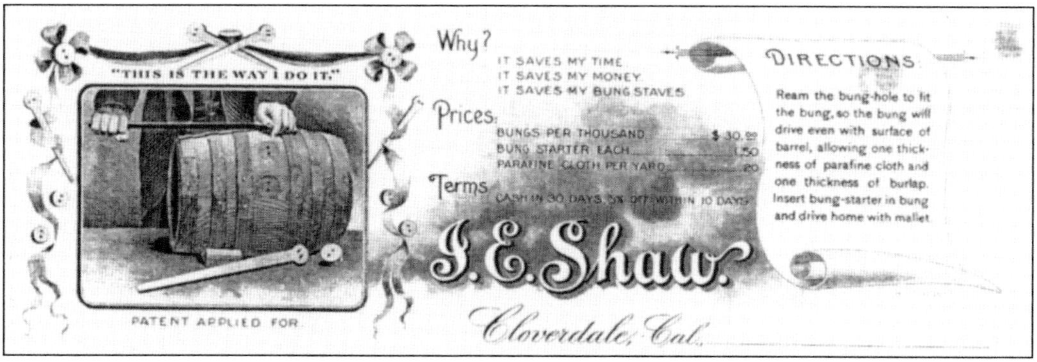

One of the items marketed by I. E. Shaw was a complete bung starter kit, which included bungs, along with the necessary bung "starter" and paraffin cloth. A bung is a stopper for the hole through which a cask, keg, or barrel is filled or emptied.

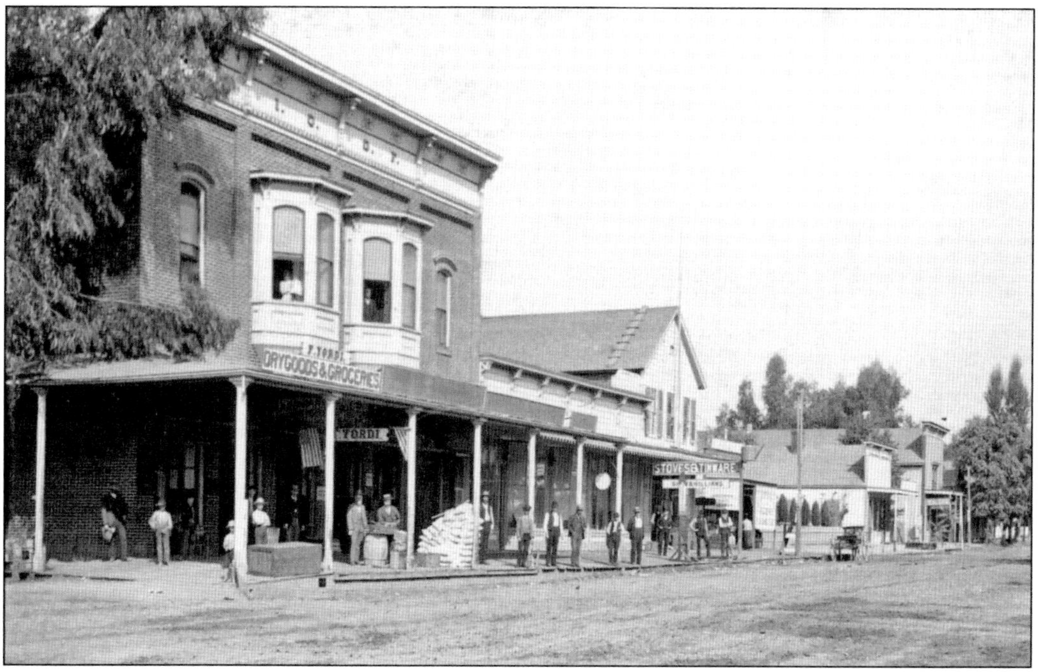

In 1888, Shaw sold his mercantile business to Fred Yordi to focus on the bank he had helped start. By the time of this photograph, around 1905, the Shaw Bowman Building had been enlarged to two stories and bore the sign "F. Yordi Dry Goods & Groceries." The building later passed into the hands of Imrie McClelland before it was sold to John Holloway. North of the Shaw Bowman Building was Pinschower's Emporium, known as the White House.

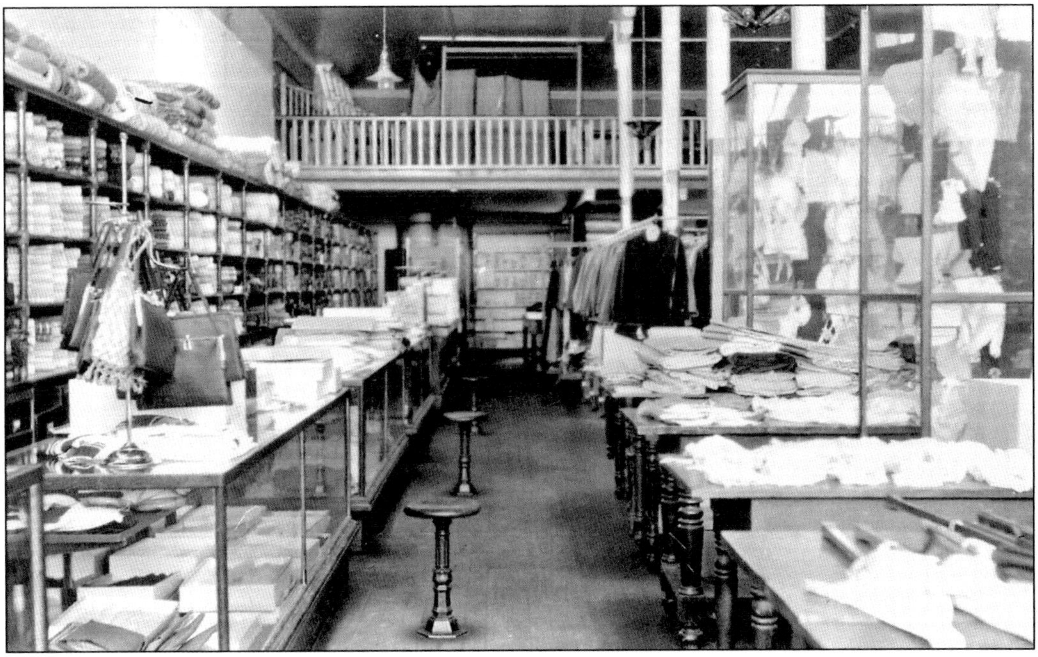

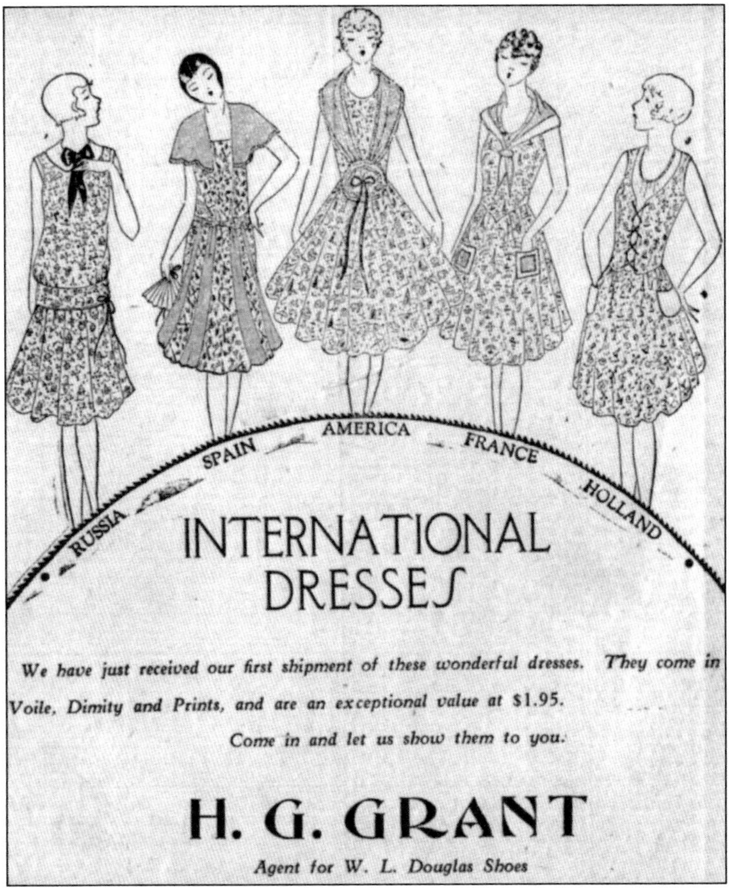

The Shaw Bowman Building changed names again in 1915 when hardware businessman H. G. "Gus" Grant purchased Yordi's dry-goods business. The name of the business was changed to reflect the new ownership—the H. G. Grant Department Store. In 1943, the business was taken over by Gus's daughter Bernice and her husband, Ray Donnelly, who operated the business under the name of the Donnelly Department Store until 1971. The once grand building was razed in 1975 to make room for a parking lot. The top image shows the interior of the store during the Grant years, and the image to the left is a *Cloverdale Reveille* advertisement from 1928.

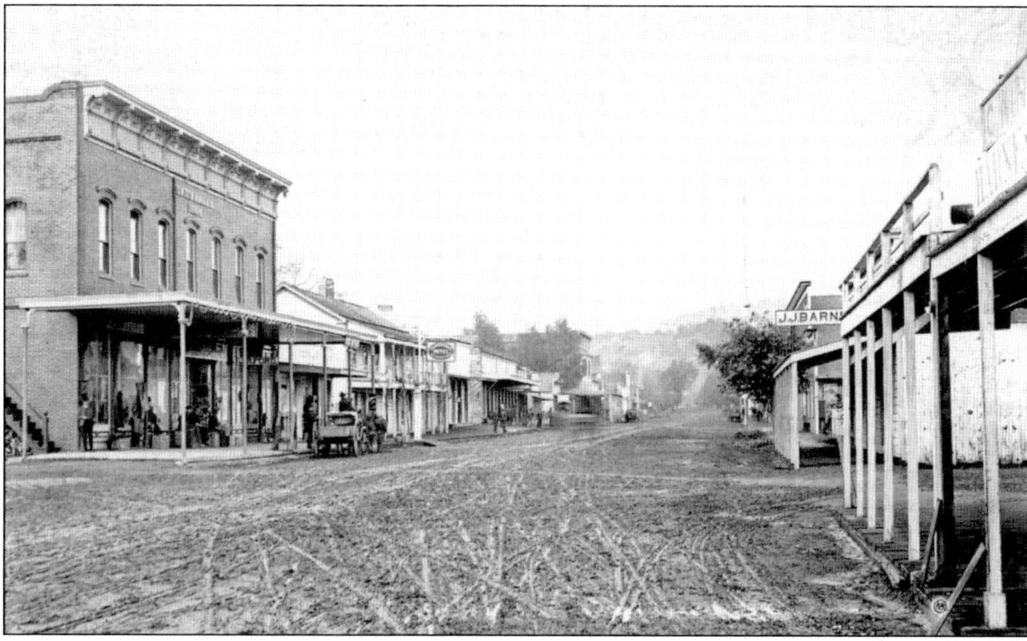

This c. 1890 photograph is of West Street looking north from First Street. On the corner is the imposing Union Hall, built in 1884 by James F. Hoadley. The next two-story wooden building is the Cloverdale Hotel, erected in 1858 by W. R. Dodge. In October 1872, the hotel was leased by Michael Menihan, who eventually gave up the Cloverdale Hotel and devoted himself to running the U.S. Hotel.

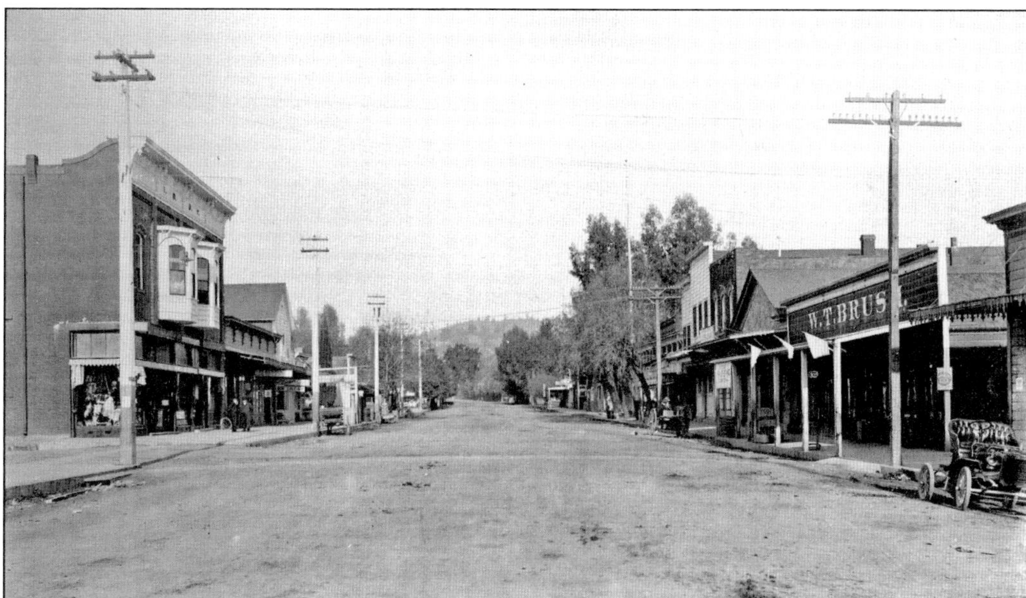

This view of West Street, looking north from Second Street around 1910, shows the W. T. Brush dry-goods store in the right foreground. The U.S. Hotel is up the street behind the row of trees. Other businesses on the east side of the street around that time included Thompson's French Laundry, Chet Byron's Saloon, Ogle Harness Shop, Brush and Son Meat Market, Will Long Hardware, and the G. F. Warren Garage.

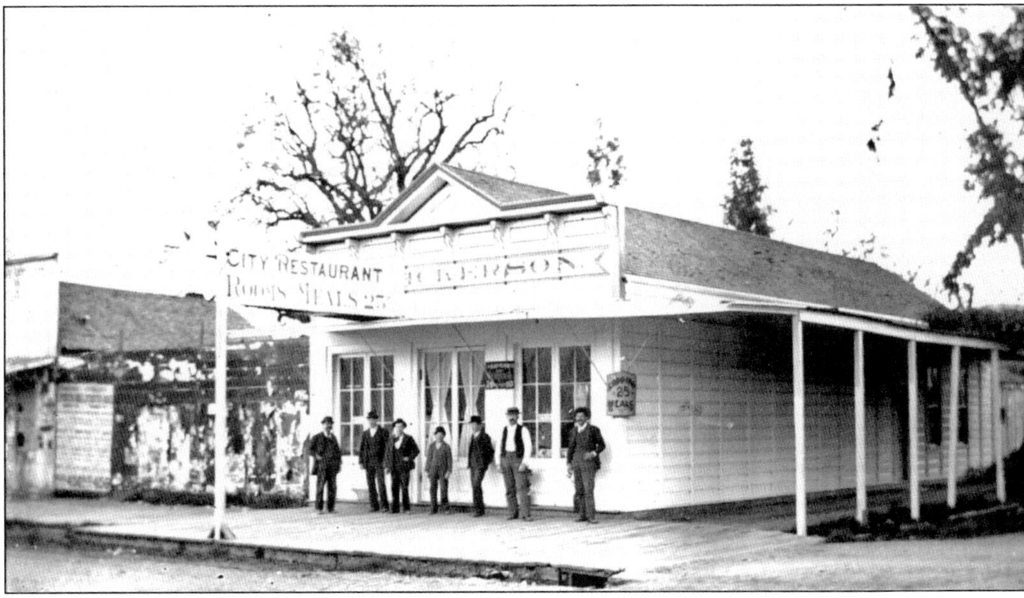

Around 1896 on the southwest corner of Second and West Streets, a restaurant was offering rooms and meals for 25¢. Prior to 1896, the building housed the Palace Saloon. The Bank of Cloverdale was built on this corner in 1907.

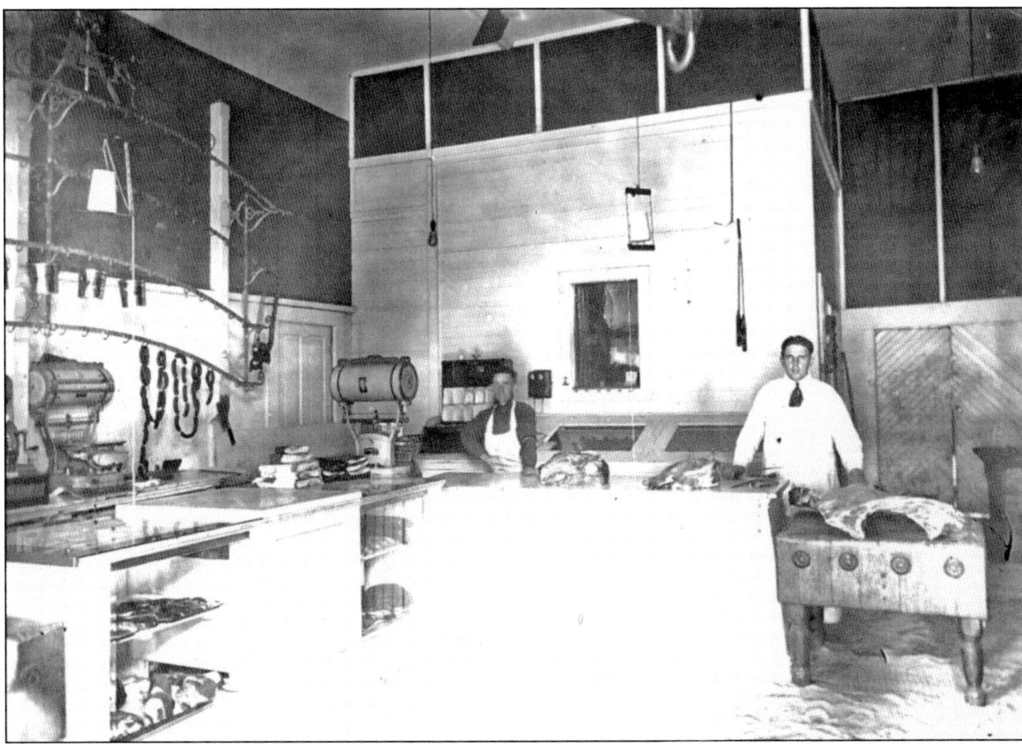

Clem Butler (right) and Pete Vassar are seen in 1918 manning the butcher counter of Butler and Zittleman's Grocery Store. In those days, there were no pre-packaged or frozen meats, just carcasses hanging in walk-in lockers waiting to be carved to order. Butler ran his own grocery from 1922 to 1946 and later worked in the meat department of the Economy Market.

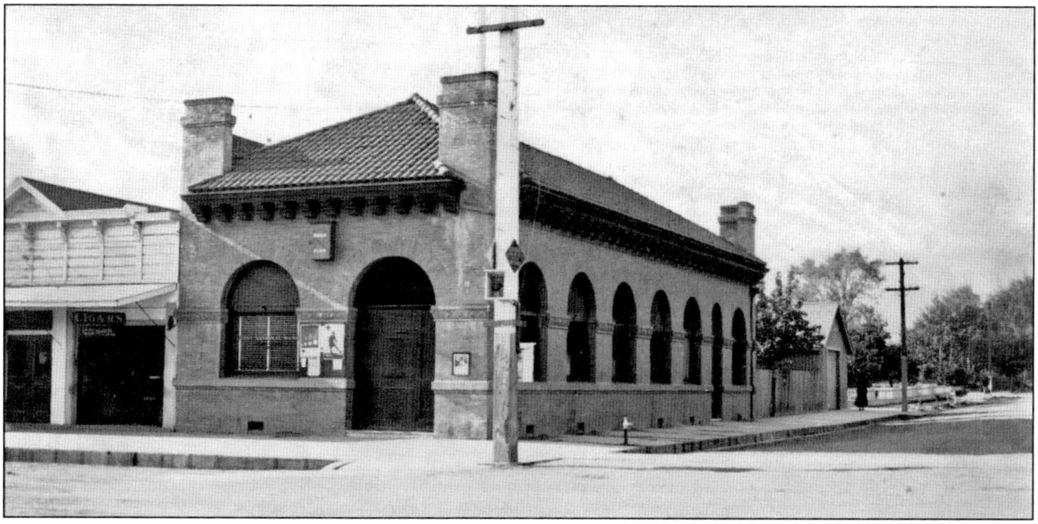

In the early 1880s, banking activities were conducted out of the Shaw Bowman Building. The operation became official on February 25, 1884, when a bank charter was obtained by I. E. Shaw and six other merchants. First called the Cloverdale Exchange Bank and later the Bank of Cloverdale, it became the First National Bank of Cloverdale when it was federally chartered in 1918. I. E. Shaw was the first president. He was succeeded in 1894 by William T. Brush and then by his son Charles Butler Shaw in 1907. That same year, the bank moved to its own building (pictured above) on the corner of West and Second Streets. C. B. Shaw served as president for more than 43 years. Together with his able cashier, Charles L. Sedgley, Shaw guided the bank through the Great Depression. Seen below around 1910 are C. L. Sedgley (right) and director Walter Sink.

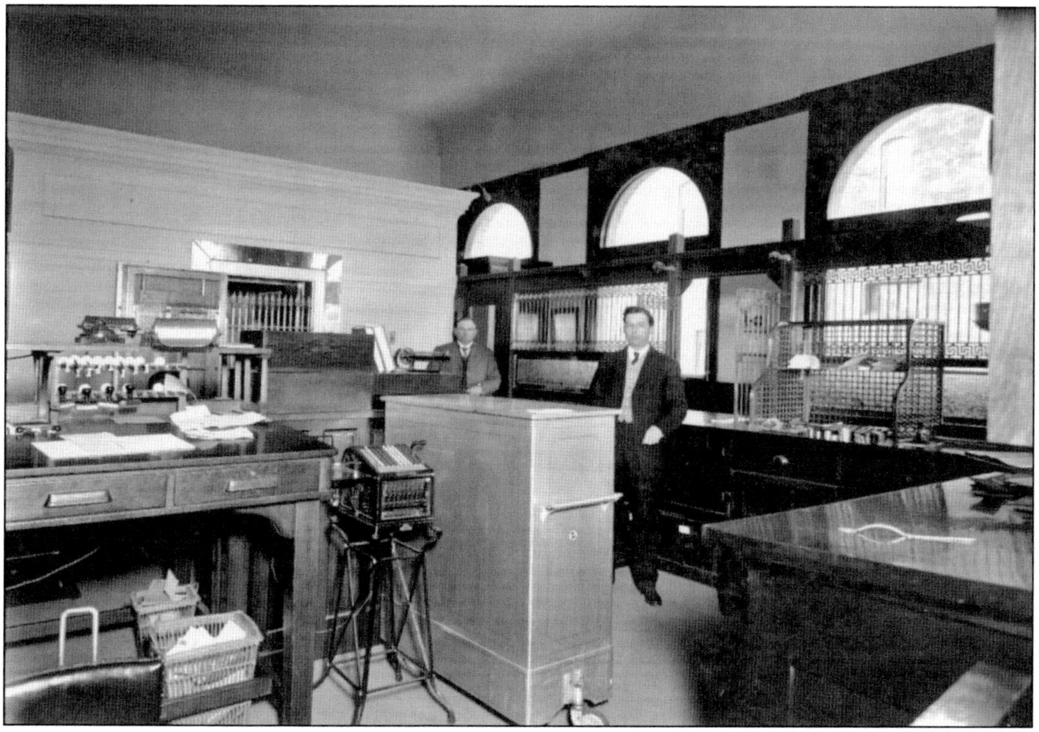

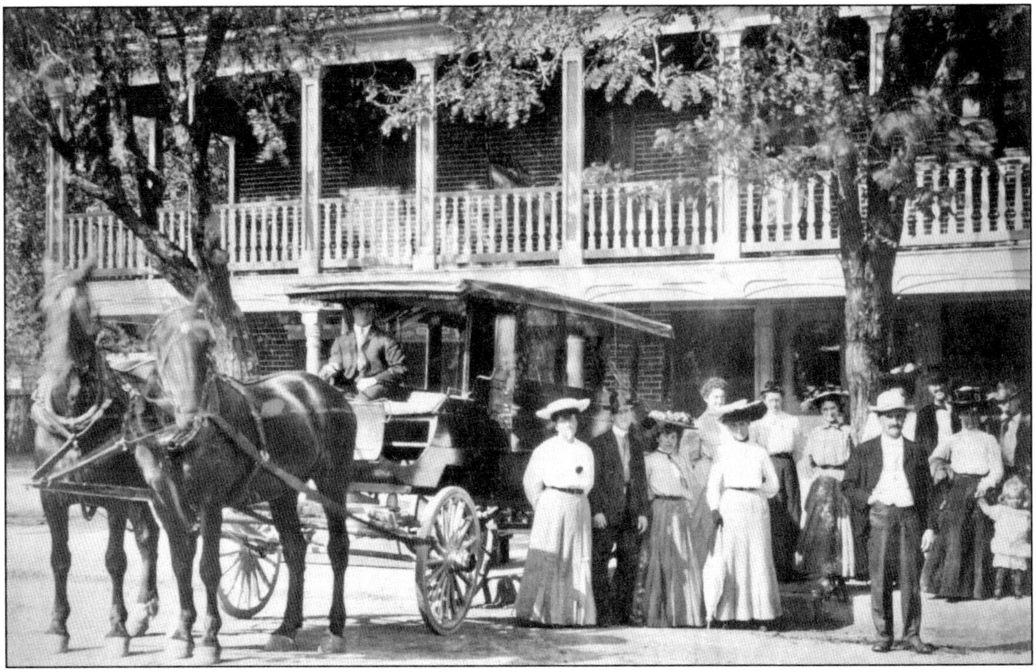

The United States Hotel, popularly referred to as the U.S. Hotel, which occupied the southeast corner of Second and West Streets, served as the stagecoach stop in Cloverdale and also operated its own stages to the railroad depot. It was built of native brick by one of the town's early settlers, Fred Gerkhardt, around 1860.

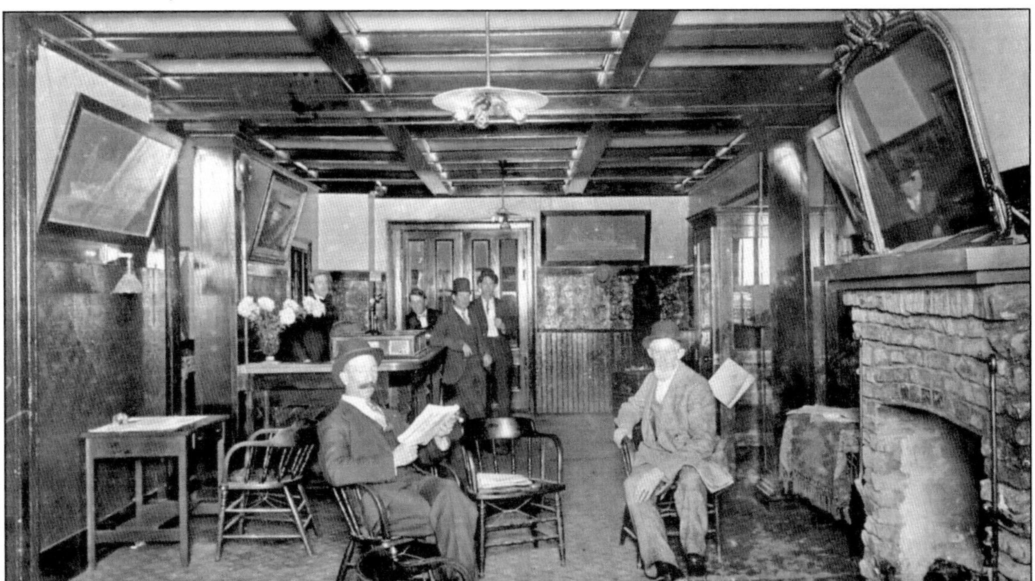

Proprietor Michael Menihan (right) sits with an unidentified man in the lobby of the U.S. Hotel around 1880. Menihan was born in Ireland, made his way to California in 1869, and two years later came to Sonoma County, where he participated in the construction of the Northwestern Pacific Railroad. Menihan was instrumental in establishing St. Peter's Catholic Church in Cloverdale. The home he built for his family still stands at 124 Broad Street.

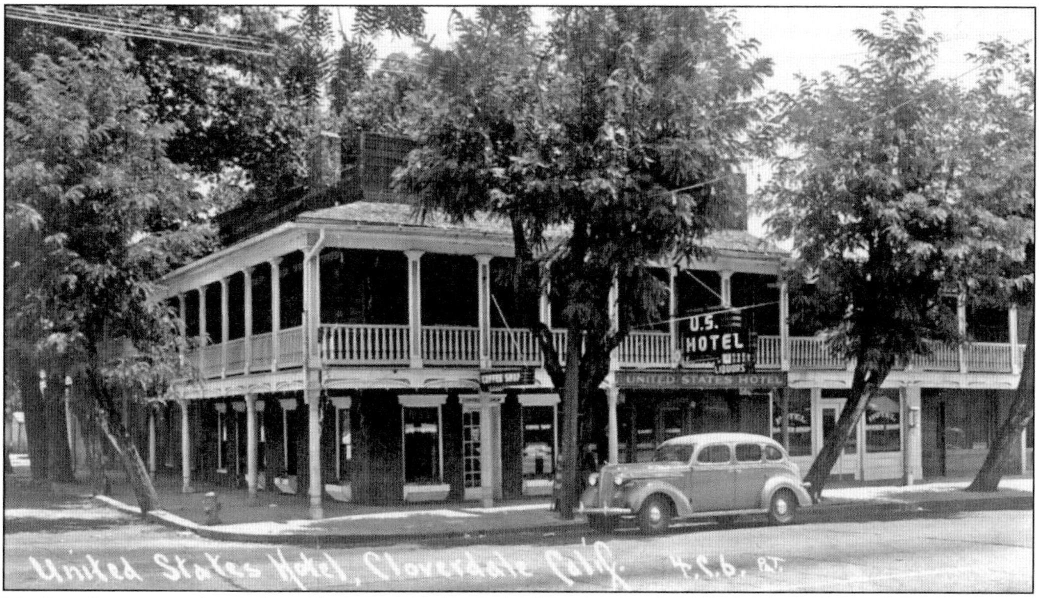

Under the ownership of Purd Ingram, who bought the hotel in 1919, the U.S. Hotel continued to enjoy popularity. It underwent a major renovation in the mid-1940s only to be destroyed on July 25, 1947, in one of Cloverdale's most spectacular fires. This photograph shows how the hotel looked in the 1930s.

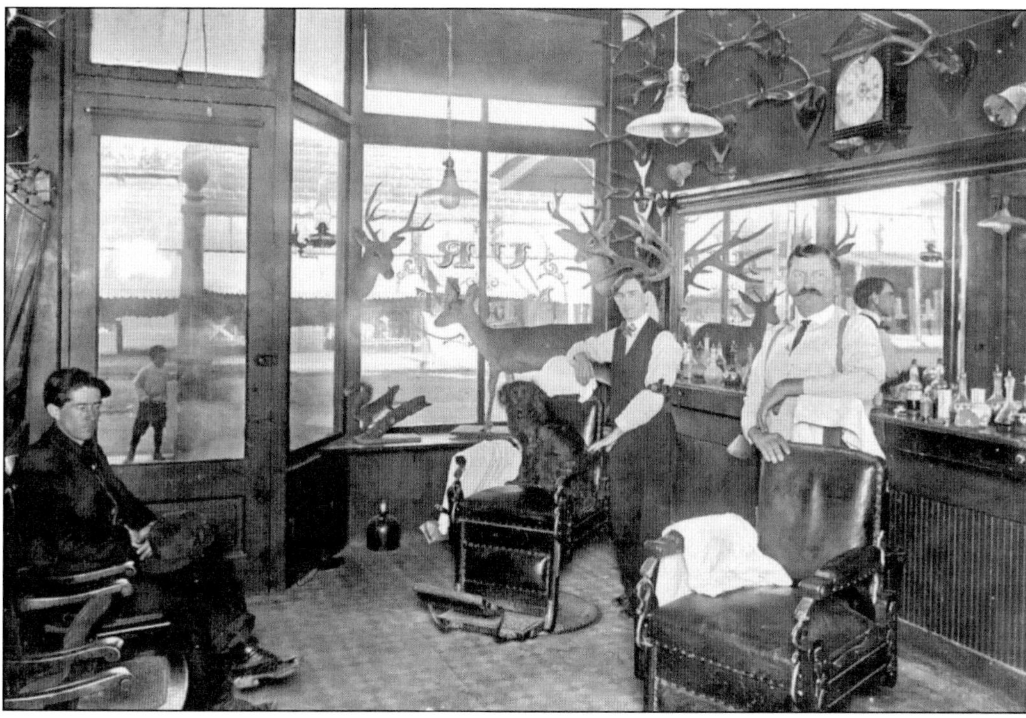

Two barbers pose and a customer waits at the U R Next Barbershop around 1910. The shop was located on the west side of West Street between First and Second Streets. Next door was Nick Ahren's tobacco stand, just south of the National Bank (now Westamerica). The brick building housing the barbershop was deemed earthquake unsafe and was torn down in 2007.

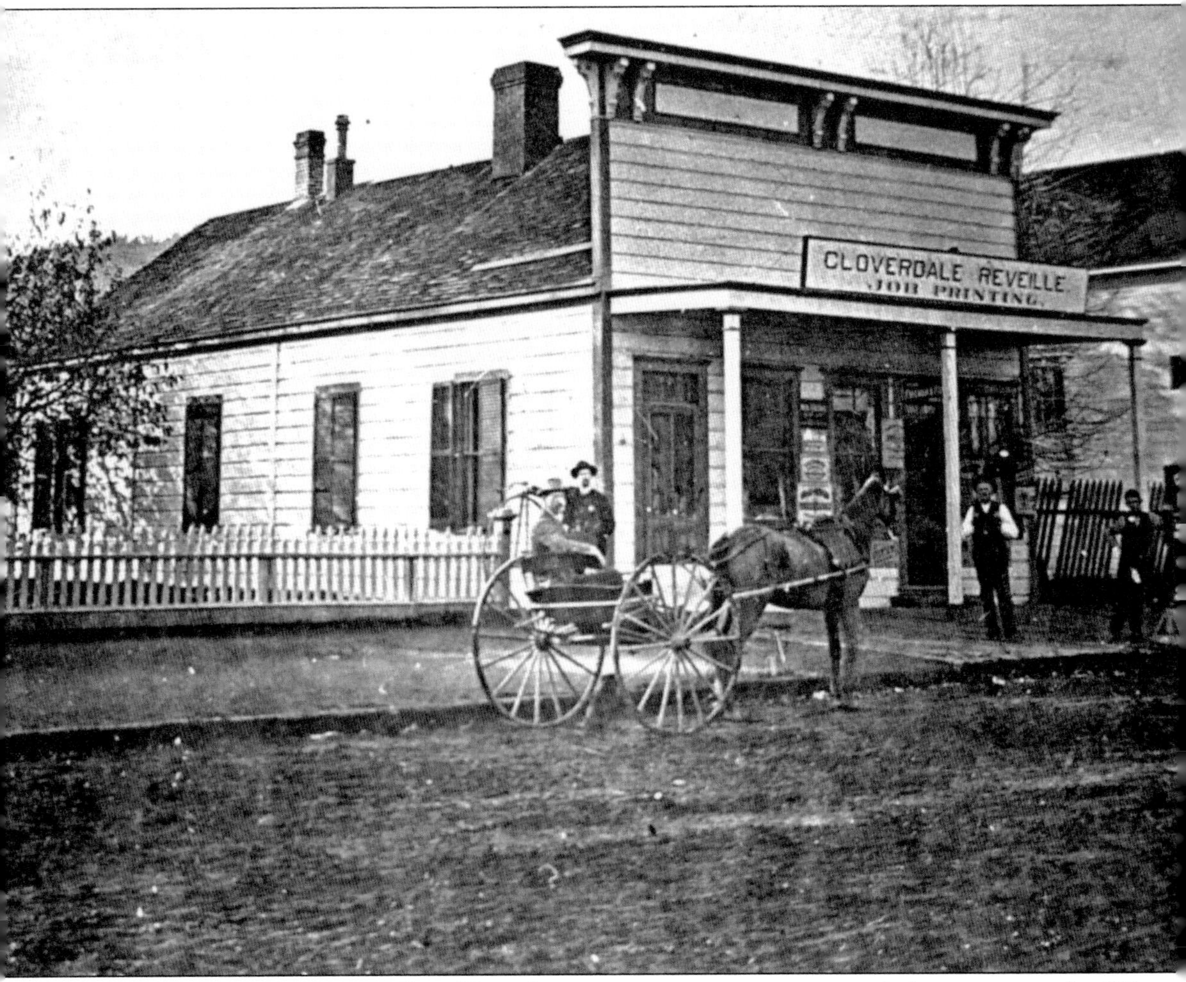

In 2008, the *Cloverdale Reveille* will have been in continuous operation with the same name for 129 years, longer than any other weekly newspaper in California. The *Reveille* was reportedly born in a two-room house on the corner of West and Third Streets. The building that housed its first plant (pictured above) still stands at 219 North Cloverdale Boulevard. Before the founding of the *Reveille* by W. S. Walker in 1879, there had been several short-lived newspapers, including the *Cloverdale Review*, started by W. J. Bowman in 1872, and the *Cloverdale Bee*, in business for just six months. George Baer bought the *Reveille* in 1885; Rev. Clem Bradshaw introduced linotype and press in the 1920s. Other owners included Bruce and Stella Wells, Carl Simmons and Leinad Simis, and the Dewarts. The most recent transfer of ownership occurred in 1988 when Bonny Jean Hanchett purchased the *Reveille* from Dean DeVries. (Courtesy Photo Graphix.)

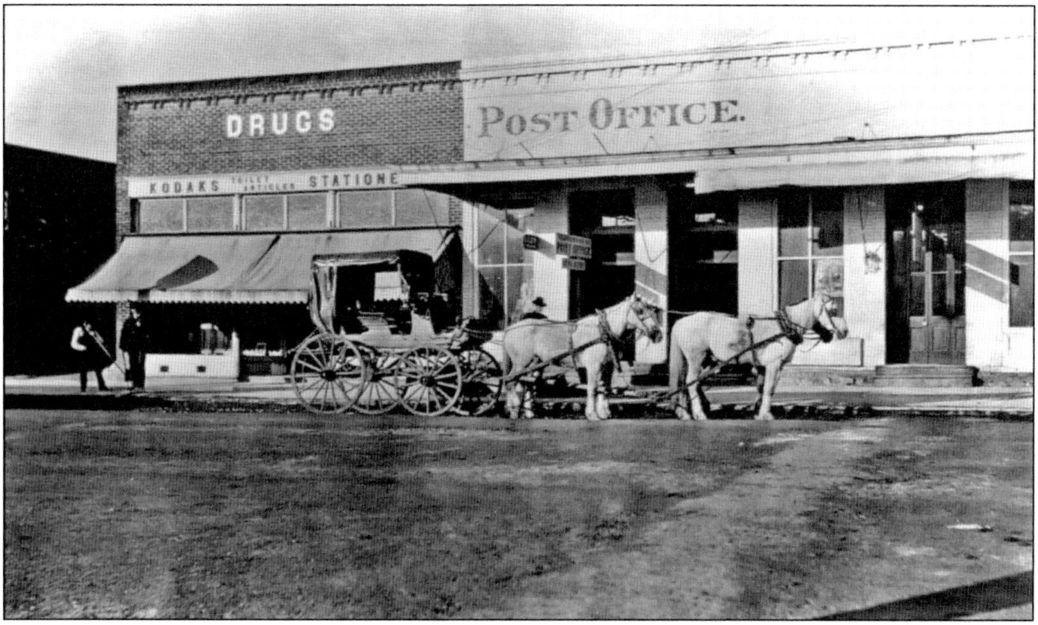

Cloverdale got its first post office and postmaster, John Hartman, in 1857. In 1878, Jasper Linville kept a post office at 229 North West Street. The post office was moved to the Carrie block (seen above) in 1914 and to the Druids Building after 1923. The present facility on Broad Street dates from 1951, when Fred Zittleman was postmaster. (Courtesy Sonoma County Library.)

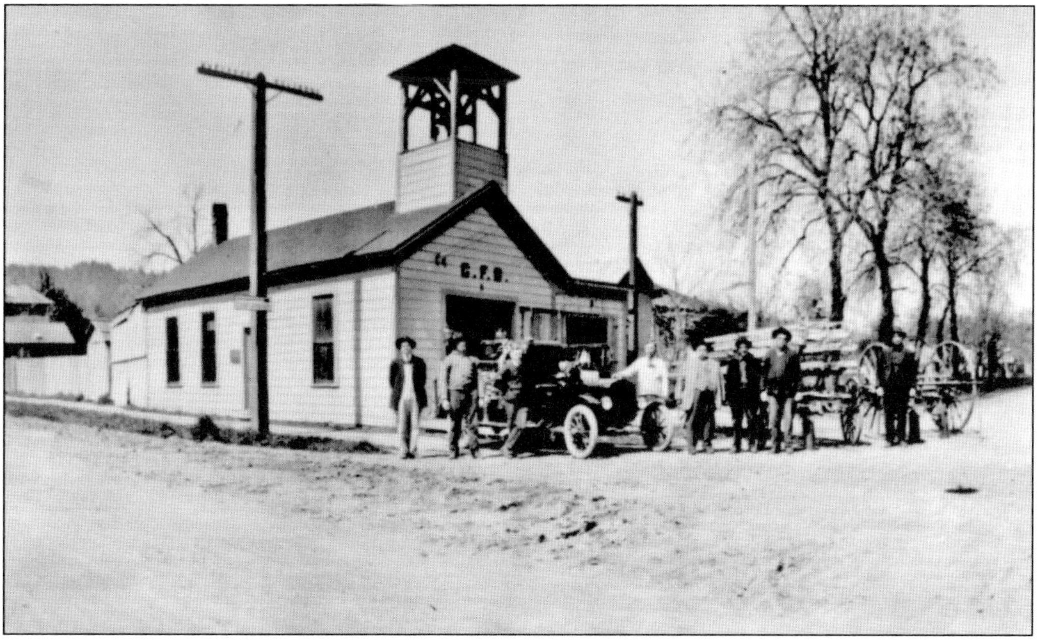

Cloverdale firemen pose in 1923 in front of the station, built in 1887 on the corner of Second and Commercial Streets, the current site of the Grange Hall. They were probably showing off their recently purchased used Model T fire engine. The motor-powered engine replaced the hand-pulled hose cart that had been in use since 1886. In 1929, Cloverdale upgraded again to a new American LaFrance pumper truck. (Courtesy Marie Hill.)

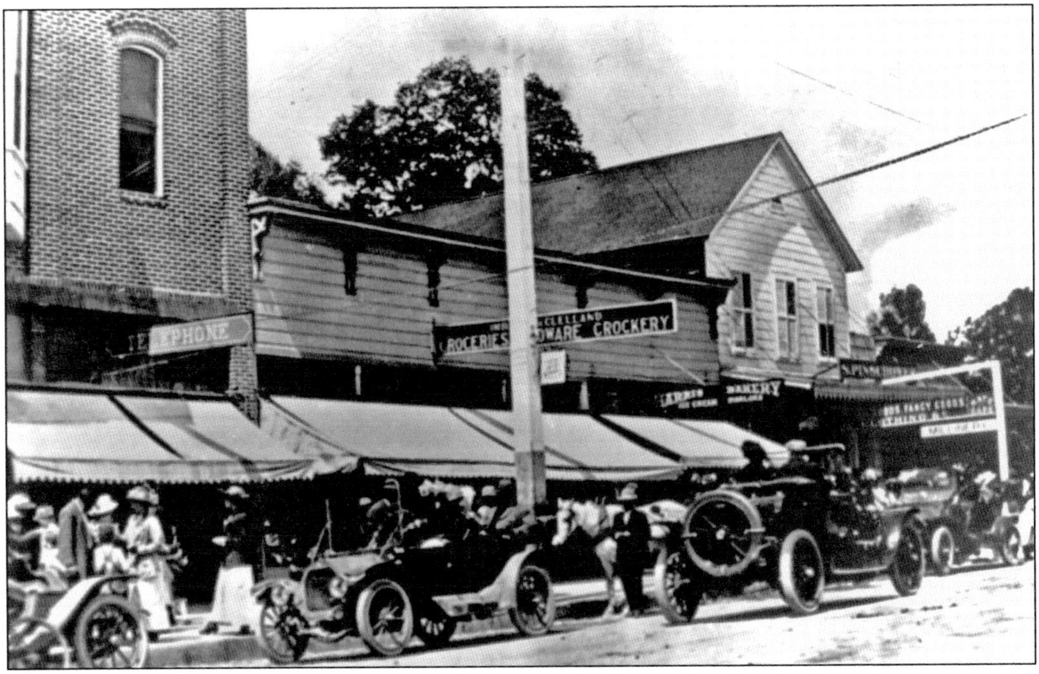

Telephone service came to town around 1883, when the first and only telephone for years was in the bakery. If an important call came in, clerk Mary Sedgley would have to rush out in search of the recipient. The bakery, first owned by William Leist and later by C. W. Harris, is seen to the right of the pole in this 1915 photograph.

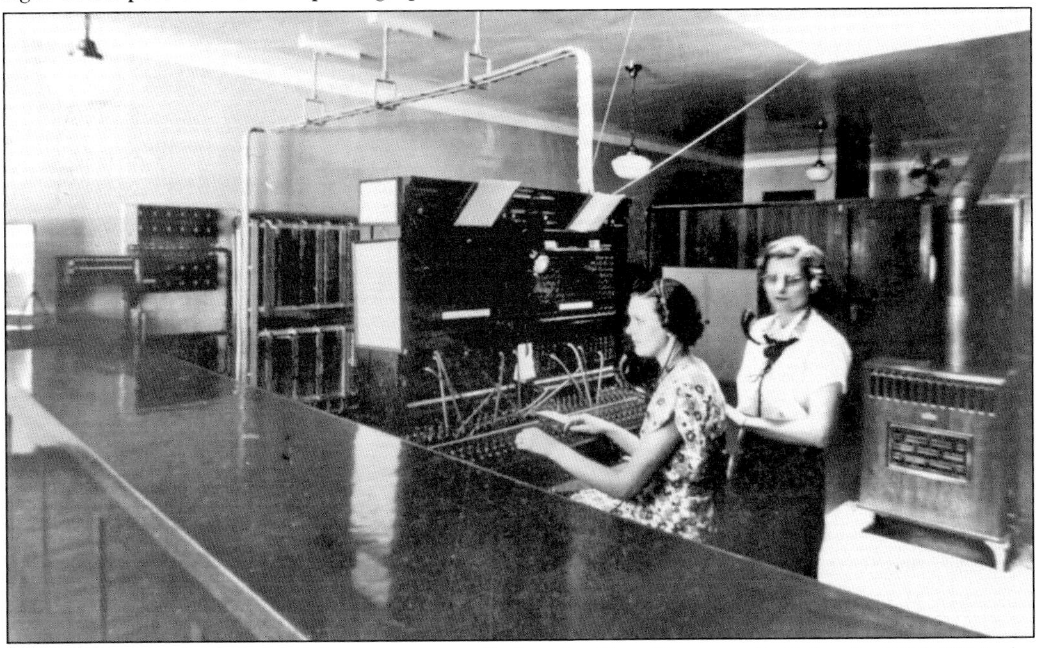

Cloverdale's first telephone exchange was installed in the Shaw Bowman Building in 1907. With the growth of telephone use, a new exchange was built by Thomas and Edna Mitchell at 112 West First Street. Operators around 1935 included Viola Kubberness Groves (at the switchboard) and Elsie Ferrari Karr (standing). The exchange was closed in September 1953 when Cloverdale "went dial."

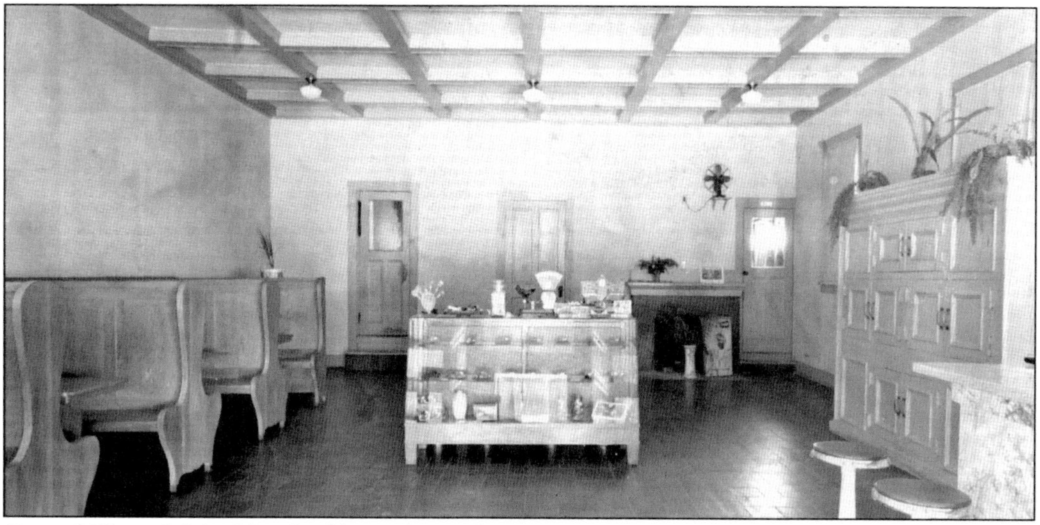

One of Cloverdale's oldest buildings, located at 117 North Cloverdale Boulevard, was purchased in 1865 by Charles Mitchell, who operated a saloon there. Charles's sons Thomas and Jake ran it as the Mitchell Brothers Saloon after the start of the 20th century. It was the only building left standing after the Hoadley block fire of 1915. This photograph shows the interior when it was a restaurant run by Thomas and Edna Mitchell from 1927 until 1945.

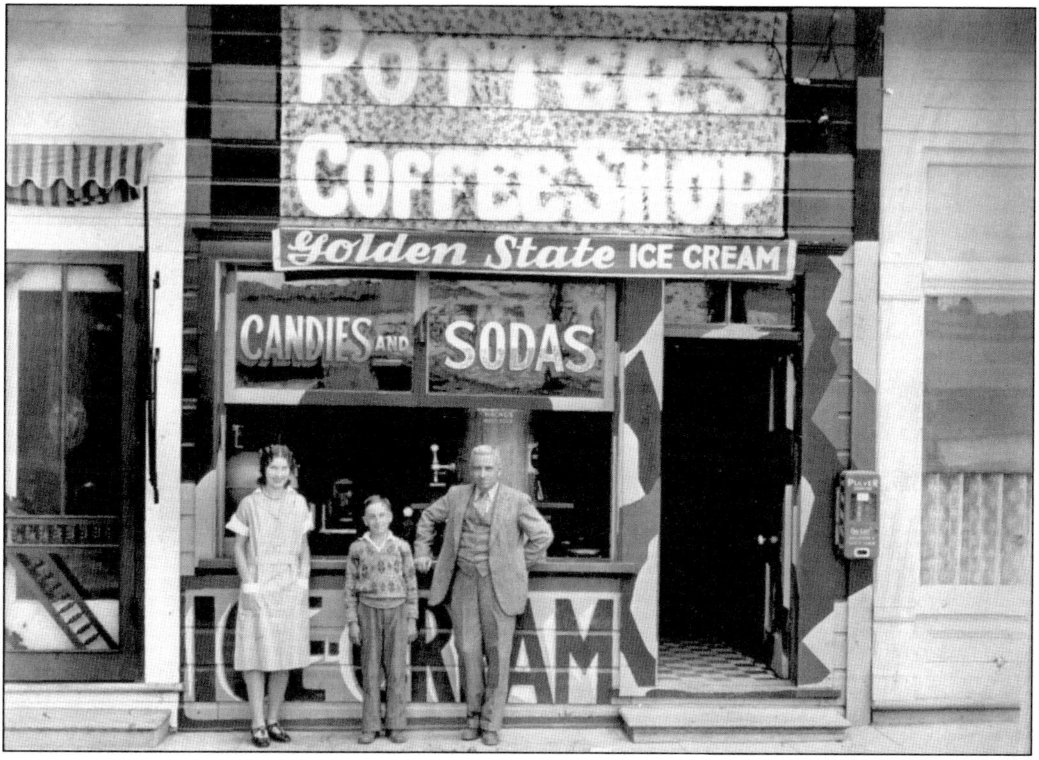

The building located at 219 North Cloverdale Boulevard, currently the site of Photo Graphix, is one of Cloverdale's oldest. The *Cloverdale Reveille* had its first office here in 1879. It was a jewelry store from 1912 into the 1920s, Potter's Coffee Shop in the 1930s, and later the site of several restaurants. From left to right are Evelyn Frost Scatena, Billie Potter, and Christo Potter.

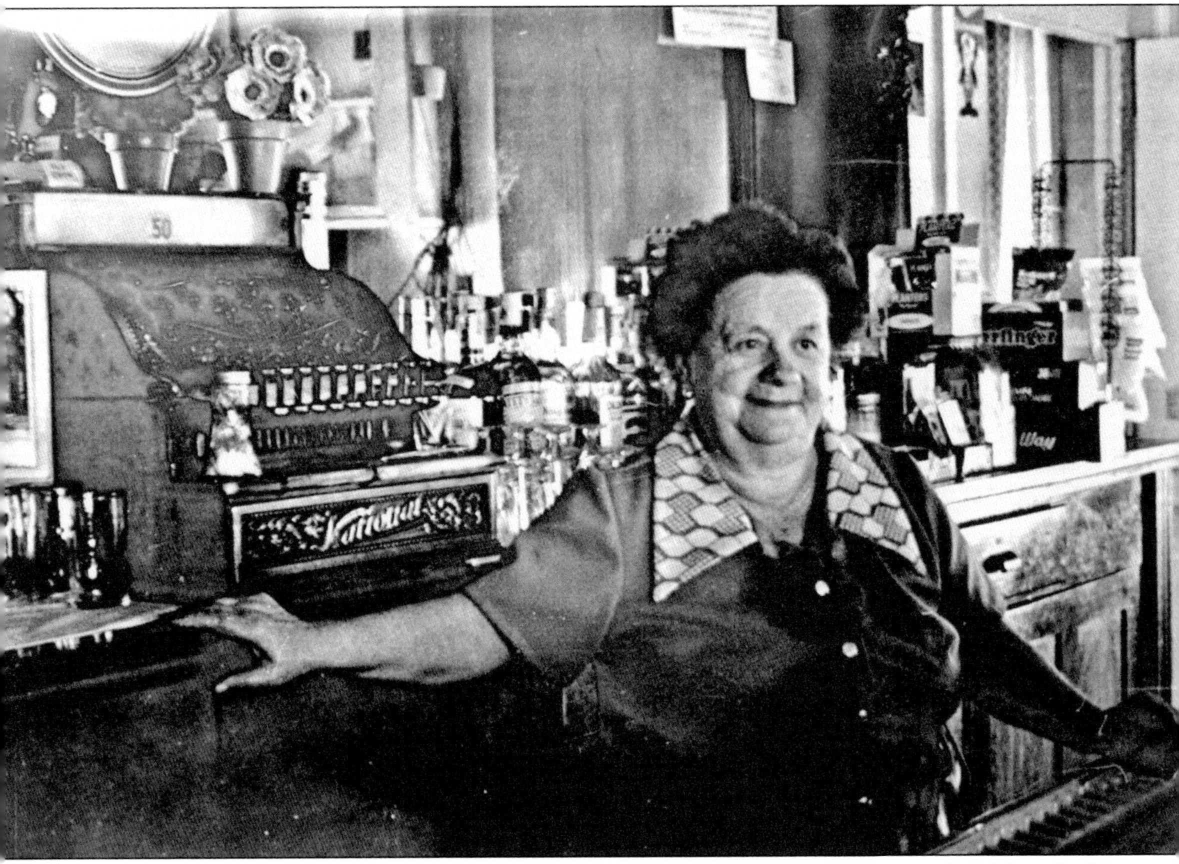

The Dante Hotel, built at the corner of Railroad Avenue and East Street around 1888 as the New Toscano, was bought in 1922 by Ermete Giannecchini, who had immigrated to Cloverdale 11 years earlier. In the 1930s and 1940s, when the railroad was running six commuter and innumerable freight trains daily, the Dante had its heyday, and in the 1950s, it enjoyed another boom serving mill workers and truckers. Ermete's daughter Tosca, seen here at the Dante bar, was 10 years old when she arrived in Cloverdale from Italy in 1922. From 1936 until they retired in 1976, Tosca and her husband, Marino Bianchini, owned and managed the Dante, where customers enjoyed "Mama Tosca's" plentiful Italian meals, prepared with her homegrown produce.

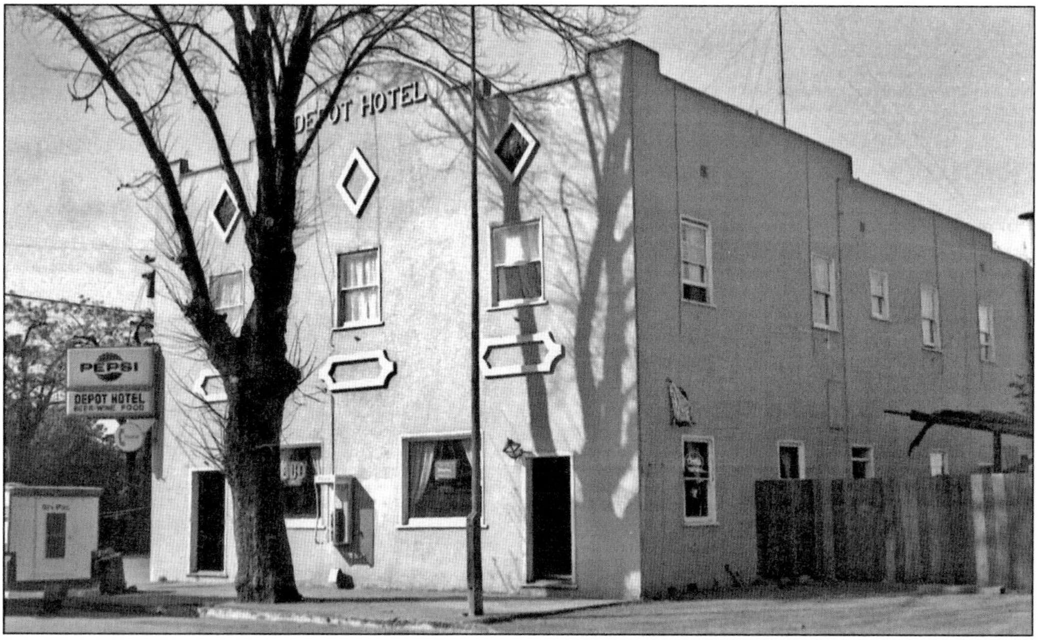

On the northwest corner of Railroad and East Streets in the 1920s was a hotel known as the Roosevelt, owned and operated by Marie Menzelli. In 1945, Curly Waitman bought the property, by then known as the Depot Hotel, and opened the popular Curly's bar. The Depot Hotel, pictured here in 1980, has recently been remodeled into offices and apartments.

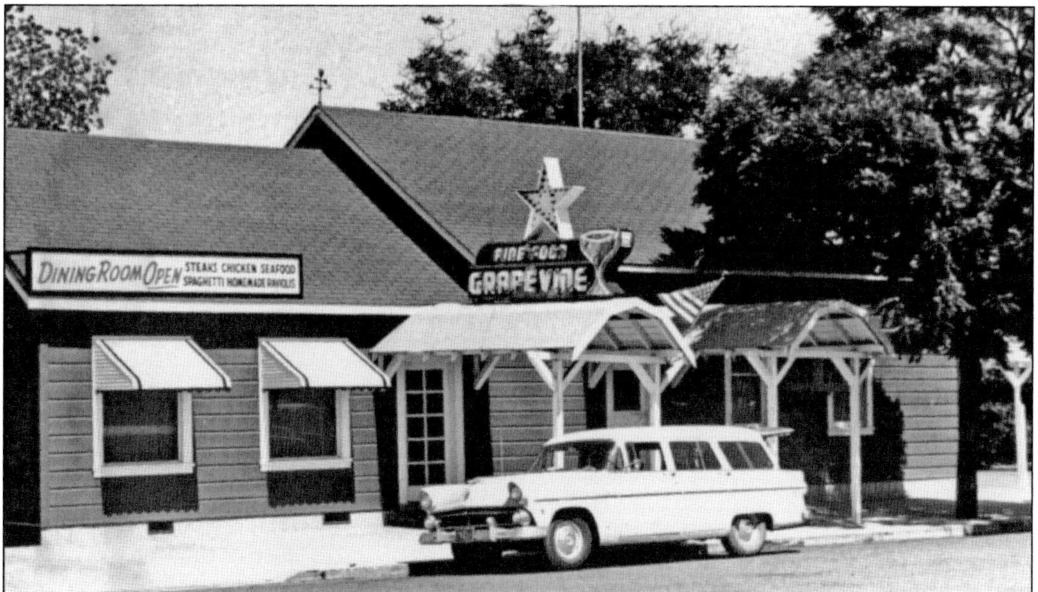

At the corner of Cloverdale Boulevard and Railroad Avenue was the popular Grapevine restaurant and bar, seen here in the 1950s when, operated by Joe and Dina Giovannetti, it was well known for Dina's delicious cooking. In the mid-1940s, co-owners were Stanley Brush, Al Giampaoli, and Bill Ritch. The property, owned for many years by Natale and Mary Bacci, served in the 1930s and 1940s as the base for Natale's business—transporting mail, groceries, and people to The Geysers. (Courtesy Paul Giovannetti.)

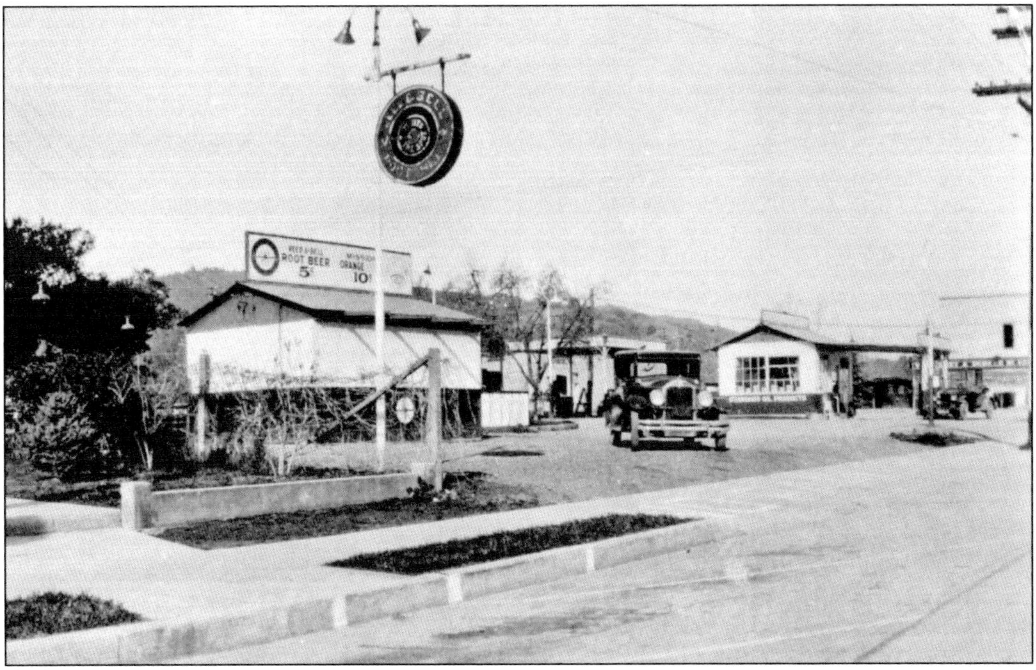

Pick's Drive-In, located at 117 South Cloverdale Boulevard, started out in the early 1920s as a Reed and Bell root-beer stand (pictured here in 1930) because of the popularity of root beer as a substitute for beer during Prohibition. The Pickards, for whom Pick's Drive-In is named, owned the stand from 1950 to about 1975. The drive-in, by some accounts the oldest in the United States, is still popular today. (Courtesy of Claudia Clow.)

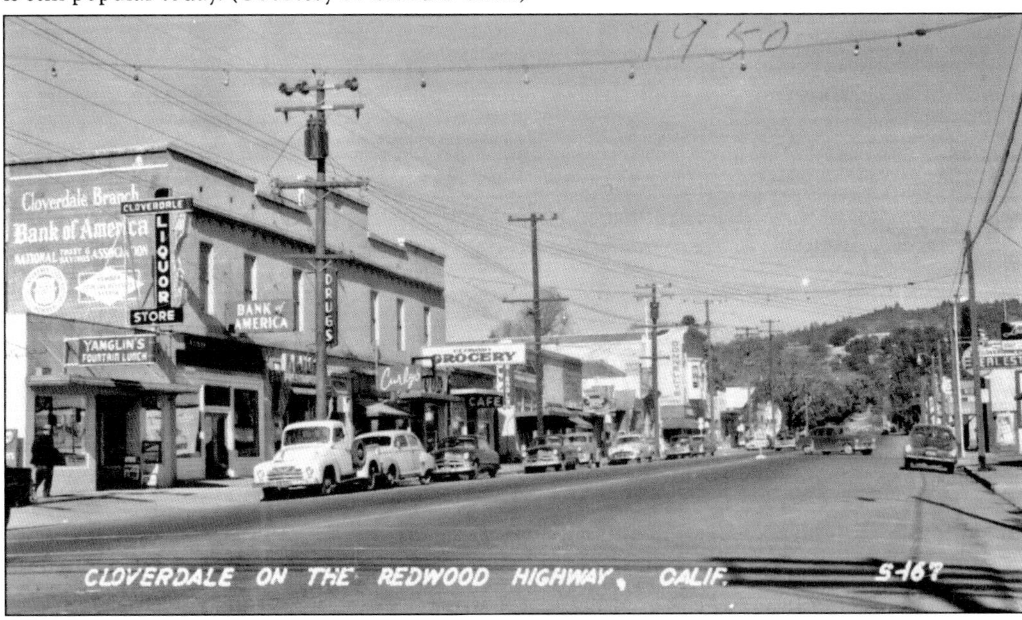

This view of West Street in the early 1950s shows the Bank of America when it was in the two-story Druids Building, where it opened in 1928. In 1956, its operations moved across the street into a new building, which today houses the Exchange Bank. Two longtime branch managers, Joe Giovannetti and Bob Galli, ran the Bank of America for several decades.

Five

Getting Here, Getting Around, and Passing Through

The story of Cloverdale cannot be told without considering the impact of developments in transportation. Stagecoaches, the railroad, automobiles, and trucks have all played roles in the history of the town.

The railroad reached Cloverdale in the same year the town was incorporated—1872. As the northern terminus of the railroad for 17 years, Cloverdale was an important transportation hub, with stagecoaches carrying passengers and mail to and from all points of the compass. Wagons hauled manufactured goods from the depot and delivered local crops and products into town for shipment to the Bay Area. Even after the extension of tracks northward to Ukiah, Cloverdale remained a regional hub. The presence of the railroad allowed the local development of commercial agriculture for markets outside of Cloverdale. Moreover, the early flourishing of nearby resorts and the popularity of the Citrus Fair had everything to do with the presence of the railroad, which made Cloverdale and the natural wonders of its environs so readily accessible.

The Redwood Highway, which eventually stretched from the Golden Gate Bridge into southern Oregon, was another major development. After the paved highway reached Cloverdale in 1926, the role of transportation in the town's economy was transformed. Over time, Cloverdale became a town that catered to the needs of travelers and truckers passing through to the north or south. After the two-lane highway to the south was converted into a freeway in the 1960s, the volume of motorists and truckers grew, as did the number of Cloverdale residents going outside of town for shopping and jobs. When the Highway 101 bypass was completed in the 1990s, with both positive and negative ramifications for Cloverdale, the impact on the town was dramatic and is still being felt today.

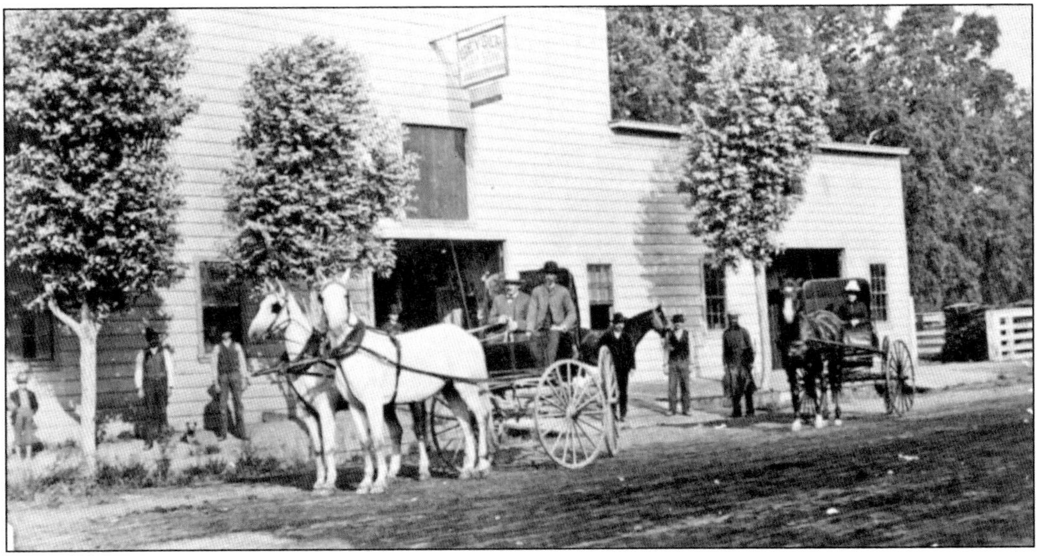

In the 1880s, John Sissingood ran the Geyser Livery Stable on South West Street (now 215 South Cloverdale Boulevard). In those days, every community had livery stables from which rigs and teams of horses were hired and where rigs and gear were cleaned and polished. The hay loft of Sissingood's stable was also the home of the 1895 and 1896 Citrus Fairs.

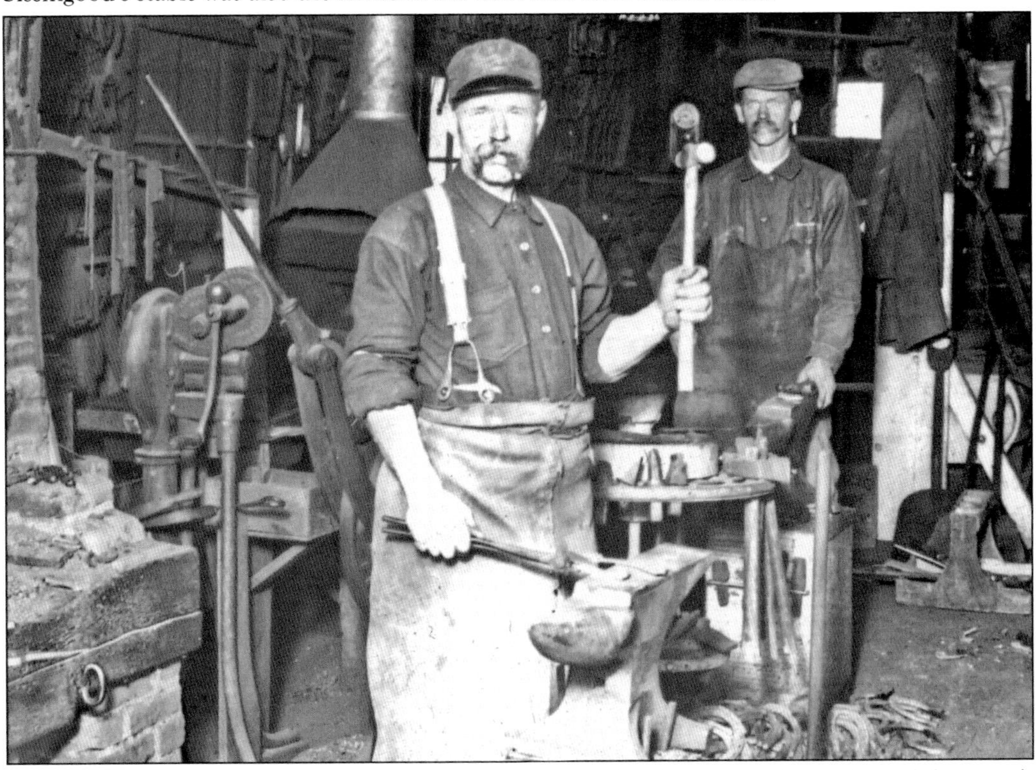

Two unidentified men are pictured in an early Cloverdale blacksmith shop. One of the town's early blacksmiths was Amos Bentley, who advertised his Second Street shop in the 1900 *Cloverdale Reveille*. Blacksmith shops were necessities in that era. Smithies shod animals, made and repaired wheels and machinery, sharpened plows, and, in general, kept the populace on the move.

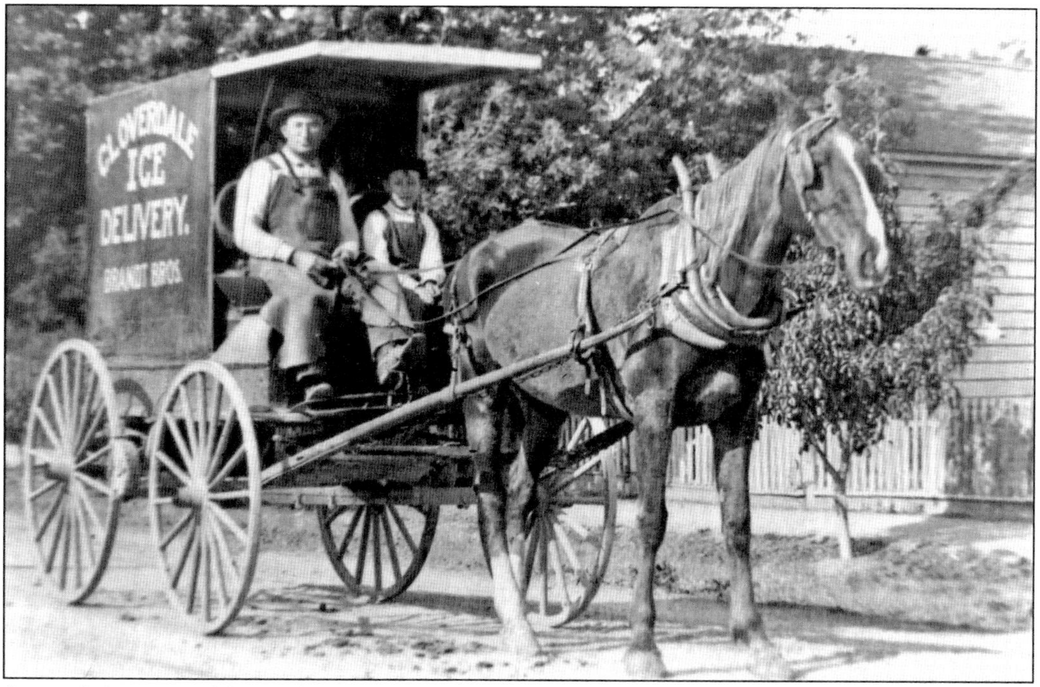

Around the cusp of the 20th century, ice was delivered to homes and businesses by horse-drawn cart, as seen in this photograph of the Brandt Brothers Ice Delivery business. Ice was stored in the Ice House, a stone building on the east side of West Street. In 1947, the fire that destroyed the U.S. Hotel and several other wooden structures was stopped at that stone building.

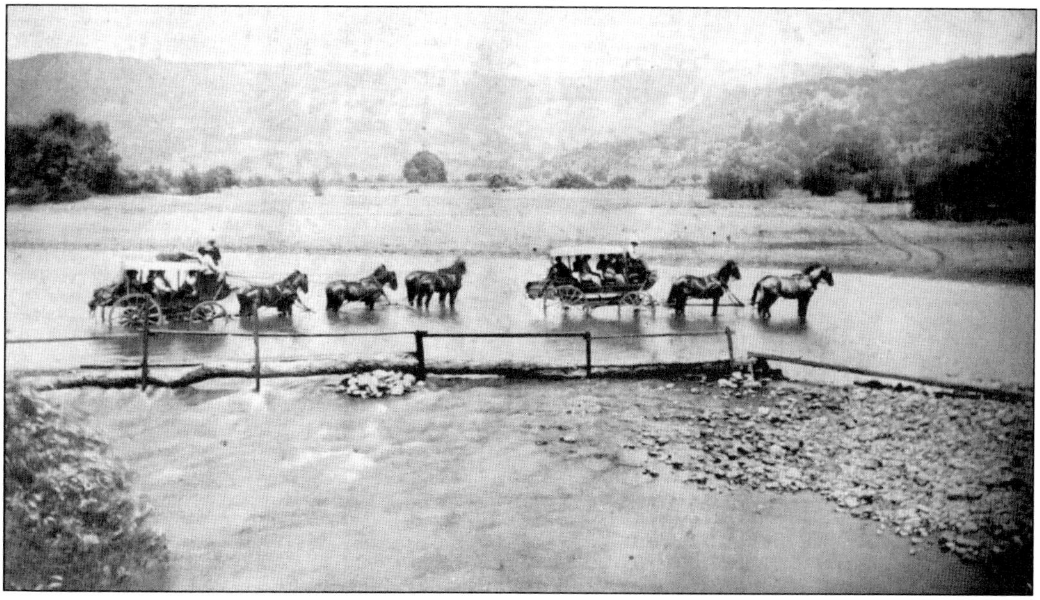

Most of the stagecoaches operating daily in and out of Cloverdale were four- to six-horse-drawn Boston and Thorough-brace coaches. The suspension was a series of leather straps up to 3 inches thick and 4 inches wide, attached front and rear, which allowed the coach body to sway. The coaches seen here crossing the Russian River were possibly headed to The Geysers. (Courtesy Lucille Sink.)

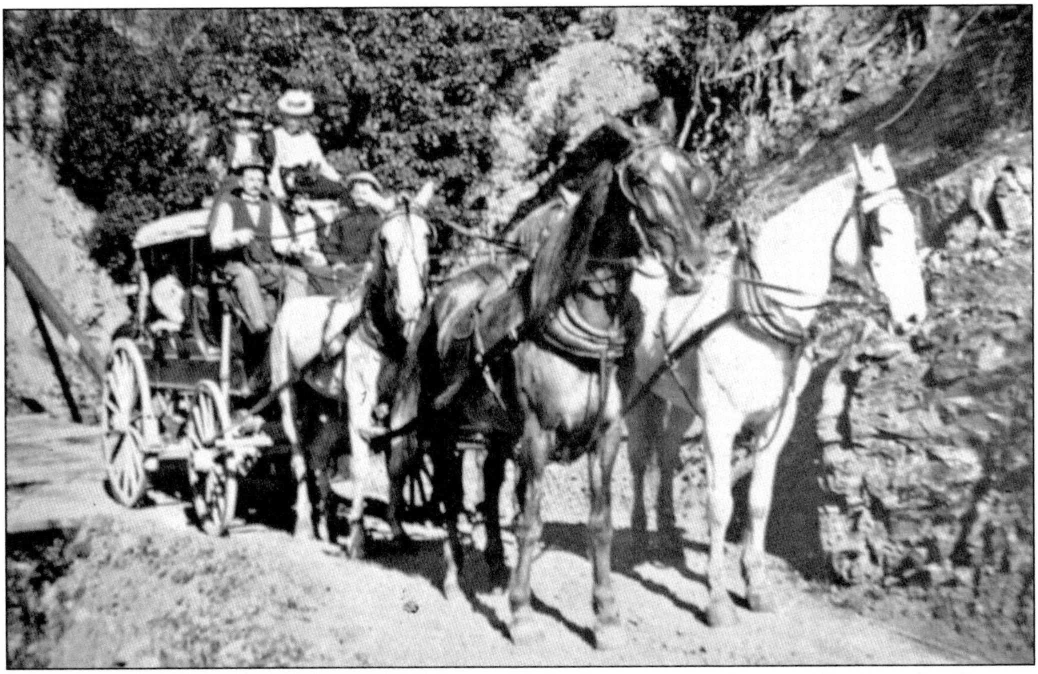

Going north from Petaluma, stage stops were established approximately every 15 miles—the distance horses could comfortably travel before teams needed to be replaced. Many stages ran from the Cloverdale hub north to Ukiah, east to Lakeport, southeast to Calistoga, and west through the Anderson Valley to Yorkville, Boonville, and Mendocino. The stage pictured here in 1899 was traveling over mountains and through canyons to The Geysers.

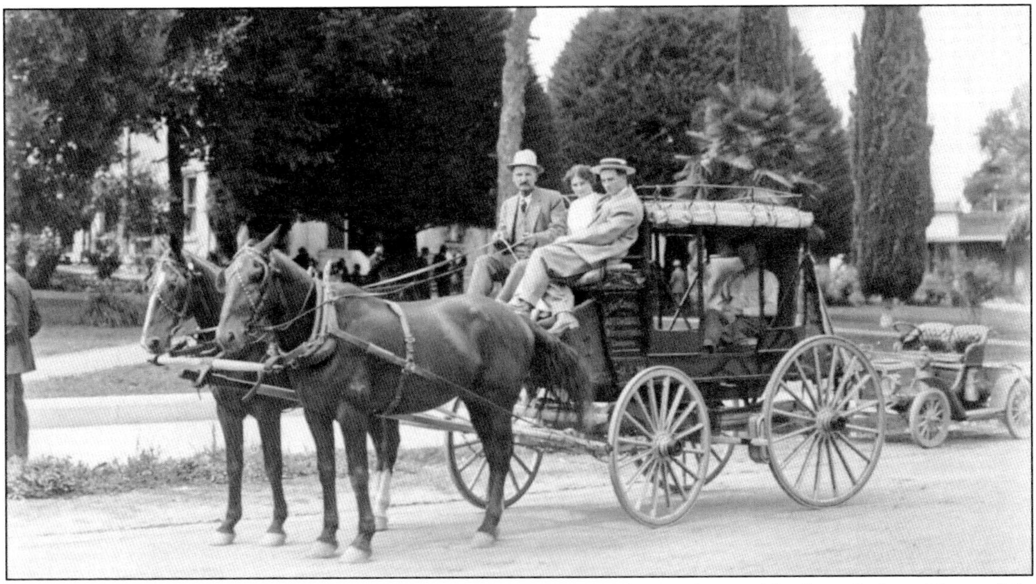

Jotham Sedgley, seen above holding the reins, came west in the 1850s and had settled in Cloverdale by 1880. Sedgley held numerous jobs, but the most glamorous was as a stagecoach driver between Cloverdale, Lake County, and other destinations within Sonoma County. During his career, he experienced numerous holdups, one of which occurred in 1883 while driving the stage to Lakeport. He eventually gave up driving to run a barbershop.

This photograph is of Charles Boles, alias San Francisco mining engineer Charles Bolton, also known as Black Bart, the notorious stagecoach robber famous for his courtesy and the poems he left at the robbery scene. Following his capture in 1883, Boles served four years in San Quentin, after which he disappeared, never to be seen again.

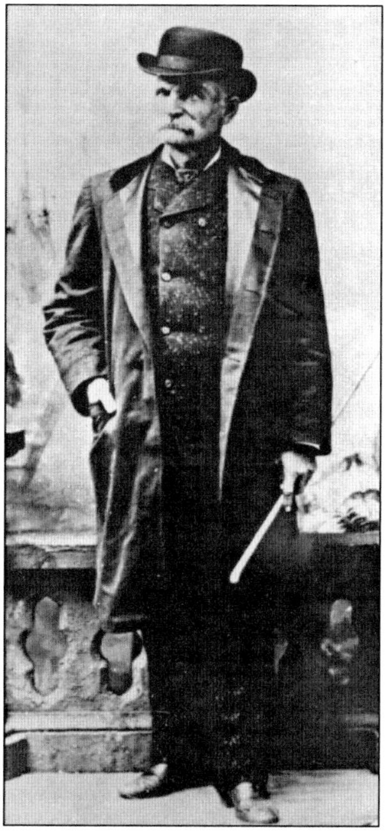

This "wanted" poster was issued by Wells Fargo and Company after Black Bart's first stagecoach robbery in 1875. Seven years later, he was still at large and wanted for robberies of Wells Fargo stages throughout Northern California. The legendary outlaw held up Cloverdale-bound stages about six miles outside of town three times between January 1882 and April 1883. Cloverdale's Wells Fargo agent at the time, Isaac Shaw, sent posses in unsuccessful pursuits of the notorious robber.

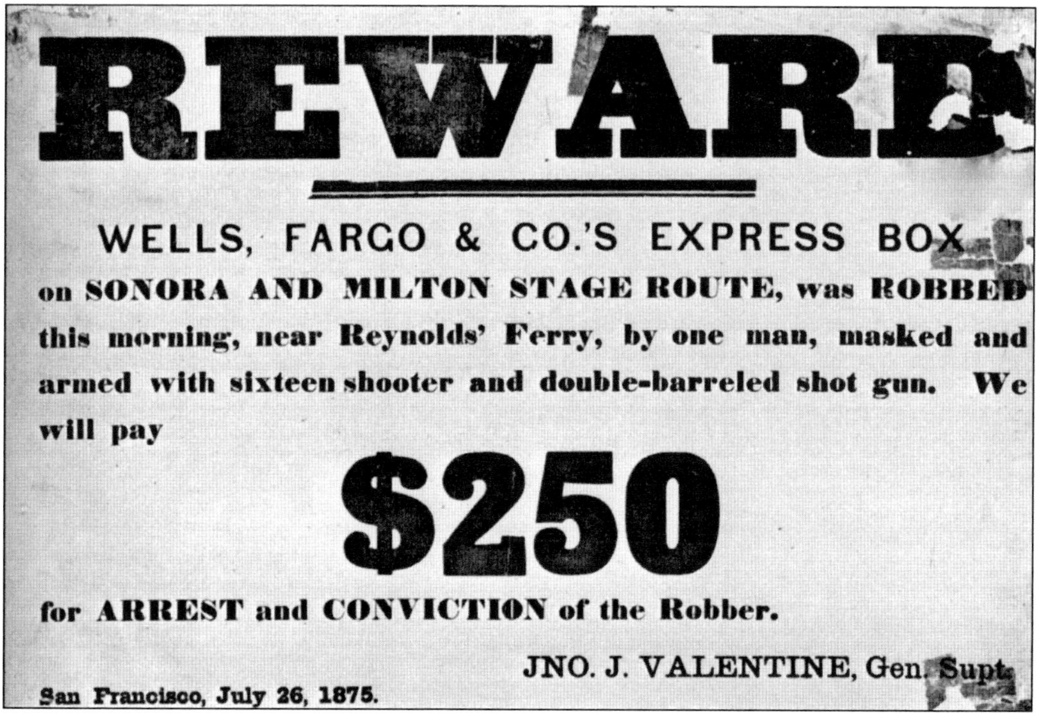

REWARD

WELLS, FARGO & CO.'S EXPRESS BOX

on SONORA AND MILTON STAGE ROUTE, was ROBBED this morning, near Reynolds' Ferry, by one man, masked and armed with sixteen shooter and double-barreled shot gun. We will pay

$250

for ARREST and CONVICTION of the Robber.

JNO. J. VALENTINE, Gen. Supt.

San Francisco, July 26, 1875.

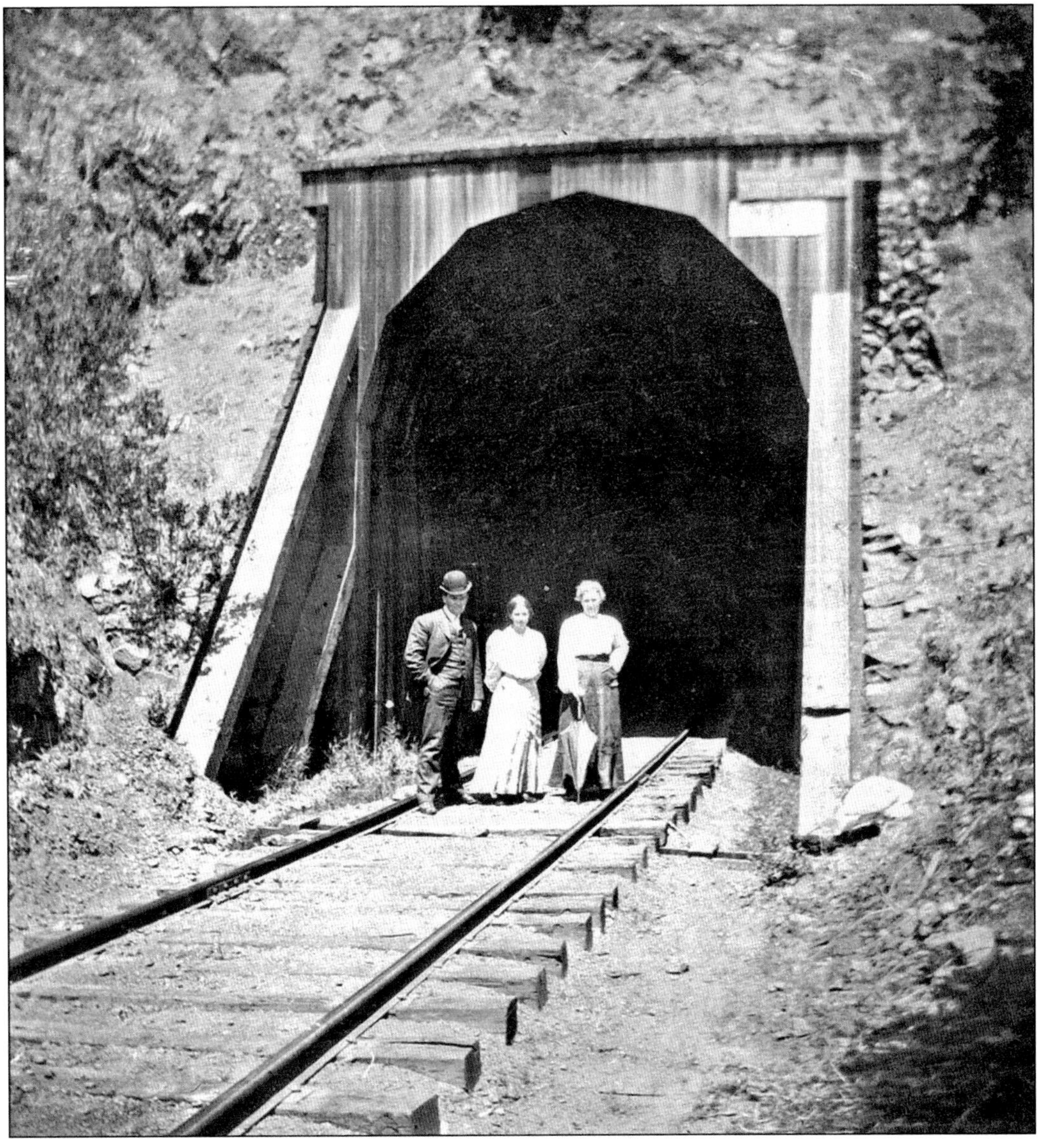

Peter Donahue, founder of the Union Iron Works in San Francisco, engineered and built the tracks that brought trains northward from Tiberon to Cloverdale in 1872. Because of the rough terrain north of Cloverdale and the lack of funding, the tracks could be laid no farther. After he and the owners had differences of opinion, Donahue bought the railroad, changing its name to the San Francisco and North Pacific Railroad. When funding became available in 1887, Donahue's son, James Mervin, took over the project. The tunnel under the cemetery to the north of town was one of four tunnels to be blasted, allowing the tracks to be extended. In the fall of 1889, the newly renamed Northwestern Pacific Railroad completed its rail line from Cloverdale to Ukiah, a distance of 28.5 miles. This photograph shows three unidentified people standing at the entrance to one of the four tunnels. As a side note, Cloverdale's Catholic church was reputedly named St. Peter's in honor of Peter Donahue, who had donated funds to furnish the church.

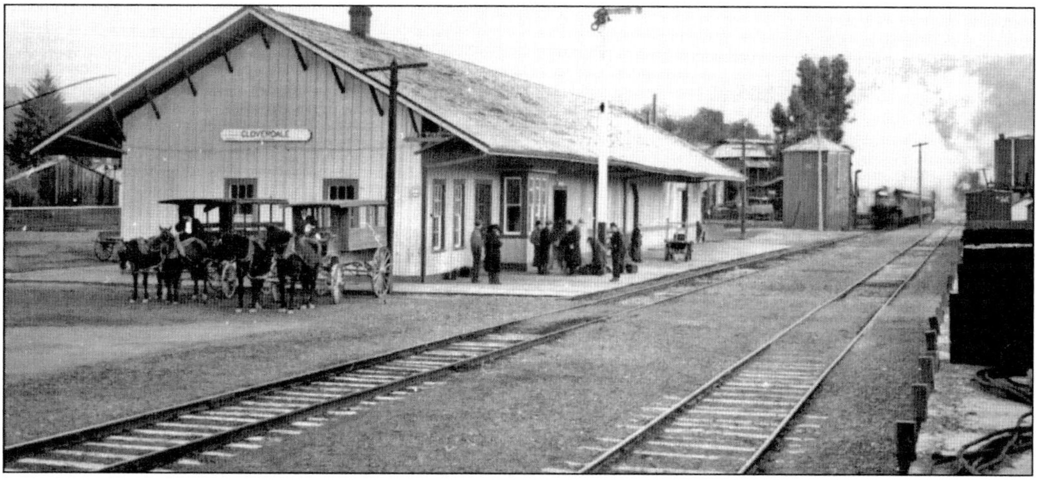

On April 15, 1872, the railroad opened passenger service to Cloverdale, and for the next 17 years, Cloverdale was the northernmost terminus of the rail line. In the 1900s, the train depot, seen below in 1911, routinely welcomed hundreds of people arriving to attend the annual Cloverdale Citrus Fair. Often fair goers were met at the station by the community's marching band. When passenger trains were discontinued in 1958, the building at Railroad Avenue and East Street became a freight office. It had been given National Register status and was to become a museum when the Highway 101 bypass was finished, but in 1991, the depot burned to the ground—the work of an arsonist.

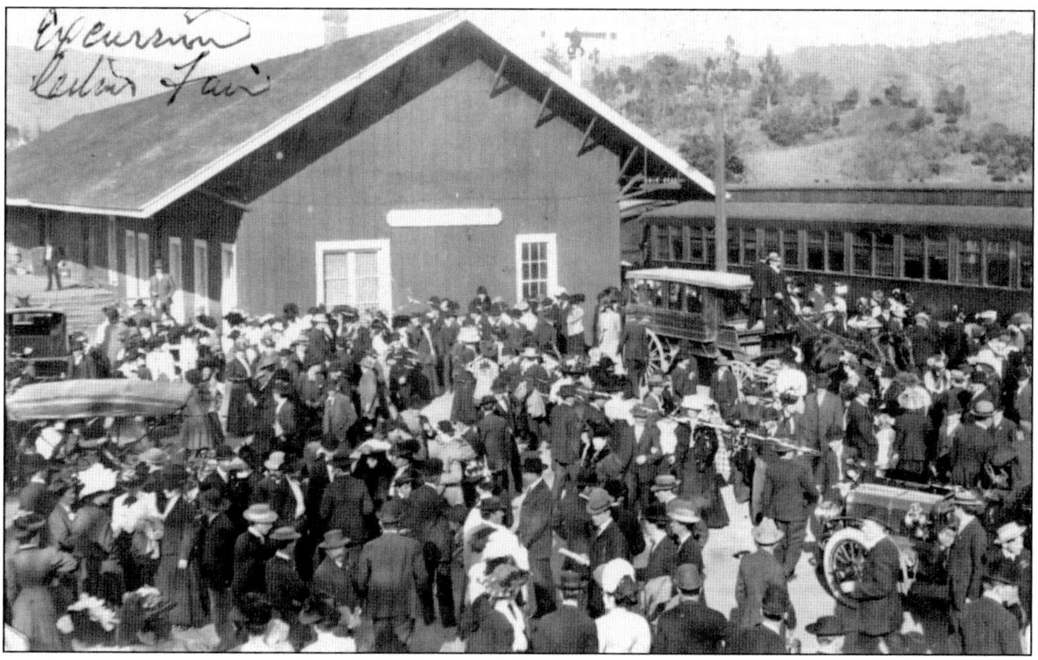

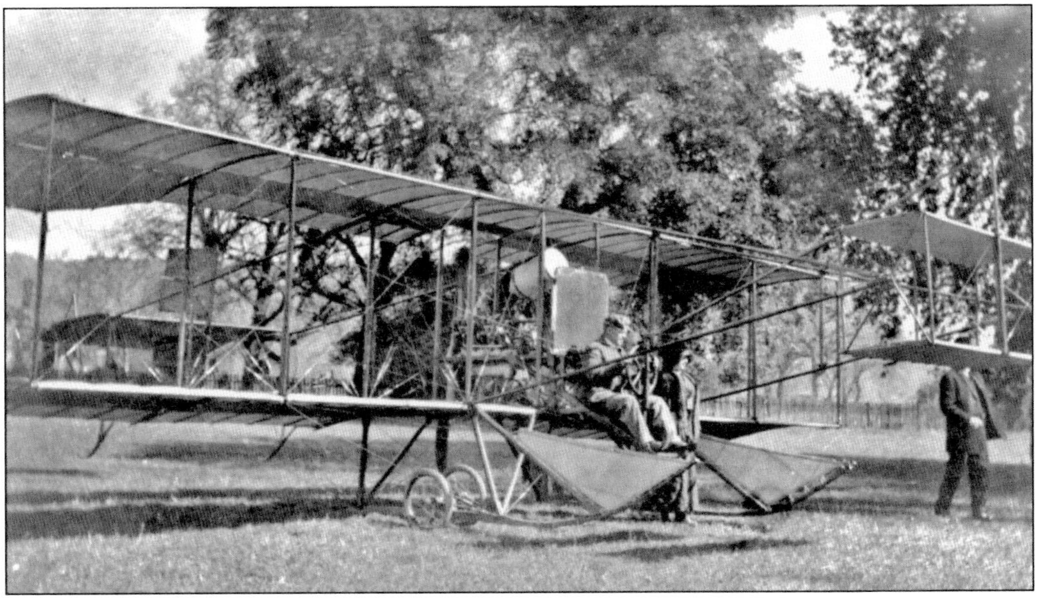

Fred Wiseman, seen above in 1911, was unofficially considered the first pilot to carry mail in the United States. The flight from Santa Rosa to Petaluma began on February 17, 1911. Because Wiseman crashed during the flight, it actually took two days to complete his delivery of 50 newspapers, 3 letters, and a sack of coffee beans. That same year, Wiseman contracted to make some exhibition flights during Cloverdale's Citrus Fair. He crash landed the day before and could not appear. The photograph below shows the crowd that gathered to look at the ruined plane. (Courtesy Sonoma County Library.)

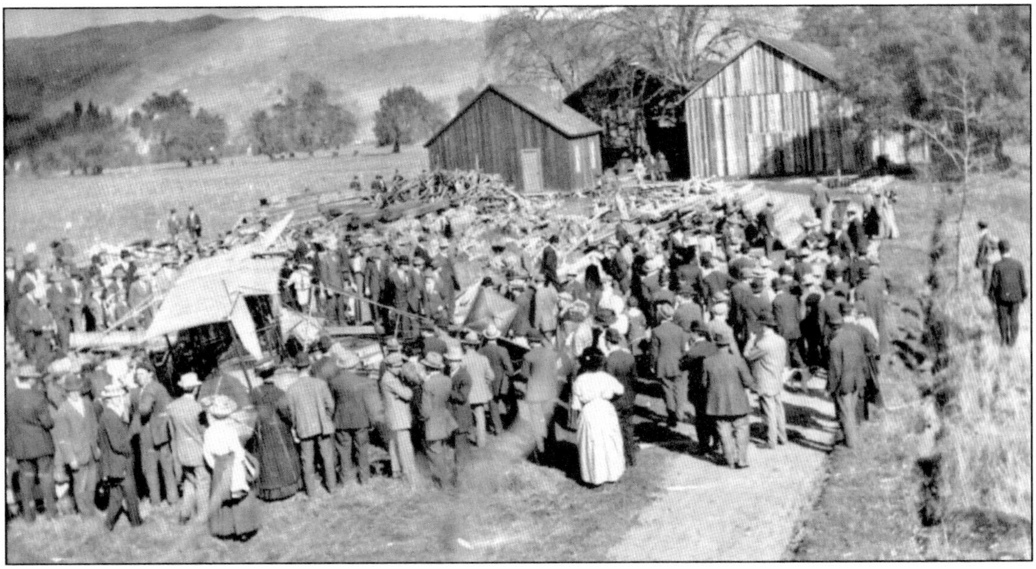

This poster, printed in the 1913 *Cloverdale Reveille*, announces the upcoming appearance of noted California aviator Harold W. Blakeley [sic]. Blakely flew from San Francisco Bay to Cloverdale, landing at Smith Field, making the 85-mile flight in 100 minutes. He traveled at 6,500 feet and dropped to 4,500 feet as he approached Cloverdale, landing easily in front of a large cheering crowd.

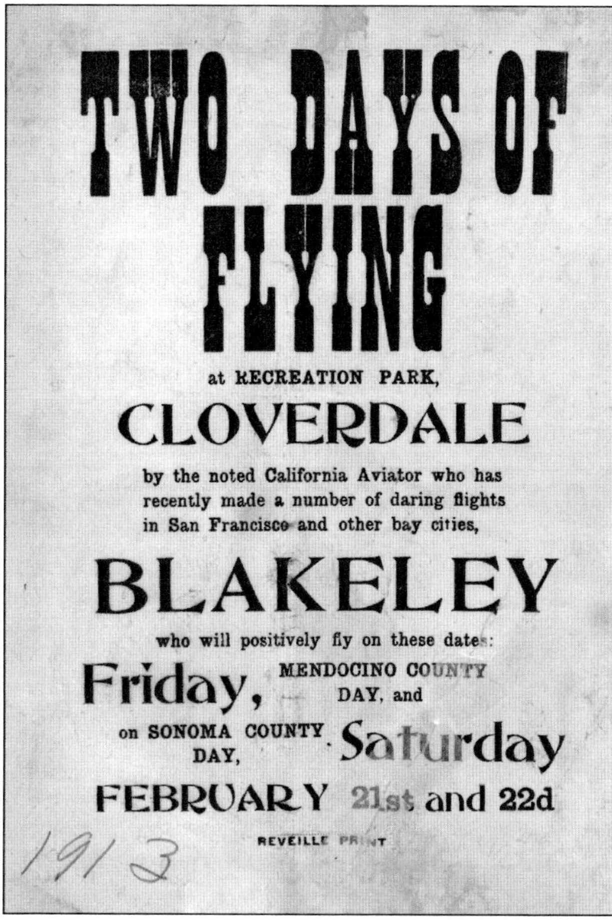

During his four days in Cloverdale, Blakely demonstrated his flying prowess, doing several takeoffs and landings, and circling over the town. He returned to Cloverdale the following year as part of the pre-year celebration of the 1915 Panama Pacific Exposition. His flight back to San Francisco ended with a crash landing into the bay. He survived but was killed in 1916 while testing a new engine.

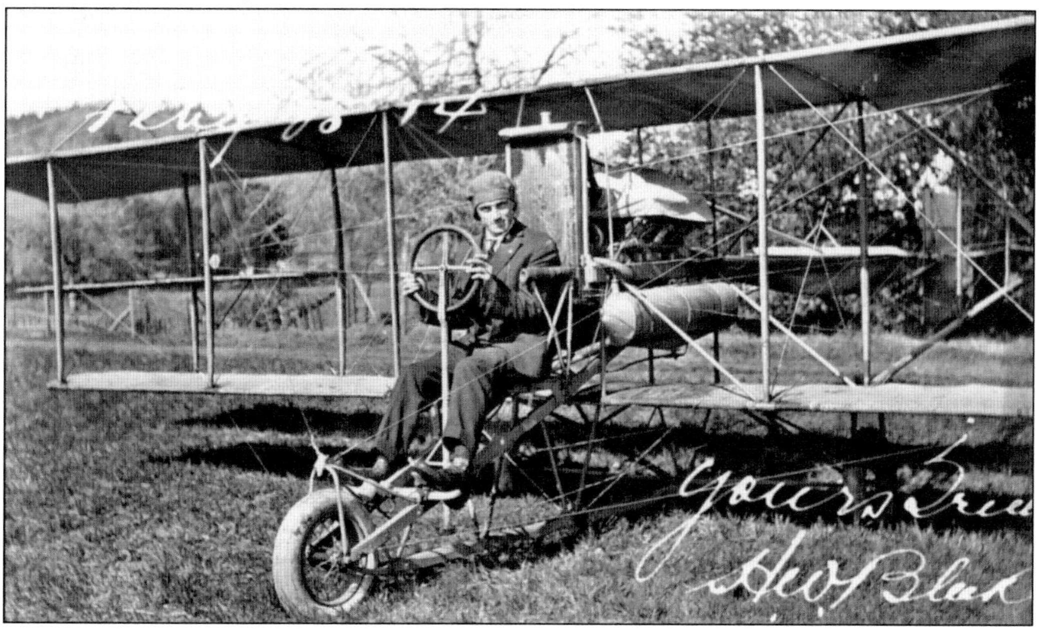

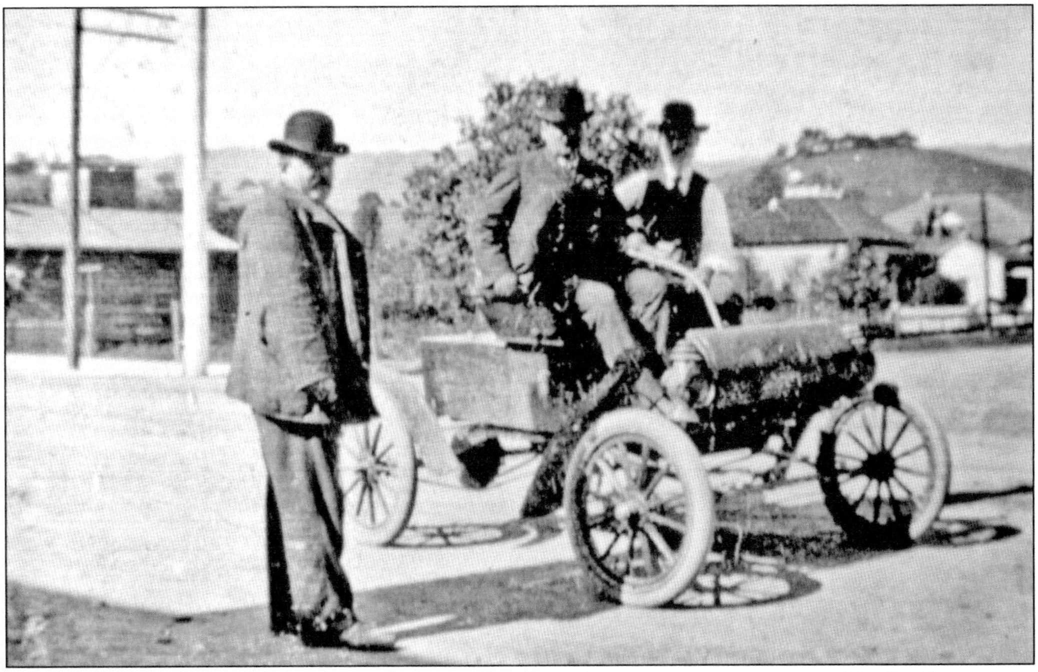

Three unidentified gentlemen are admiring this horseless carriage, quite possibly the first car in Cloverdale. The first owner of an automobile in Cloverdale was reportedly Harry Kleiser. His car was an Orinet Buck Board built by the Waltham Watch Company.

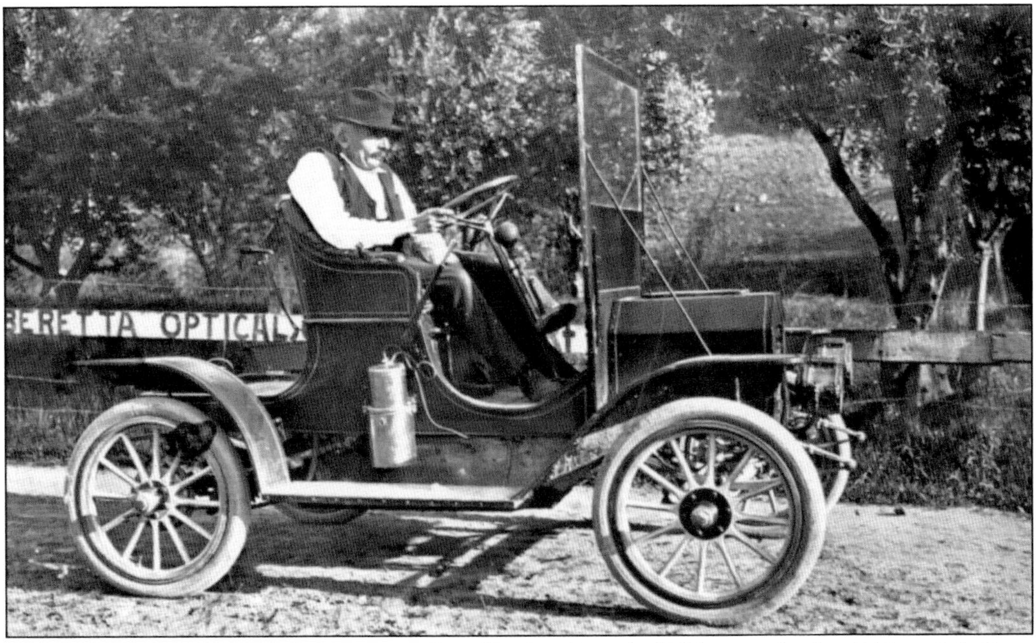

Freddie Reichers is seen here sitting in Dr. Charles Grant's 1905 one-cylinder Oldsmobile Reo, bought from Oliver Williams. A story is told that Williams was driving a Reo down the Redwood Highway when he met a team of horses. He got so excited he ran into the Albertz fence, and later, when parking the car at Humbert's livery stable, he ran into a hearse that was being stored there.

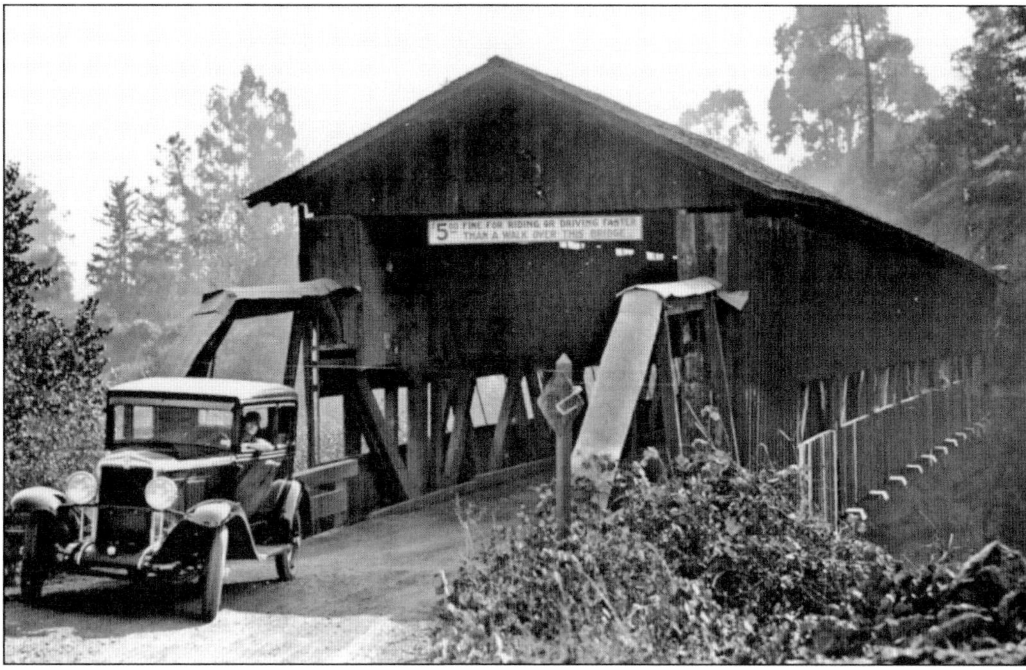

This red-painted covered bridge spanned the Russian River at Preston two miles north of Cloverdale. Built in 1872, it remained a landmark for almost 70 years until collapsing into the river. Its east footing connected with the county stage and wagon road, allowing travelers to continue northward along the river to Mendocino. It was replaced by a steel truss bridge in 1933.

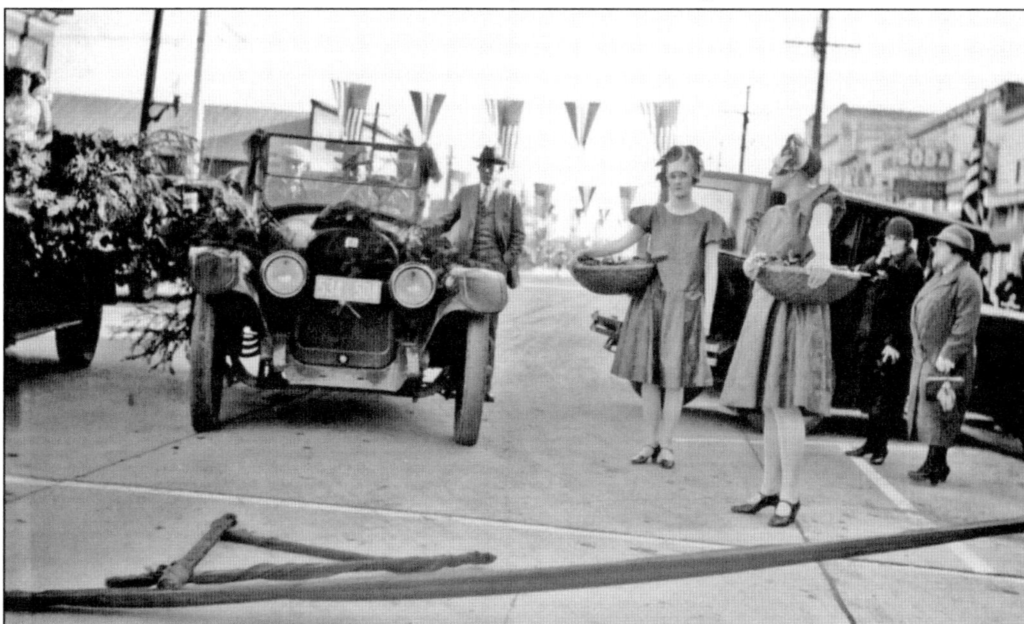

The official opening of the Redwood Highway, providing a paved road from the city of Healdsburg to Third Street in Cloverdale, took place in 1926 at Broad and West Streets. Visible in the photograph on the right are the Druids Building and the Dineen/Gothrup Drugstore. The automobile is a Buick, and the young ladies are Virginia Williams Grace (left) and Beatrice Horn (Maio).

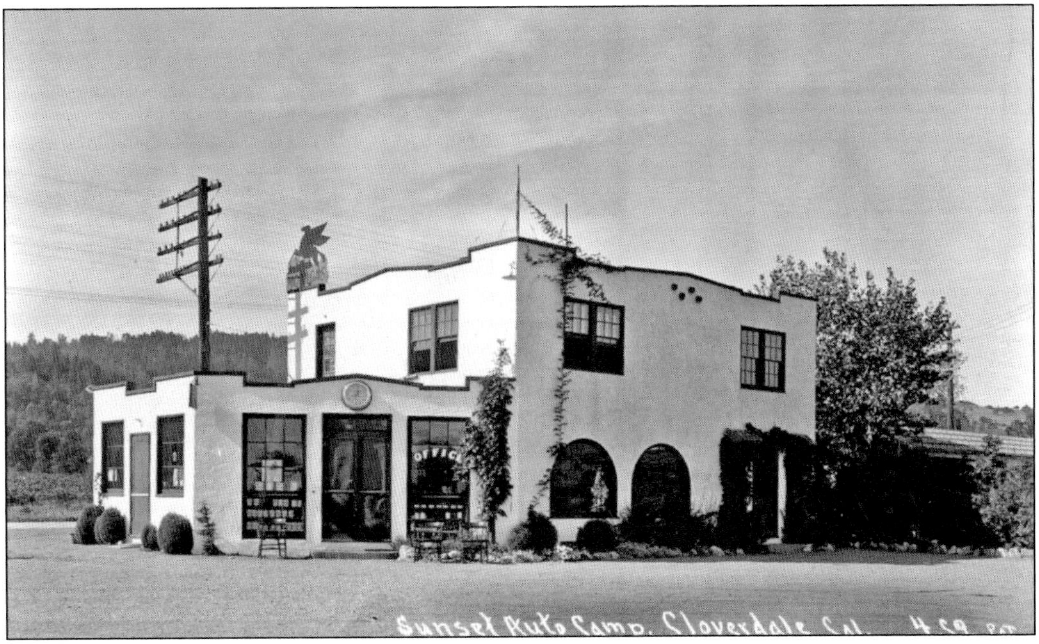

George Martensen built the Sunset Auto Court in 1925 at the junction of South Cloverdale Boulevard and Healdsburg Avenue on the property where the Owl Café now stands. For the convenience of those passing through Cloverdale, the complex provided a sandwich shop, a small grocery store, and one gasoline pump. An upstairs and several cabins in the rear were added later. In 1963, the property was purchased by Dann Halikas, who razed the motel and all but one of the cabins, which later housed the Cloverdale Chamber of Commerce. Halikas developed the business building known as the Owl Plaza, which had restaurant seating for 150 guests.

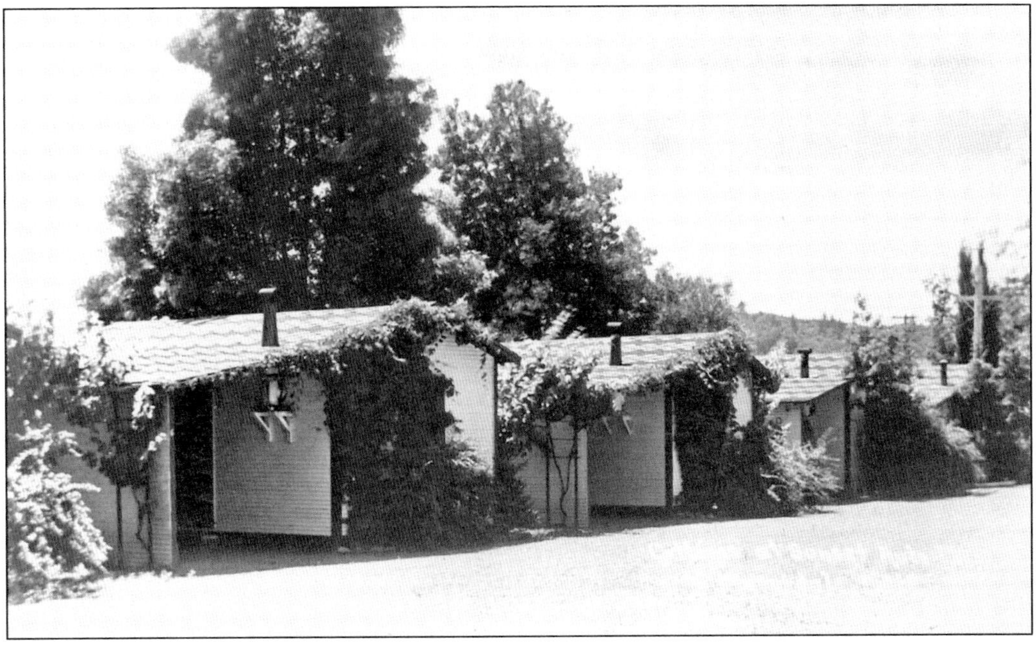

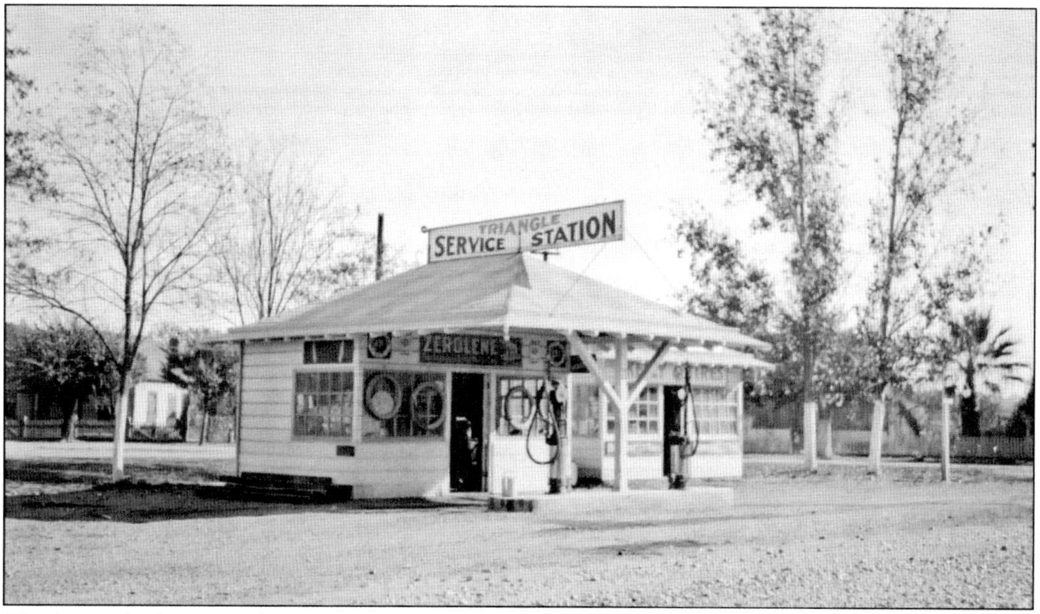

The Triangle Associated Service Station was located on West Street at Railroad Avenue. At its largest, the complex consisted of gas pumps, a tire/lube/battery shop, an office, and a café. At one time, it was the only station between San Francisco and Eureka that catered to 18-wheelers. The station was owned by George Haugsten and Louie Ottoboni in the years before World War II.

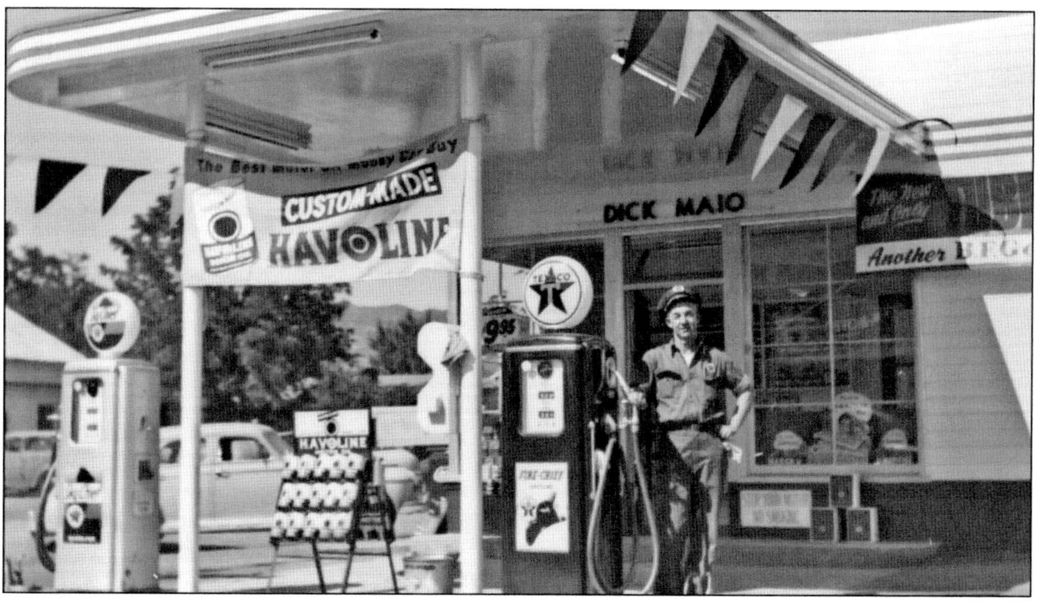

Dick Maio is seen here in the mid-1950s in front of his gas station at the southeast corner of Second and West Streets. Dick, who had married Bee Horn in 1931, moved to Cloverdale in 1950. For six years, he owned and operated the Texaco station, which was built—according to Texaco Company specifications for stations along the Redwood Highway—almost entirely of redwood.

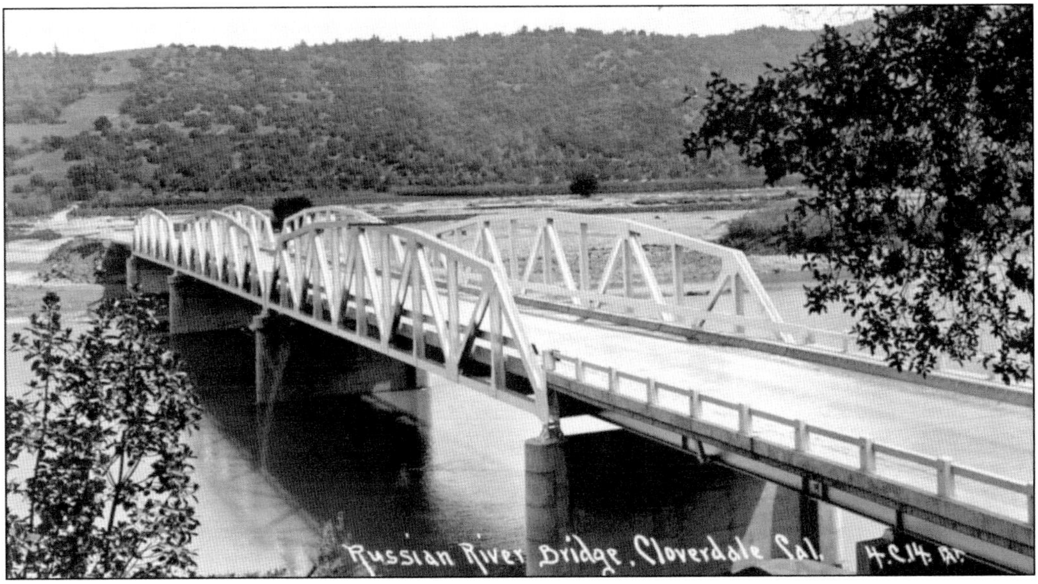

The new bridge across the Russian River at First Street was dedicated on February 22, 1939, with federal, state, and local officials in attendance. It replaced two bridges built in 1888 and 1889—one over the main channel and one over the overflow channel. The new $100,000 bridge was built as part of the federal government's farm-to-market project, addressing the needs of the agricultural district east of Cloverdale.

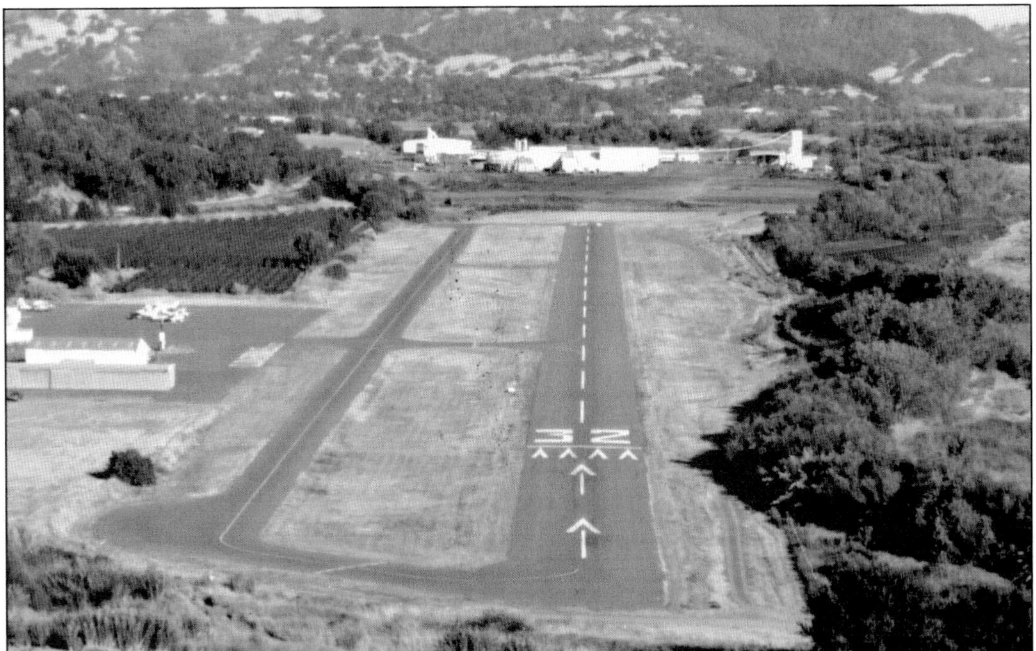

One of Cloverdale's early airstrips, located on the Albertz property south of town, was in use from 1929 to 1931. Property for the present airport (pictured above) was deeded to Cloverdale in 1952 and opened to the public 10 years later. E. G. "Bud" Groom, director of the airport commission at the time, oversaw its construction, with significant contributions of manpower, equipment, and money provided by Cloverdale's logging industry.

Six

Rest and Recreation Cloverdale Style

"One might travel far and wide, crossing many seas, before he would cast his eye over a more pleasing landscape, for truly Cloverdale is a beautiful place." This flowery language, appearing in the 1898 *Illustrated Atlas of Sonoma County,* reflects a sentiment popular for more than 100 years. Local residents as well as visitors have always appreciated the natural attributes and pleasant climate Cloverdale has to offer.

The late 1800s and early 1900s witnessed the flourishing of local resorts featuring mineral and geothermal baths and access to swimming holes on the Russian River. The resorts and Cloverdale's signature event, the Citrus Fair, benefited from the railroad, which delivered trainloads of visitors, most of who came north from the Bay Area.

After the Redwood Highway opened in the 1920s, automobile travel became increasingly common. By the late 1930s, a chamber of commerce brochure was enticing visitors with a list of Cloverdale's attractions—beaches on the coast, fishing in local rivers and creeks, deer hunting in nearby hills, The Geysers—the "eighth wonder of the world"—and the highway itself, "the most kaleidoscopic succession of enchanting vistas ever concentrated in one single tour."

Ironically, the freedom afforded by the automobile eventually contributed to the demise of the local resorts, a decline exacerbated by the Great Depression and by fuel rationing during World War II. The local economy still relies heavily on tourism, but the focus has shifted to the attractions of Lake Sonoma and the charms of the Wine Country, giving rise to a more recent promotional slogan, "Cloverdale—Where the Vineyards meet the Redwoods."

Of course, recreation has also included those activities typically found in any small town—sports, drama, music, movies, dancing, and seasonal events. In fact, residents and visitors looking for rest or recreation in Cloverdale find that the only shortage is enough time to enjoy all the options.

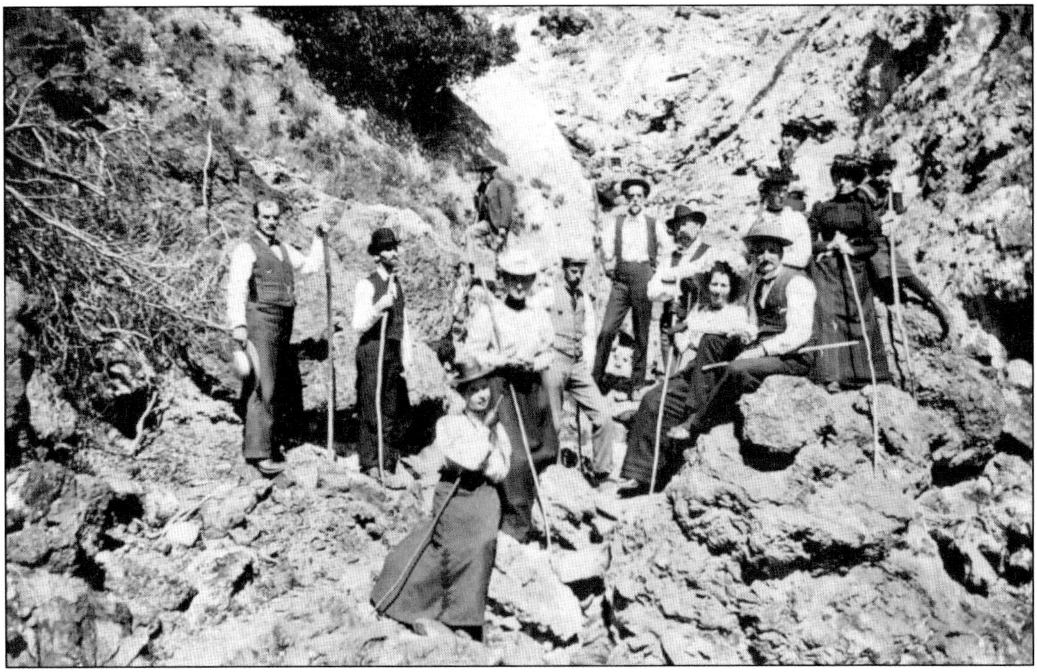

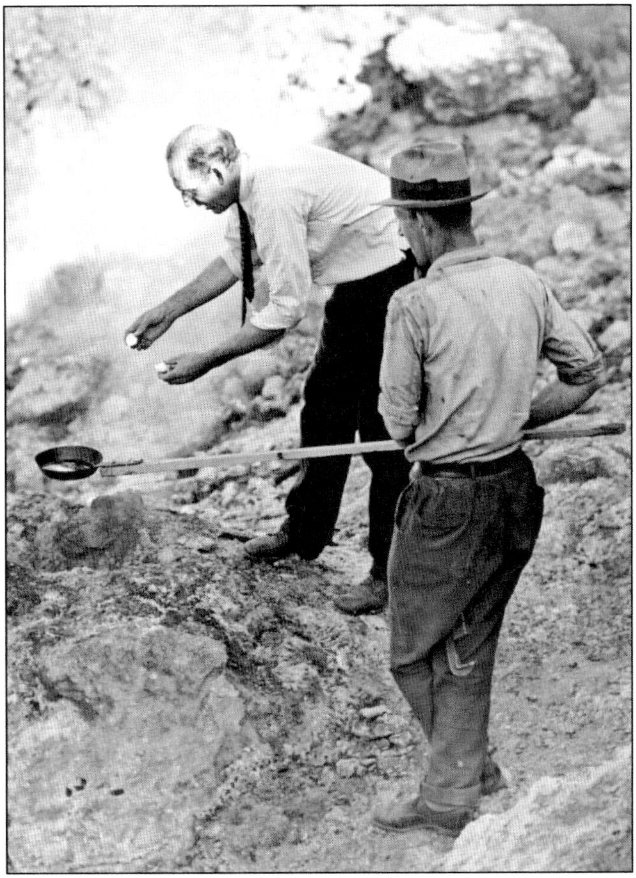

On April 7, 1899, a group of visitors were enjoying the sights at The Geysers, the most famous of Cloverdale's turn-of-the-20th-century resorts. The Geysers, located on Big Sulfur Creek about 16 miles east of Cloverdale, were first seen by a white man in 1847. William Bell Elliott was hunting bear in the area when he noticed a strong smell of brimstone and saw a cloud of steam emanating from a seemingly bottomless pit.

Although referred to as "The Geysers," they are actually steam fumaroles, and the effort to cook eggs over one was probably successful. Research by a Captain Davidson in 1859 estimated the temperature of one boiling spring known as the Witches' Caldron to be 500 degrees, sufficient to reduce a man to broth in two minutes should he happen to fall in. (Courtesy Redwood Empire Association.)

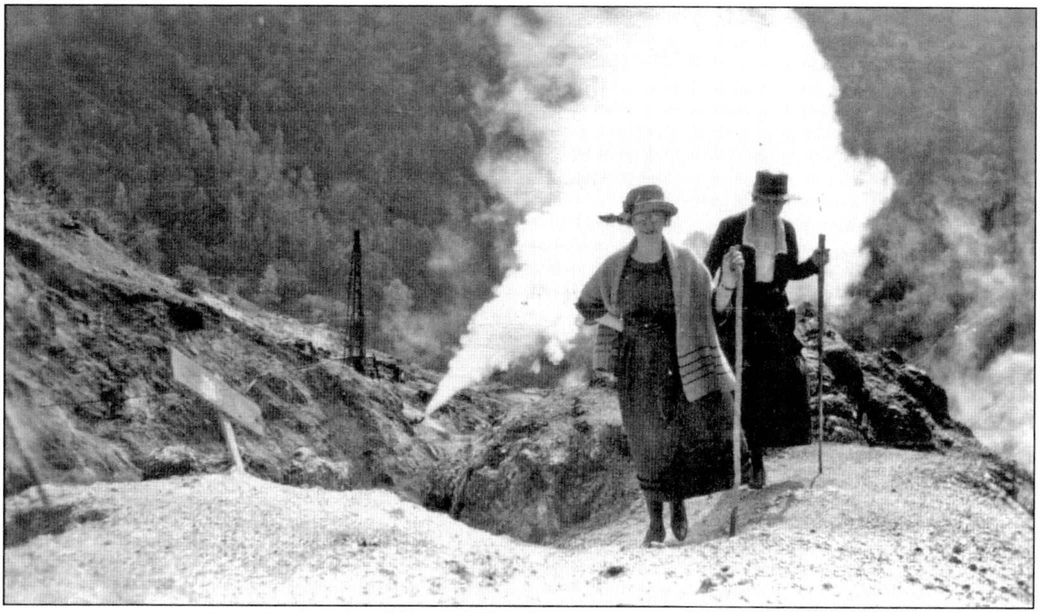

From the lean-to shack built by William Bell Elliott in 1848 grew a famous spa whose hissing steam and bubbling springs attracted visitors from all over the world, including the Prince of Wales, Guiseppe Garibaldi, Mark Twain, and presidents Ulysses S. Grant, Theodore Roosevelt, and William Howard Taft. These unidentified women were exploring the fumaroles in the 1920s.

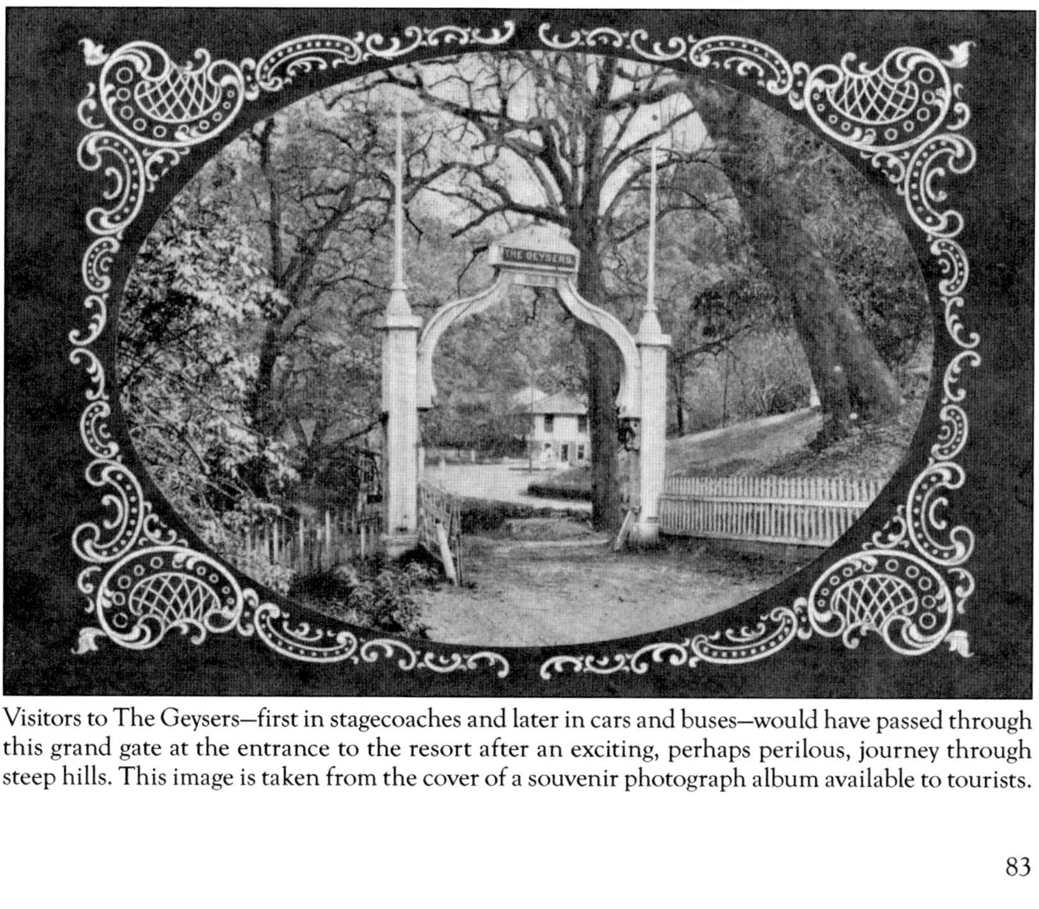

Visitors to The Geysers—first in stagecoaches and later in cars and buses—would have passed through this grand gate at the entrance to the resort after an exciting, perhaps perilous, journey through steep hills. This image is taken from the cover of a souvenir photograph album available to tourists.

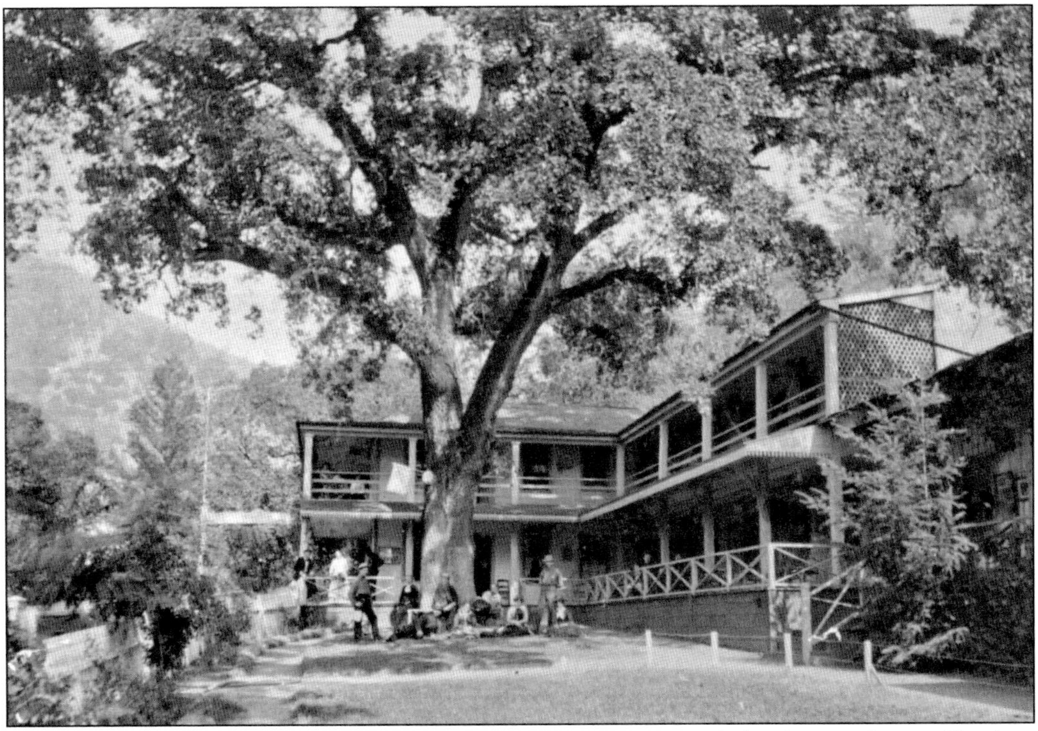

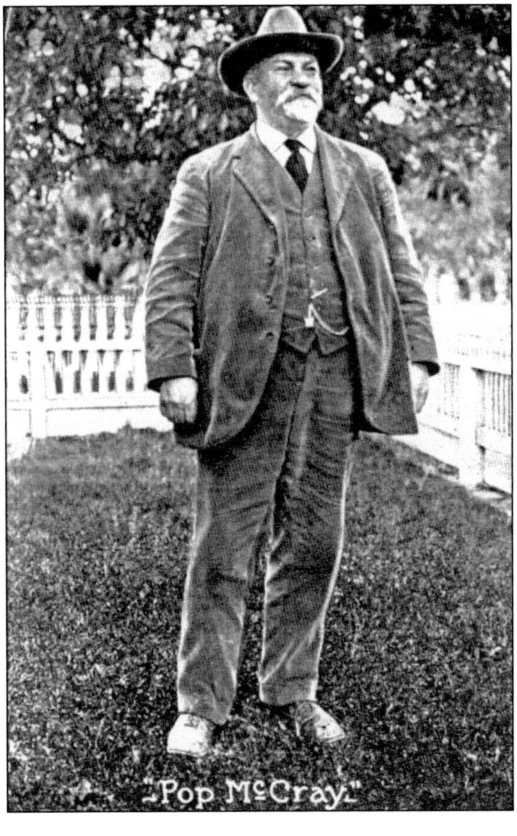

Construction of The Geysers Resort Hotel began in 1854. The register grew from only 20 names in that first year to 3,500 in 1875. A catastrophic landslide and fire destroyed the main building in 1938, but cabins, a swimming pool, and a restaurant remained until 1980, when everything was dismantled, leaving no trace.

William Lafayette "Pop" McCray was one of Cloverdale's most picturesque characters. McCray traveled from Missouri to California by oxcart at the age of 16. He operated a stage line in Lake County and is credited with the start of the town of Upper Lake. In 1900, he settled in Oat Valley on 236 acres originally owned by his mother-in-law, Rachel Cyrus Elliott, near what is now Hamburger Ranch. There he developed a resort called the Old Homestead.

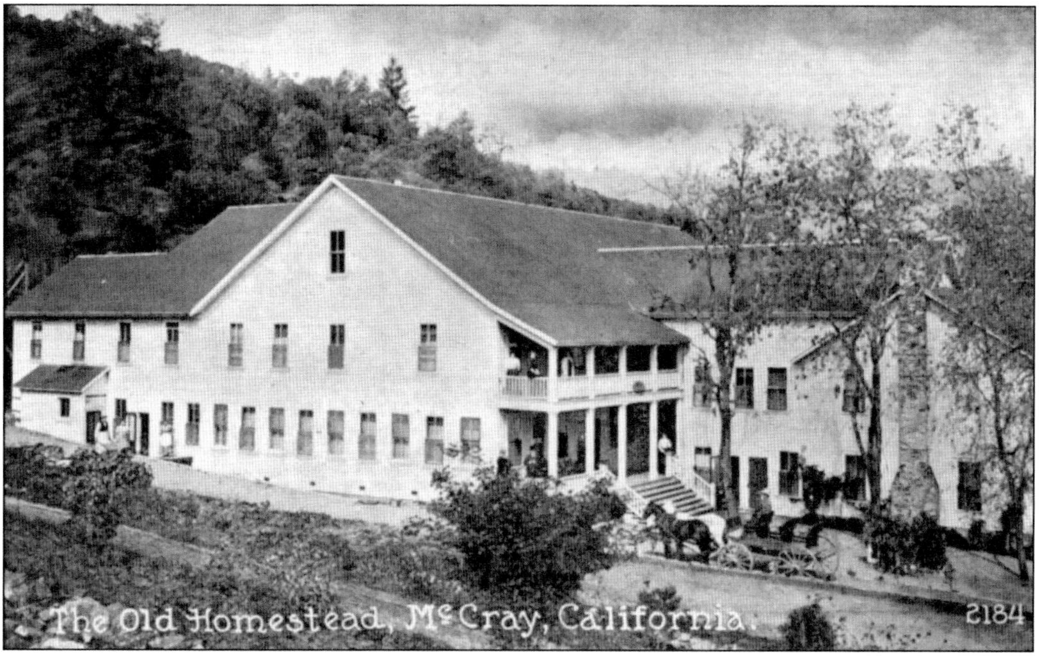

McCray's resort was extremely popular in the early decades of the 20th century, when people from the Bay Area traveled by train to Cloverdale seeking relief from city life or summertime chill. The resort had facilities to sleep 300 and a clubhouse that could feed 1,000. Fire destroyed the Old Homestead in 1928, and the resort's popularity was in decline by the mid-1930s.

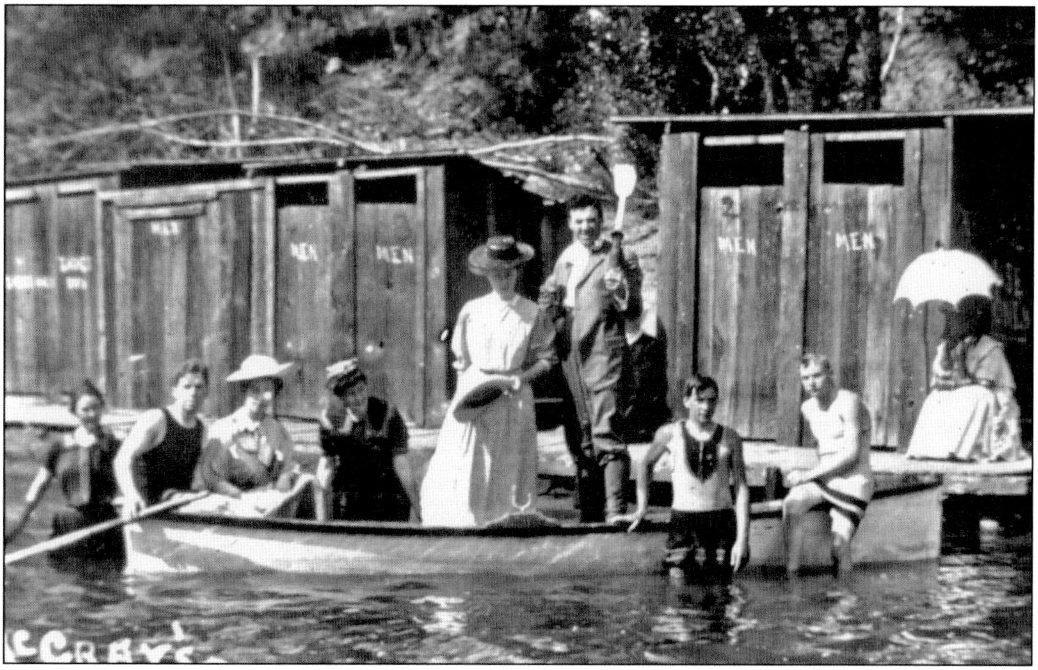

One of the major draws of McCray's resort was a beach area along the Russian River where guests could relax and take advantage of Cloverdale's sunny summer weather.

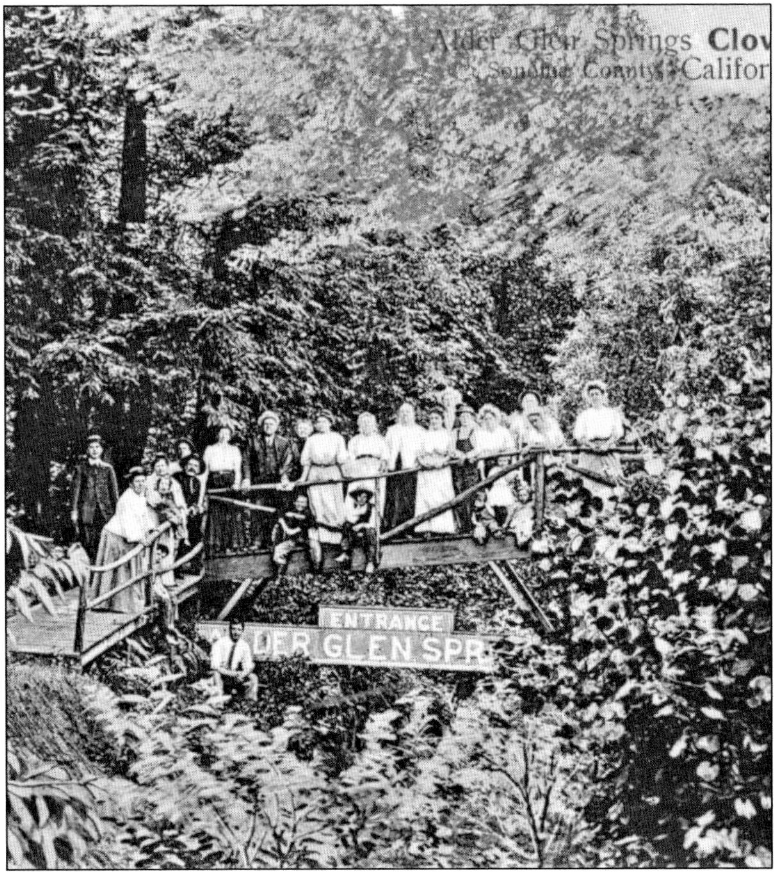

The Alder Glen resort, which opened four miles northwest of Cloverdale in 1897 with a hotel, bar, and cabins, lasted into the 1950s. Its mineral water springs, discovered by R. J. Shipley in the early 1870s, were located in a secluded glen surrounded by large rock outcroppings. The waters were considered medicinal and were said to have different flavors, including lemon-lime.

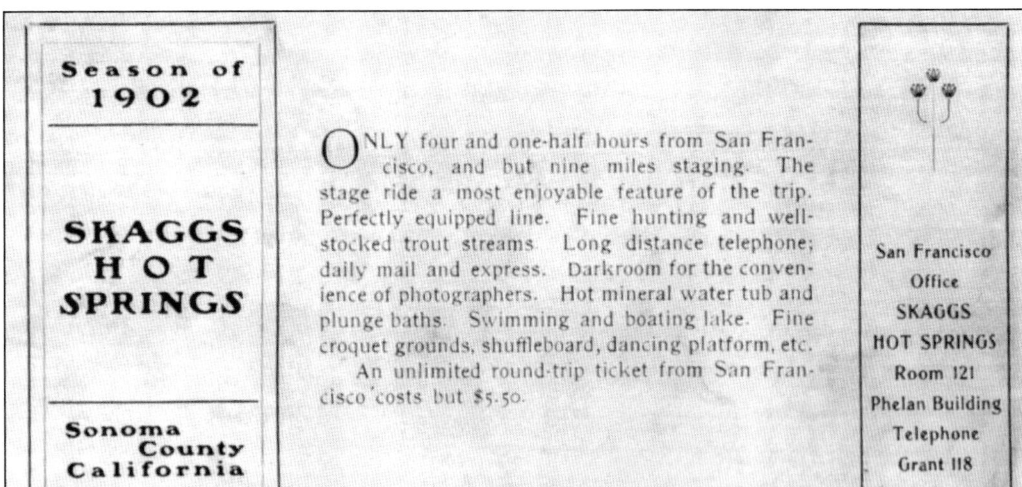

Another early resort was Skaggs Hot Springs, southwest of Cloverdale on the Stewarts Point Road. The hotel, opened in 1864 by Alexander Skaggs, was accommodating up to 300 guests a night by the 1870s. The resort experienced a serious decline in visitors during the Depression and closed permanently in 1942 after World War II gasoline rationing took effect. Today the site lies below the surface of Lake Sonoma.

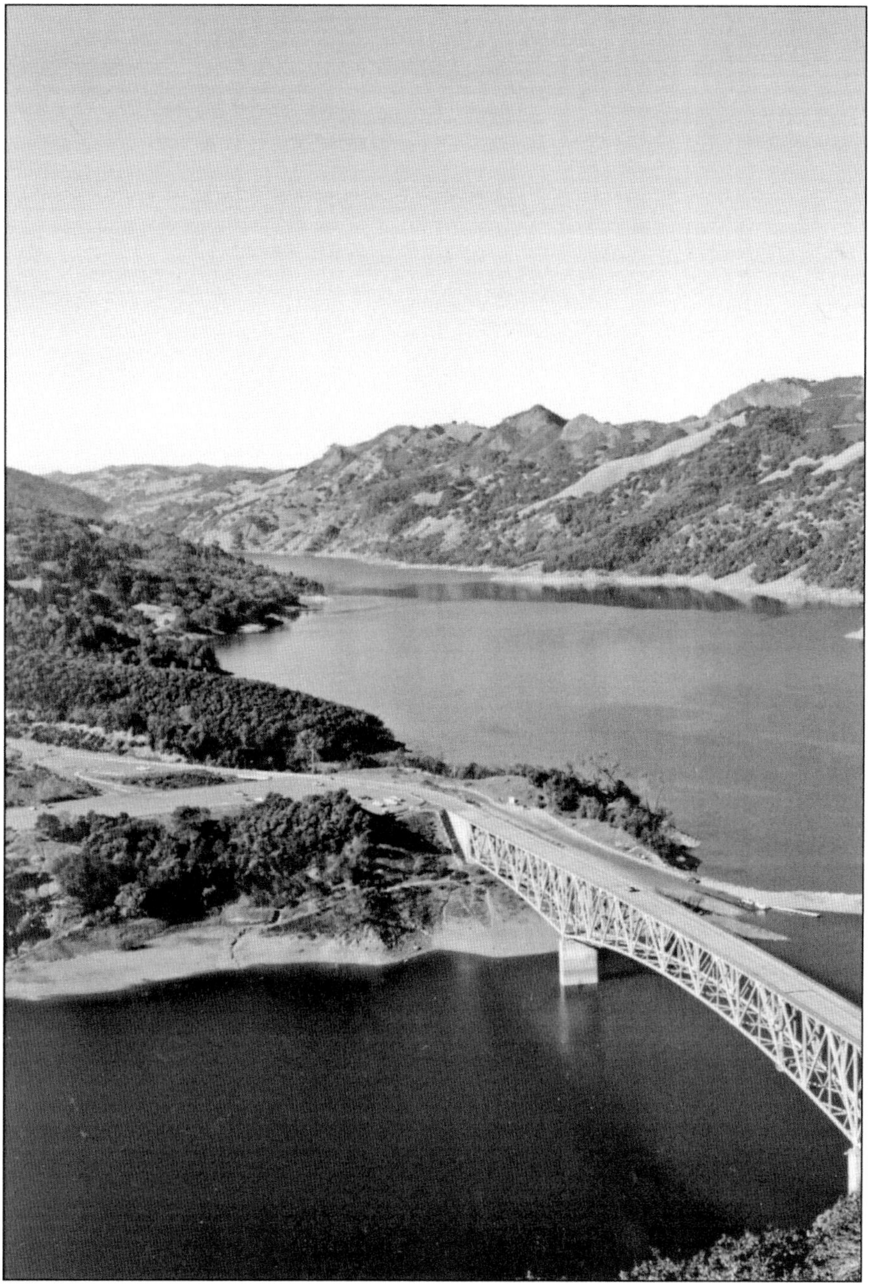

The compacted, earth-fill Warm Springs Dam was completed in 1983 by the U.S. Army Corps of Engineers to serve three purposes: flood control, domestic water supply, and recreation. By 1985, the valley was fully drowned, creating Lake Sonoma. Extending nine miles on Dry Creek and four miles on Warm Springs Creek, the lake offers more than 2,700 surface acres of water for boating and water sports, as well as 40 miles of hiking and horseback riding trails. Visitor center exhibits focus on the culture of the original inhabitants of the Dry Creek Valley, the Pomo Indians, and fish hatchery displays describe the life cycle of the coho salmon, steelhead, and chinook. Hot Springs Road leads from Cloverdale to the Yorty Creek Recreation Area, with a swim beach, picnic areas, and car-top boat launch.

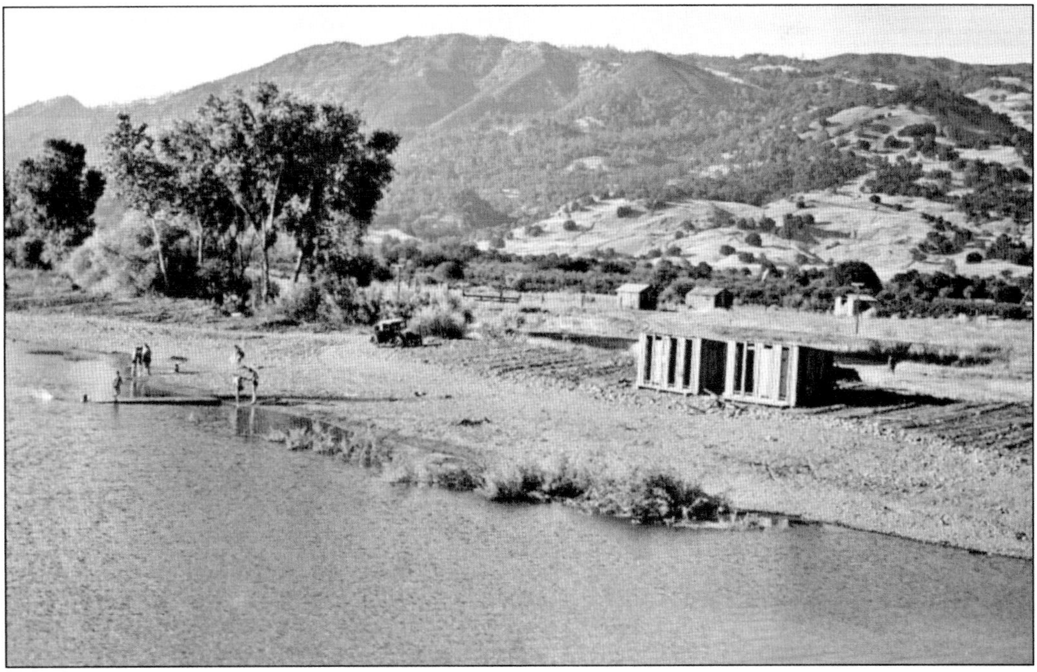

The Russian River has always been a popular spot for those seeking relief from the heat on Cloverdale's typically hot summer days. This group is enjoying the water at the river's bathing beach just north of the First Street Bridge in 1939. Changing rooms were provided at the water's edge for the convenience of bathers.

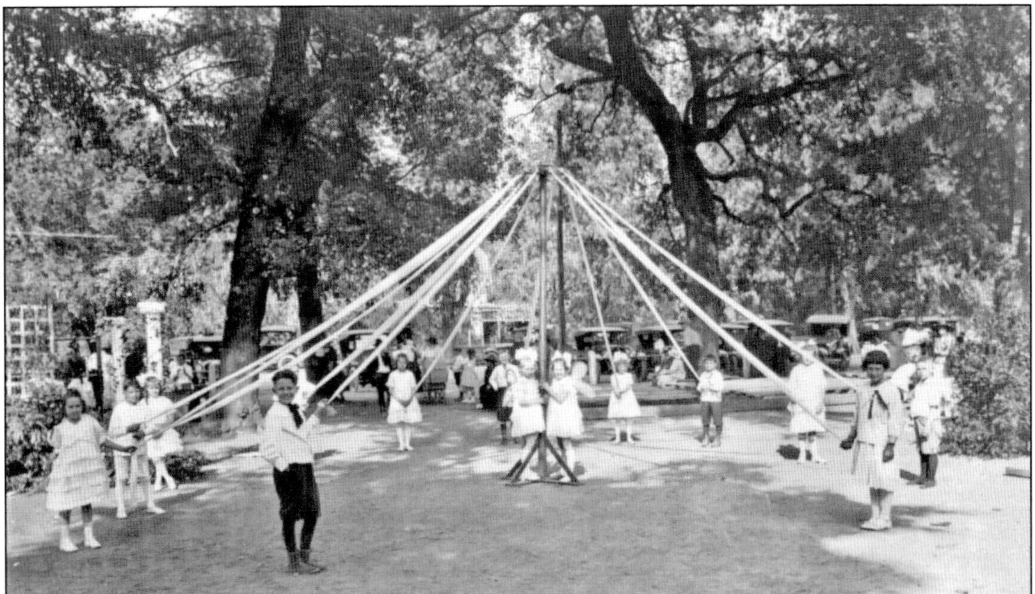

These children are dancing around the maypole in the park known as the Grove. This beautiful stand of oak, pepperwood, and madrone trees, located at the west end of Second Street, was purchased by Cloverdale Trustees in 1924 to be developed into a city park. The Grove was a popular spot for picnics and reunions, and the pavilion at its center was the site of countless dances well into the 1950s.

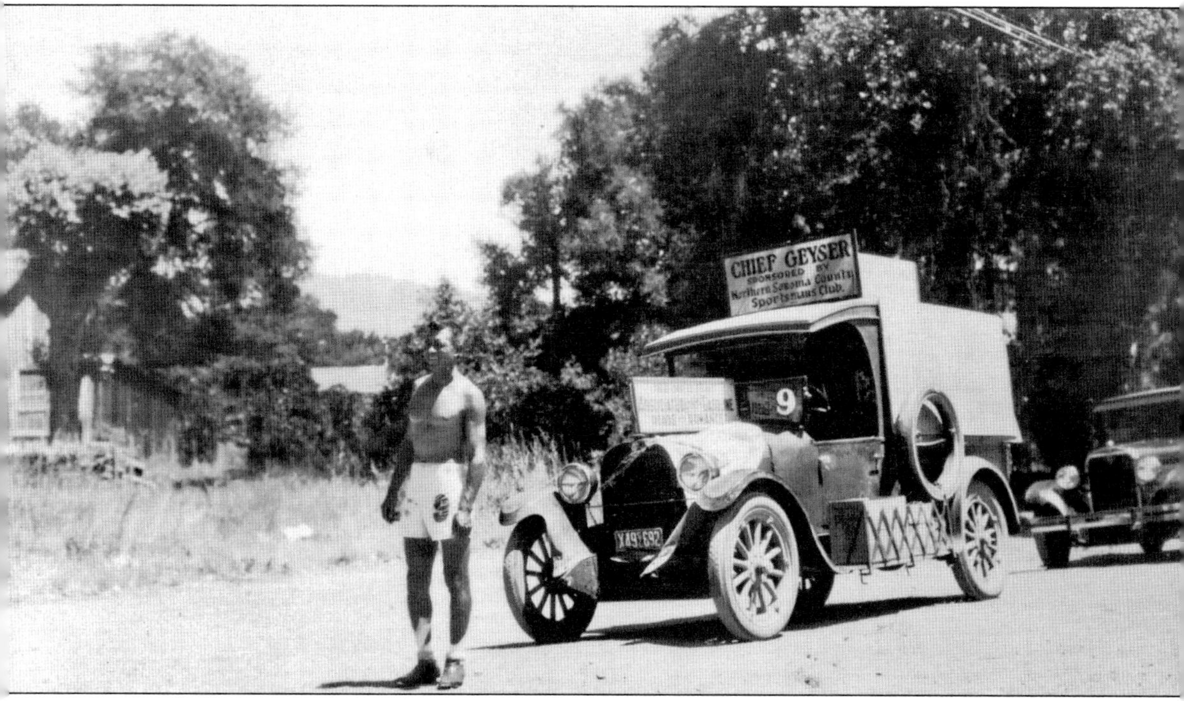

Nationally publicized Indian Marathons were held in 1927 and 1928 to promote the newly completed Redwood Highway, which stretched from San Francisco through Cloverdale to Grants Pass, Oregon. The races, a distance of 462 miles, offered $10,000 in prize money. They attracted American Indian runners from counties along the highway and from as far away as Arizona. Cloverdale's entry in the 1928 race, "Chief Geyser," is seen in the photograph here. That same year, Cloverdale sponsored its own marathon with $75 in prize money. The winner of the 15-mile race of July 1, 1928, was Fabni Luna, paced most of the distance by Chief Geyser. The following year's Healdsburg-Cloverdale race was won by a 56-year-old American Indian known as Chief Ukiah, who ran a slow little trot of short mincing steps. The Druids-sponsored marathon of 1930 attracted several of San Francisco's Olympic-caliber amateur distance runners. All of Cloverdale's marathons were huge "front-page-news" events.

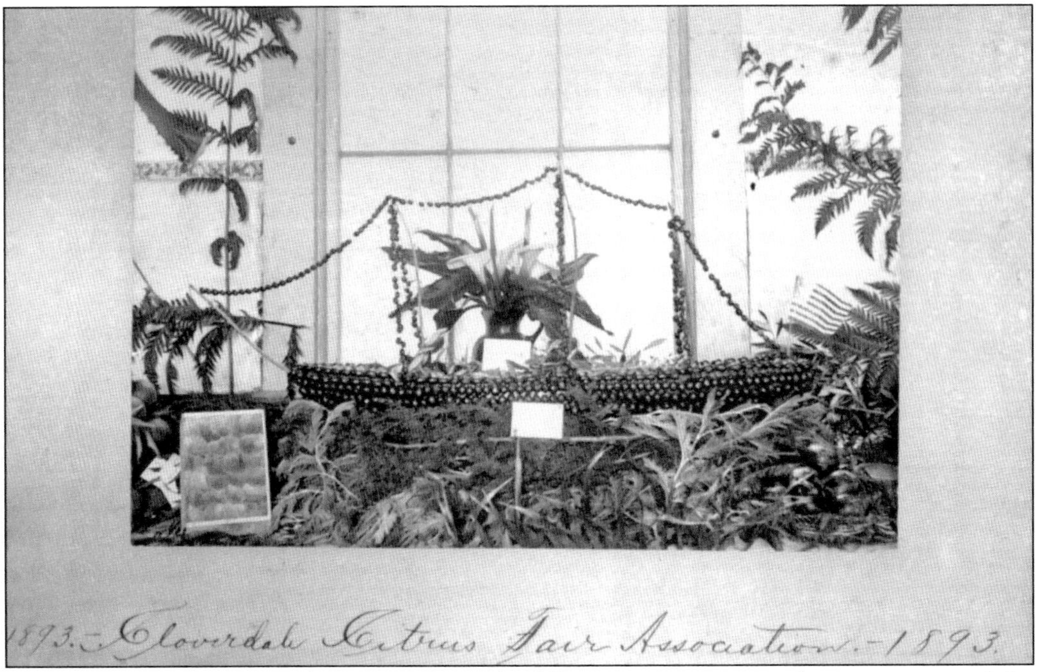

The idea for a citrus fair was born in 1892. In the following year, a group of citizens organized the Citrus Fair Association. The first Citrus Fair was held in January 1893 at Library Hall, a two-story wooden building on West Street. Thirty-five exhibitors created displays; the one pictured above, by Pauline Brush, took first place. The second Citrus Fair was also in Library Hall, but in 1895 and 1896, the fairs were held in Sissingood's Livery Stable on South West Street. The stagecoach barn was decorated with potted palms and bamboo screens, with the hayloft serving as a dance floor. In 1897, the large wooden pavilion seen below was constructed on West and First Streets. It housed the annual fairs until it was destroyed in 1909 by a fire that leveled the whole block south of First Street.

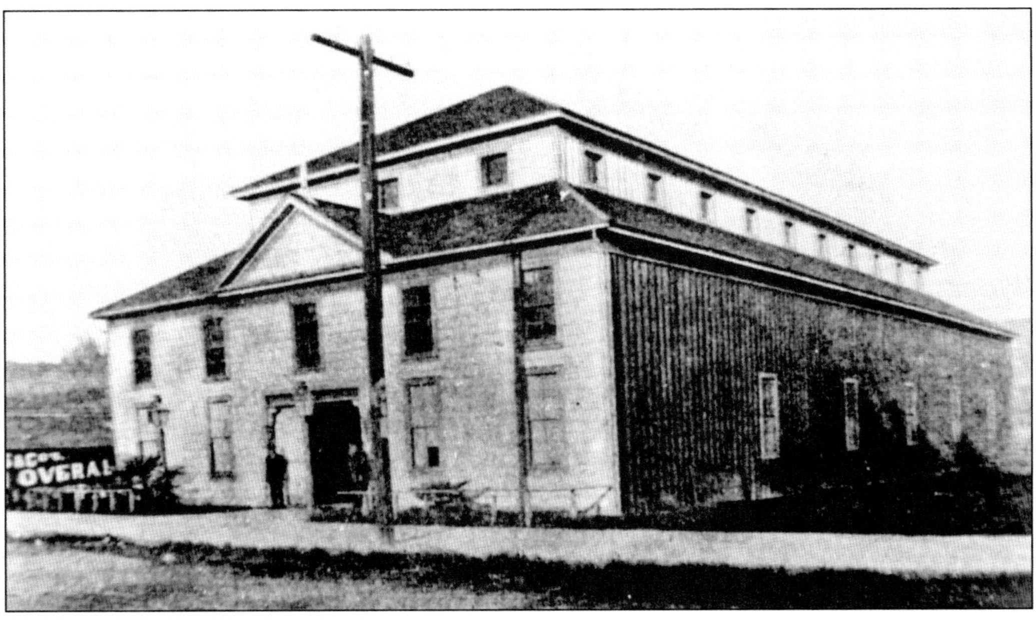

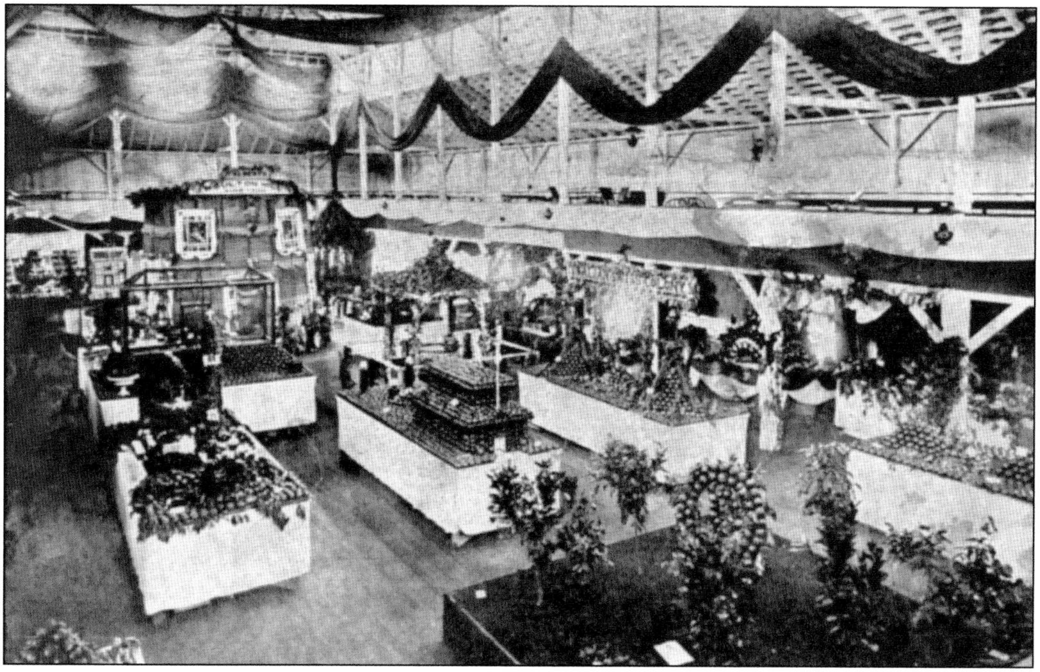

This photograph of the 1897 Citrus Fair shows the interior of the first pavilion. One of the exhibits was created by the Italian Swiss Colony and another by the Moulton Hill Winery. After the 1909 fire, a new "fireproof" pavilion (pictured below) was constructed at the same location out of reinforced concrete. For the 1910 fair, a uniformed band met every train, and visitors were escorted to the fair in carriages and automobiles. After the Citrus Fair moved to its present location in 1951, the old pavilion was used for commercial purposes. It was gutted by fire in 1968. Today this is the site of the parking lot north of Exchange Bank.

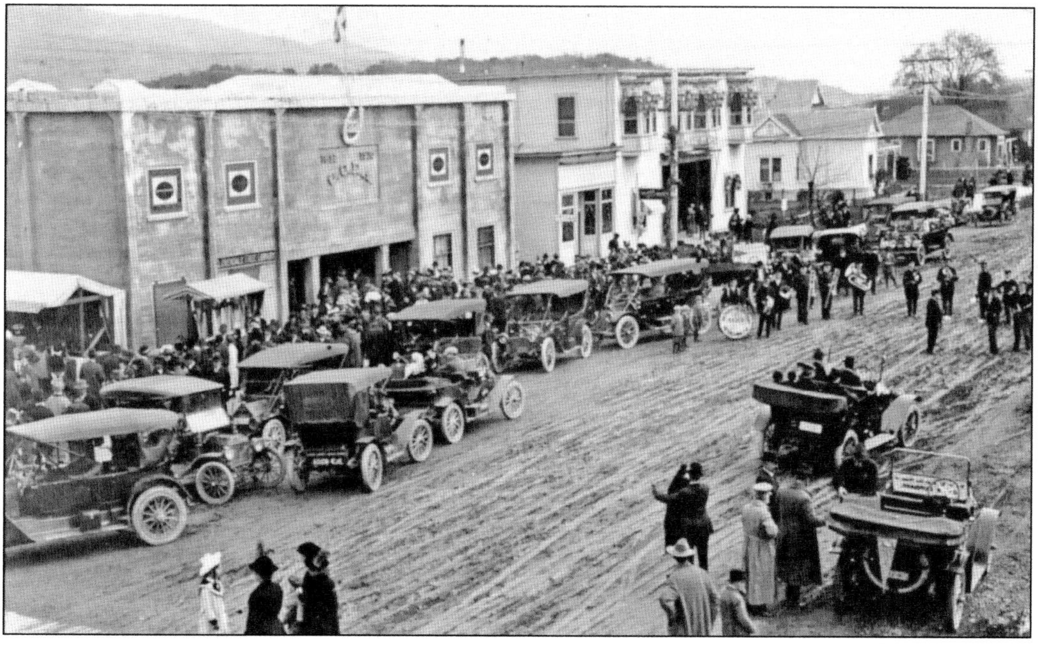

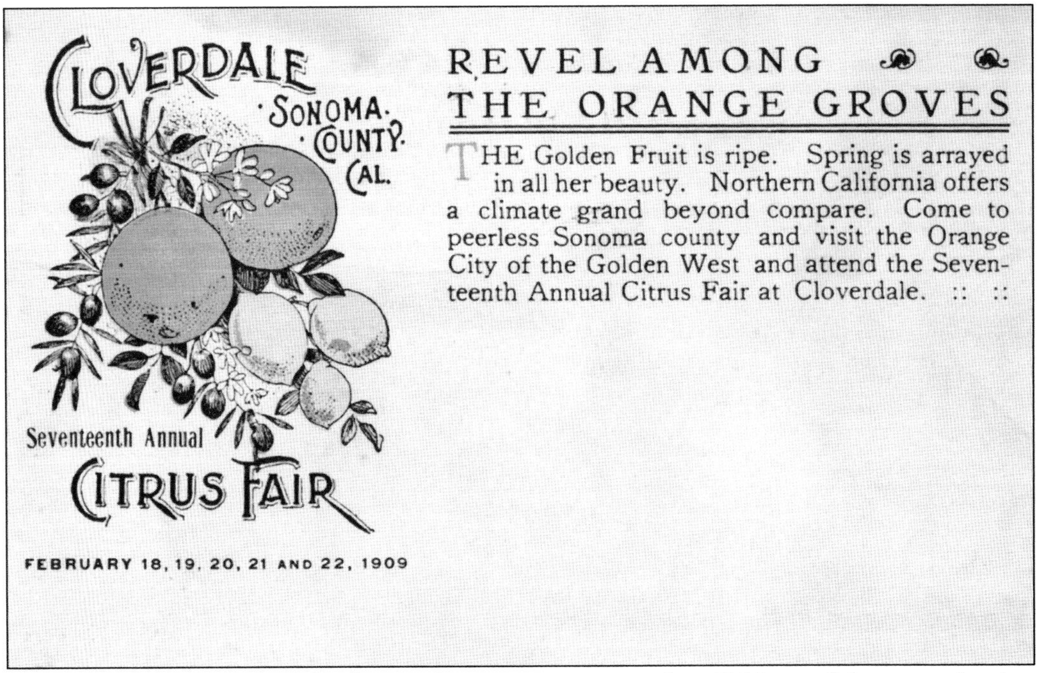

This logo, printed in colorful yellow and orange on a postcard in 1909, is still being used today, almost 100 years later, to promote the annual Citrus Fair.

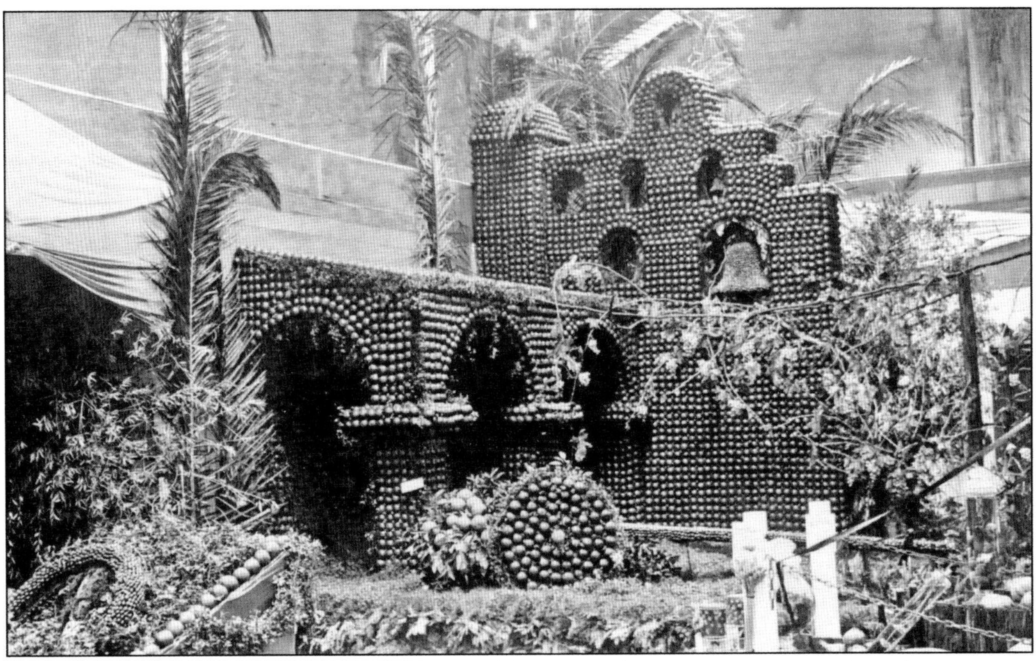

Early Citrus Fair exhibits tended to be more elaborate and to use more citrus than those seen in recent years. Early exhibitors included Fidelia Furber, whose display featured a boxer made out of citrus and prunes, and I. E. Shaw, who created a lighthouse. The display seen here of a California mission, created by the Rotary Club, won first prize at the 1914 fair.

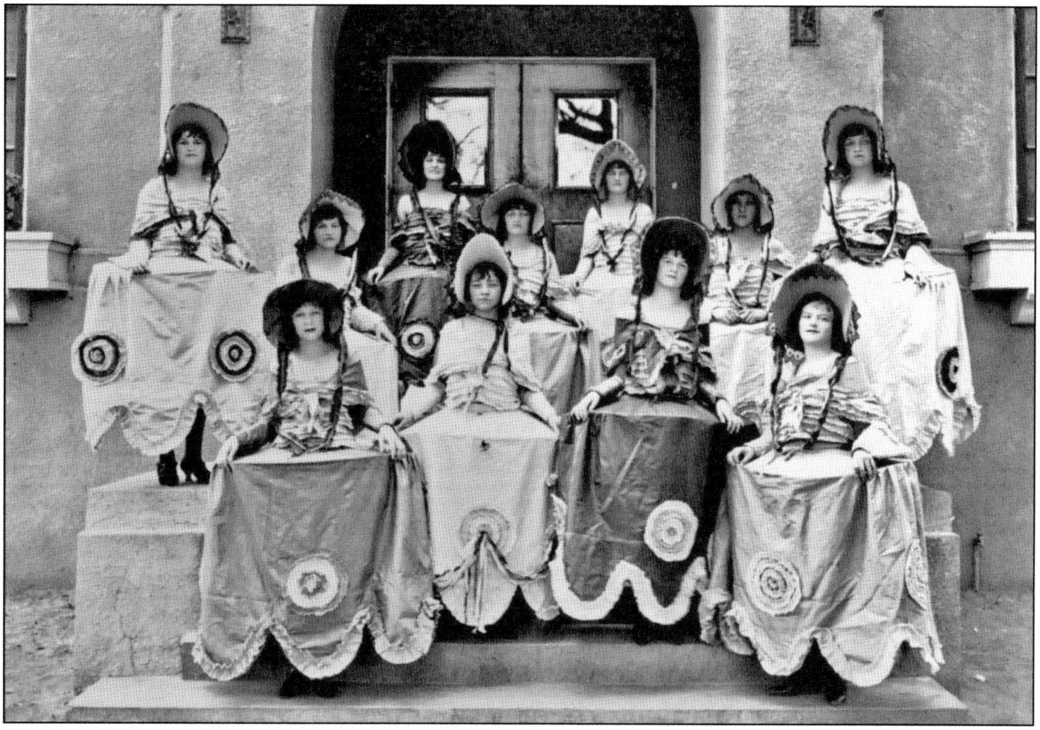

Entertainment at the Citrus Fair is a long-standing tradition. These young ladies posing on the school steps performed a play for the 1924 fair. From left to right are (first row) Maurine Bradford, Alice Grace Yordi, Virginia Williams, and Jane Whitaker; (second row) Ann McMichael, Hazel Gianoli, Isabelle Murray, Evelyn Cook, Celia Smith, Jane Kleiser, and Pauline Domini.

Cloverdale, Calif.
May 25th, 1926.

Chamber of Commerce,

Gentlemen:

Herewith I submit full and final report of 1926 Fair and all paid vouchers are enclosed:

Report of 1926 Citrus Fair

Received

Door receipts	$4239.75	
Concessions	555.00	
Dance	415.30	
Donation	1.00	
		$5211.05

Disbursed

Printing and advertising	$323.75	
Music and entertainment	620.55	
Exhibits	353.28	
Decorations	135.00	
Rent	527.00	
Miscellaneous	411.45	
		$2371.03
Profit from Fair		$2840.02
		$5211.05

Note:--$159.98 was taken from the General Fund of the Chamber of Commerce and added to the profit of $2840.02 and $3000. deposited to interest account.

Respectfully submitted,

C. L. Sedgley
Chairman Finance Committee.

In 1926, Charles L. Sedgley, cashier of the First National Bank of Cloverdale, also served as chairman of the finance committee of the Citrus Fair. That year, Sedgley reported the fair made a profit of $2,840.02 after expenses of $2,371.03. The chamber of commerce contributed an extra $159.98 to make the deposit a nice round $3,000.

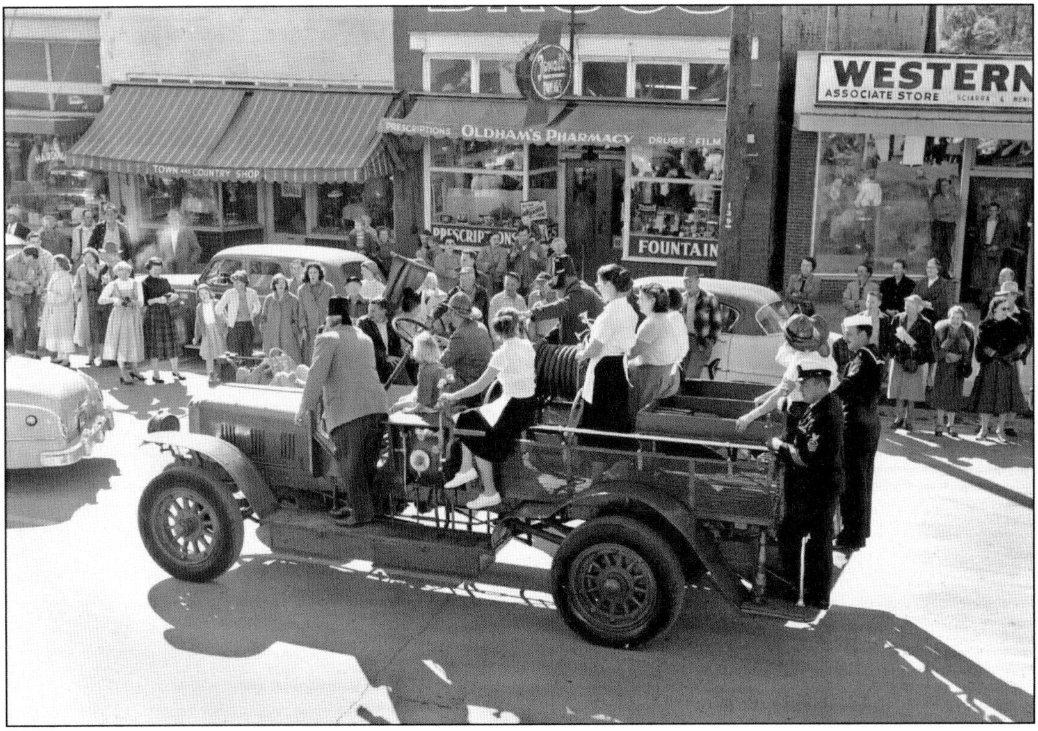

An antique fire truck, the float sponsored by the Rainbow Room, moves south down West Street in the 1956 Citrus Fair parade. Spectators are lined up in front of the local businesses: Western Auto, Oldham's Rexall Pharmacy, and the Town and Country clothing store. The brick building housing the latter two businesses, constructed sometime before 1884, was deemed earthquake unsafe and torn down in 2007.

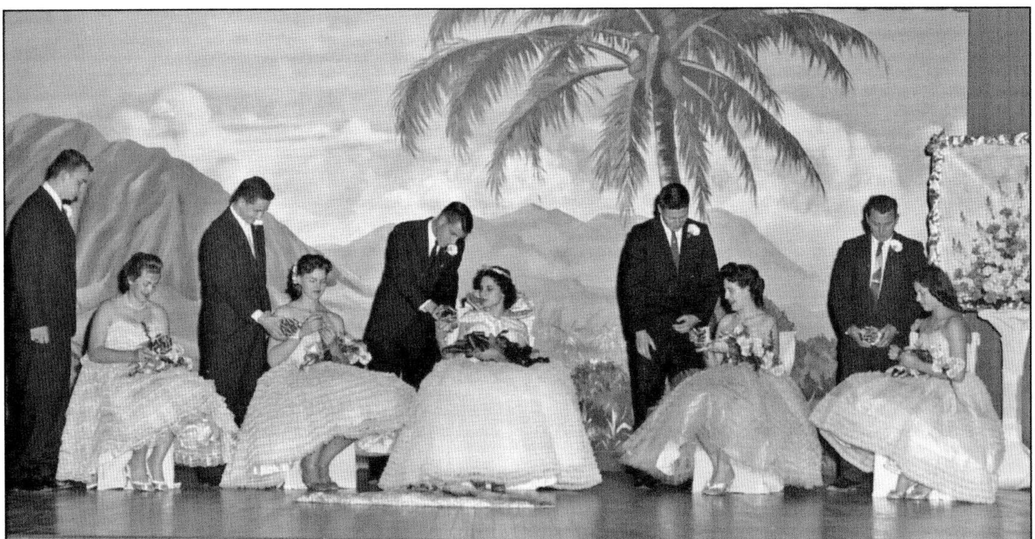

In 1960, five young ladies competed to become queen of the Citrus Fair. Seated in the center, wearing her crown, is Citrus Fair queen Virginia Giovannetti. On either side, receiving corsages from their escorts, are (from left to right) Princesses Sharon Denman, Ilene Raines, Lynn Richardson, and Janet Sauvageau.

With no television, movies, or video games to provide amusement, Cloverdalians happily created their own forms of entertainment, one being the performance of theatrical productions. These three actors performed the melodrama *Hickry Farm* in Union Hall on May 17, 1897. George Hoadley (left), the owner of the building, played Larry McKeegan of the Tenth Ward. Mrs. Fred Conner played Mrs. Priscilla Dodge, a susceptible widow. Charles Sedgley, later the cashier for the First National Bank of Cloverdale, played Uriah Skinner, a miser.

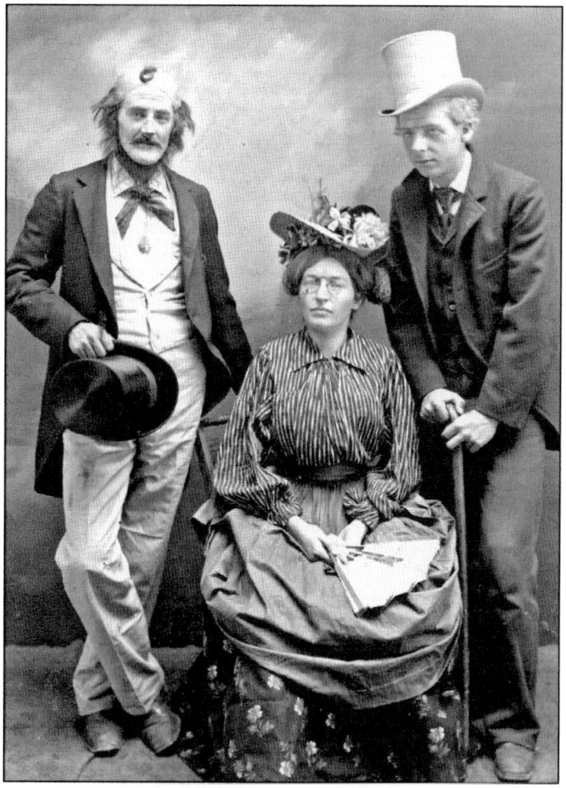

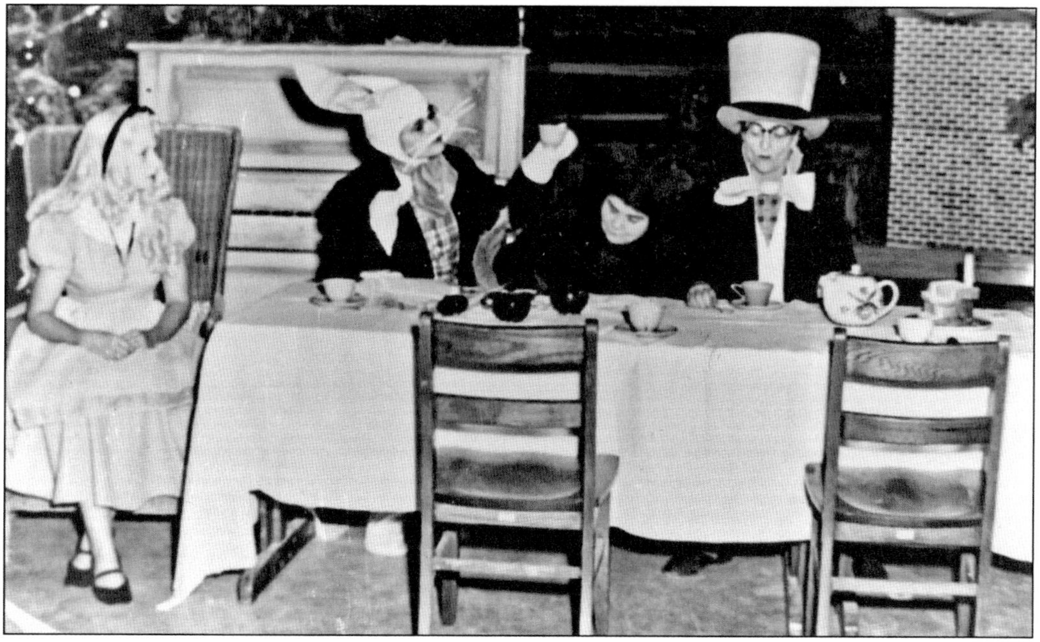

The Redwood Players were a popular theatrical group in Cloverdale going back to the 1930s. In December 1932, the group performed a skit from *Alice in Wonderland* at the Rounds and Kilpatrick (a local sawmill) Christmas party. Performers are, from left to right, Judy Hewitt (Alice), Dena Gambetta (Rabbit), Helen Butts (Doormouse), and Bee Horn Maio (Mad Hatter).

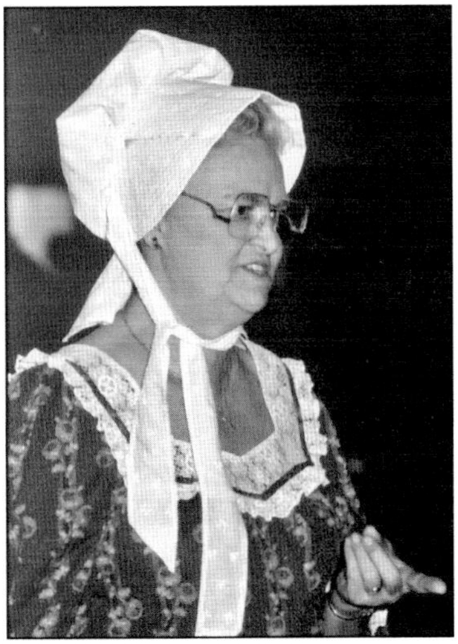

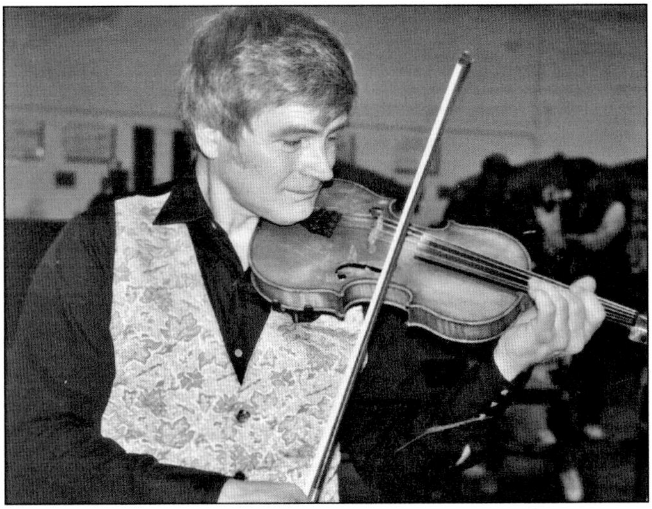

In January 1975, the Cloverdale Historical Society sponsored its first Old Time Fiddle Contest. Since then, people have come to this annual competition to perform and celebrate the music that was enjoyed across America before the advent of radio. Early competitions were emceed by "Aunt" Edith Thompson (left) and promoted by local chiropractor and master fiddler Dr. Robert Quam.

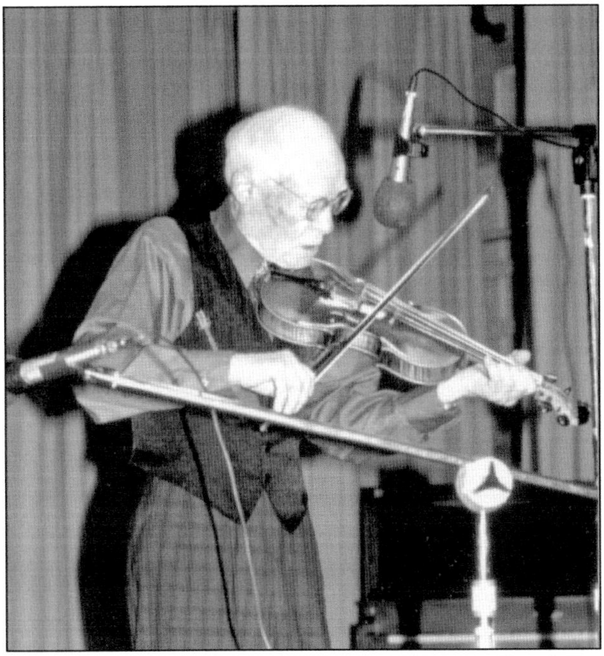

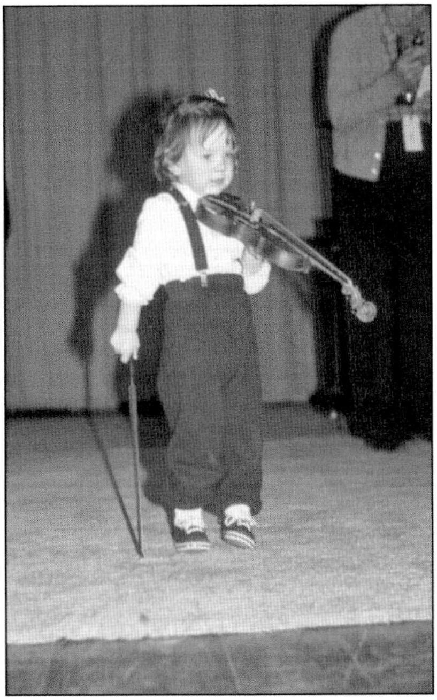

Alva Ingram (left) got his fiddle around 1900 when he traded a horse for a handmade instrument that had come across the plains in 1839. Ingram played this fiddle at the annual fiddle contest for many years, the last time when he was 91 years old. The contest also attracts the "Pee Wees," including the unidentified little fiddler (right) performing here in 1989.

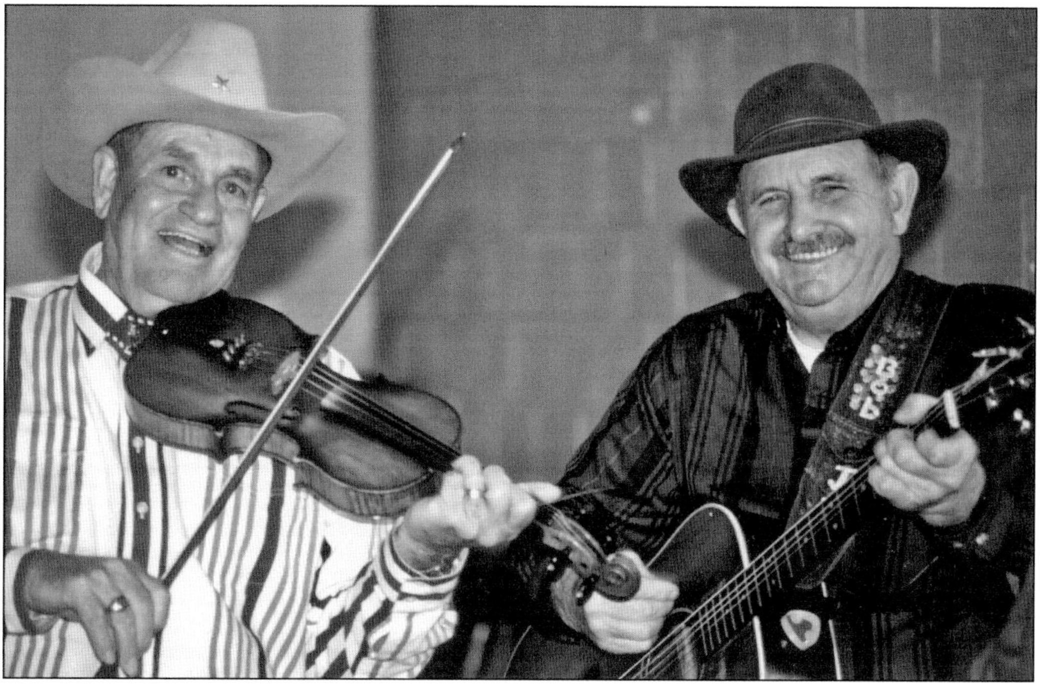

Master performer Art Deems (left) and his sidekick Ernie Hunt were crowd favorites at the fiddle contest for many years. Art could play his fiddle behind his back and upside down. Art and Ernie are pictured here jamming at the 1998 contest.

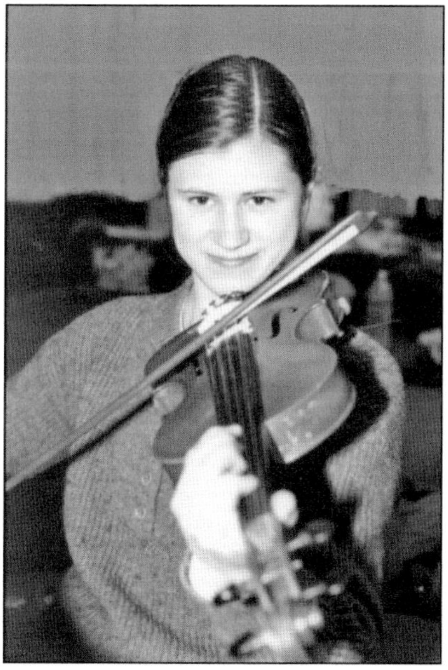

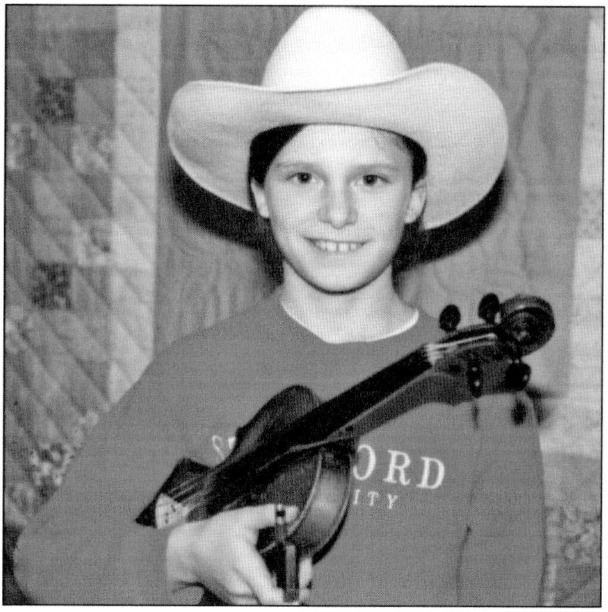

Siblings Tashina (left) and Tristan Clarridge, pictured here in 1998, first competed in the Junior-Junior Division of the Old Time Fiddle Contest. The youngsters amazed the audience and the judges with their style and skill. Their dedication to fiddling brought them back to Cloverdale year after year and took them to venues throughout the state and the nation. Both have gone on to win national championships.

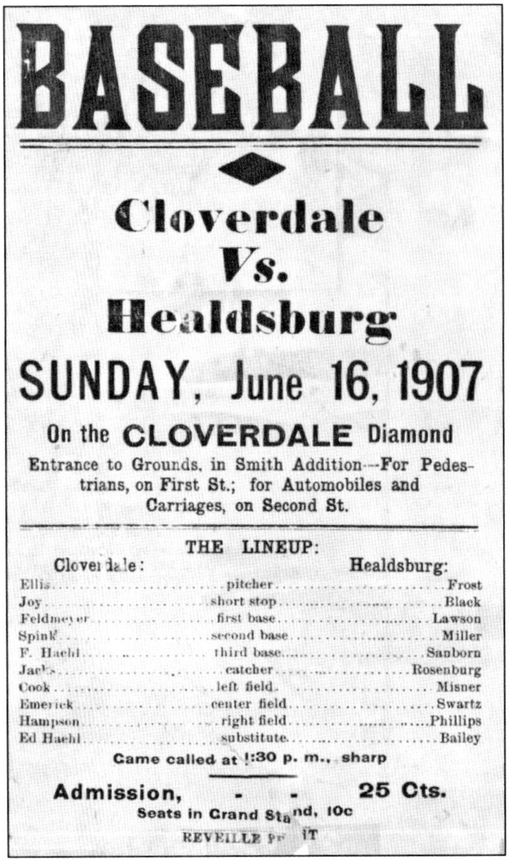

BASEBALL

Cloverdale Vs. Healdsburg

SUNDAY, June 16, 1907

On the CLOVERDALE Diamond

Entrance to Grounds, in Smith Addition—For Pedestrians, on First St.; for Automobiles and Carriages, on Second St.

THE LINEUP:

Cloverdale:		Healdsburg:
Ellis	pitcher	Frost
Joy	short stop	Black
Feldmeyer	first base	Lawson
Spink	second base	Miller
F. Haehl	third base	Sanborn
Jacks	catcher	Rosenburg
Cook	left field	Misner
Emerick	center field	Swartz
Hampson	right field	Phillips
Ed Haehl	substitute	Bailey

Game called at 1:30 p. m., sharp

Admission, - - 25 Cts.

Seats in Grand Stand, 10c

REVEILLE PRINT

Whether it is 1907 or 2007, Cloverdalians do love their baseball. On June 16, 1907, the Cloverdale baseball team hosted their rivals from Healdsburg. Spectators arrived on foot, in automobiles, and in carriages. Admission was 25¢, but one could sit in the grandstand for only a dime.

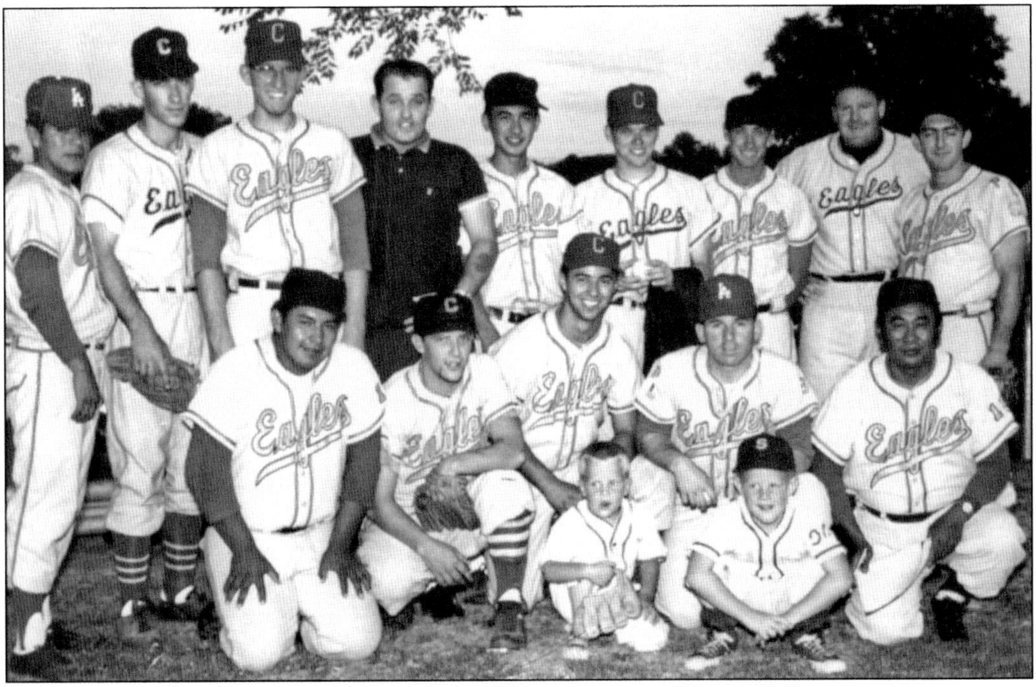

These young men, wearing "recycled" high school jerseys, enjoyed playing on the 1965 adult league team sponsored by Cloverdale merchants. The team competed with Ukiah, Lakeport, and other towns. From left to right are (kneeling) Carl Fred, Charley Ricard, Wayne Menicucci, Robert Davis, John Santana, and D. Magnussen's two boys; (standing) Pat Dollar, Dick Tucker, Leo Giovannetti, Pat Daly, Jerry Santana, Ed Bowen, Johnny Uselton, D. Magnussen, and Jim Wirt. (Courtesy Paul Giovannetti.)

Seven

Places and Faces through the Years

In small towns, citizens from the mayor to the youngest 4-H member often play more than one role. In 1930s Cloverdale, Judge Estelle Gibbons, also the city clerk, city treasurer, and the town's only notary, held court and performed weddings. At the same time, legendary marksman Jim Ledford was Cloverdale's one-man police force as well as its water-meter reader. For much of Cloverdale's history, fire protection was provided by an all-volunteer fire department with assistance from the town's switchboard operator, who activated the fire siren on the roof of the telephone office.

Cloverdale's organizations and clubs have always provided much of the town's active social life. The first was the Masons, which started in the year of the town's founding, 1859. Many others followed, among them the Odd Fellows in 1886, the Druids in 1908, and the American Legion following World War I. These groups frequently engaged in civic improvement projects. The Women's Improvement Club, for example, built Cloverdale's first library in 1921, and the Grange during World War II sponsored Cloverdale's first blood drive, an event to which Italian Swiss Colony manager Enrico Prati sent 32 men up from Asti to give blood.

Individuals such as doctors, teachers, and bankers have also played essential roles. Determined to encourage financial prudence, Bank of America manager Joe Giovannetti in the 1940s reportedly refused to let a young man withdraw his savings to buy a car unless he first went home and "slept on it."

A picture history of Cloverdale is rightly replete with images of street scenes, vintage buildings, memorable events, and people who came together to create community. Here are a few of Cloverdale's places and faces through the years.

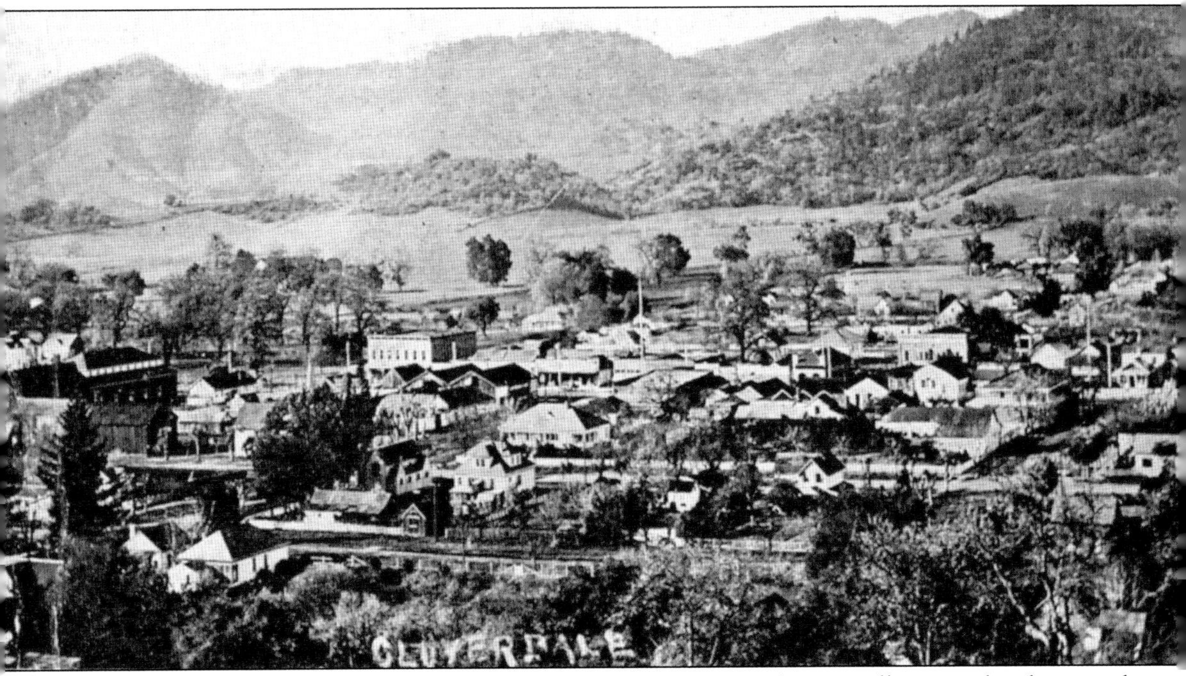

This c. 1907 panorama of Cloverdale shows Main Street running horizontally across the photograph with the Episcopal Church of the Good Shepherd on the left and the Pinschower residence (now Vintage Towers Bed and Breakfast) on the right. From left to right along West Street are the old

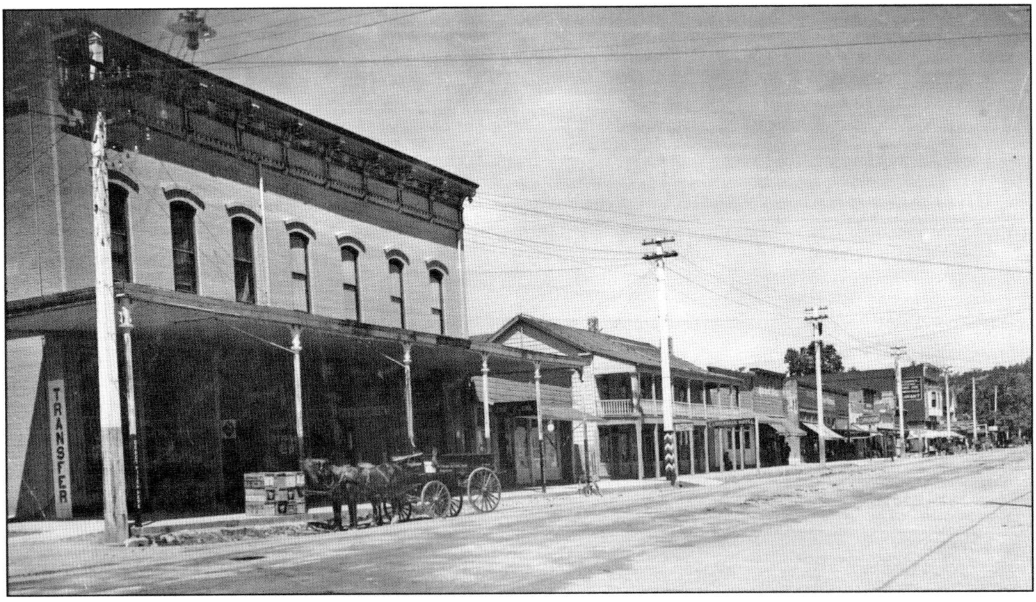

This view of West Street from First Street was taken some time before the disastrous fire of 1915. The headline of the Santa Rosa *Press Democrat* of October 15, 1915, reported, "Cloverdale's Big Fire—Early Morning Blaze Takes Toll of 3 Lives." The fire wiped out the Union Hall (far left), Humbert's Opera House, an ice cream parlor, a barbershop, a jewelry store, the Cloverdale Hotel, and two saloons—the Grape Vine and the Owl.

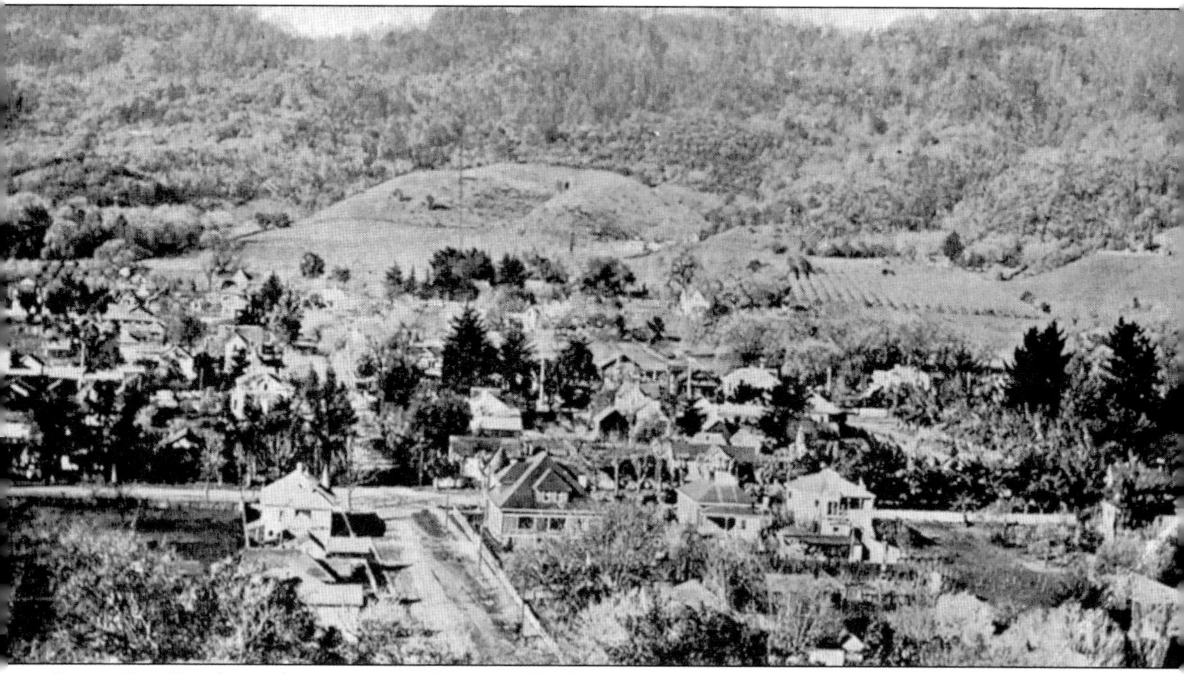

Citrus Fair Pavilion, the two-story Union Hall, the First National Bank, the U.S. Hotel, and the Isaac Shaw house. Much of the surrounding area was planted in grapes, including the Haehl property located west of Jefferson.

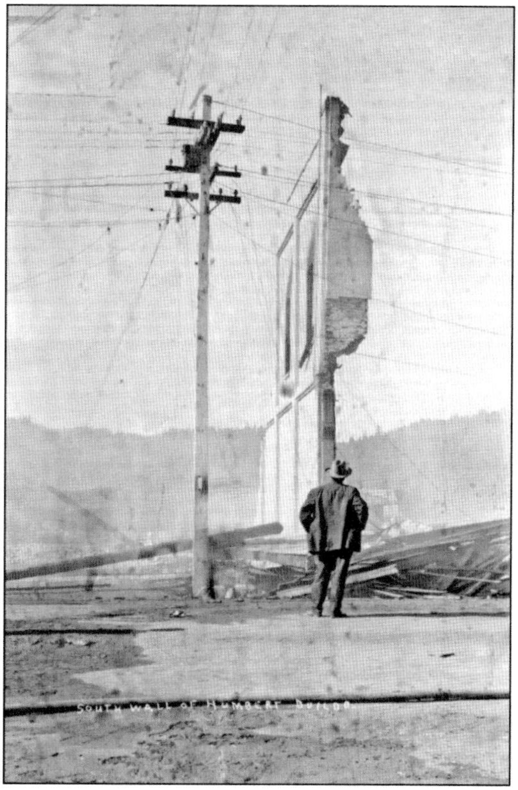

Charles Humbert is seen gazing at the burned-out remains of his opera house. The fire started in a restaurant at the front of the Cloverdale Hotel. Hotel manager Joe Swindell had left the restaurant to check the fuel supply after lighting his gasoline stove. When he returned, he discovered the stove had exploded. The fire destroyed the entire block of buildings, stopping just short of the Mitchell Brothers' Saloon at 117 North Cloverdale Boulevard. Humbert, who ran a stage line to The Geysers and was president of the Culver-Baer Mining Company, later served as Cloverdale's mayor from 1930 to 1934.

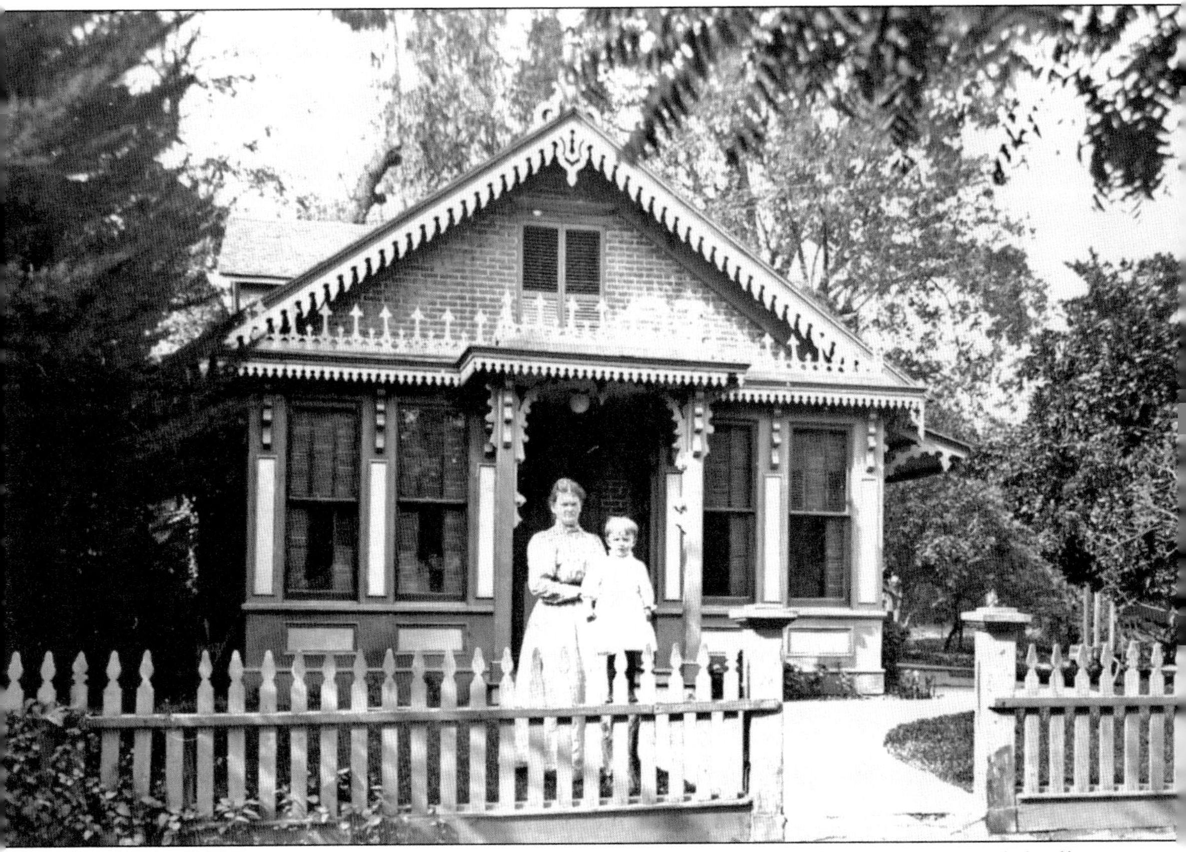

The Gould-Shaw House, built in 1862 by Thomas Gould, is the oldest documented dwelling in Cloverdale and one of the rare surviving examples of Gothic Revival, an architectural style of the Victorian era characterized by steeply pitched roofs, pointed-arch windows, elaborate trim along roof edges, and high dormers. The 1877 atlas of Sonoma County describes the building as one of the best of its style. The house was purchased in 1875 by Isaac Ellis Shaw, whose second wife, Minerva McCray Shaw, lived in the house from 1879 until her death in 1938. Minerva appears along with her daughter Gertrude in this photograph taken around 1899. The Cloverdale Historical Society purchased the house and property in 1983 and undertook a major renovation and retrofitting in the late 1990s. Today the house, which is listed on the National Register of Historic Places, is home to the Cloverdale Historical Society and Museum.

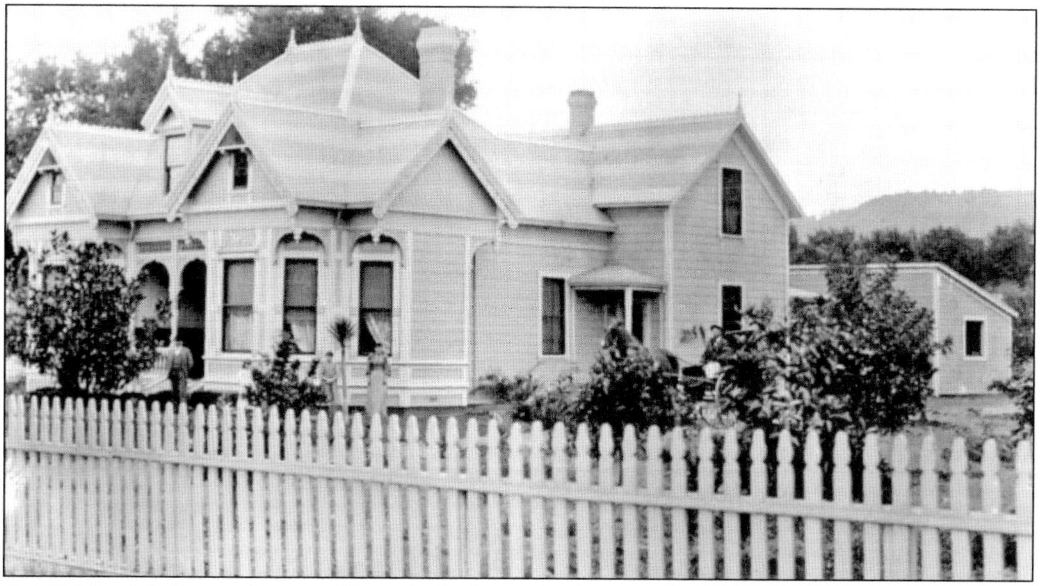

At 221 North Jefferson Street still stands the house built around 1880 for Fred Yordi, who not only had a large mercantile business in Cloverdale in the old Shaw Bowman Building, but also ran a large stock ranch four miles to the west of town. His residence was on four acres and was planted to fruit, including 200 orange trees. The misspelled Yorty Creek is named for this early business leader.

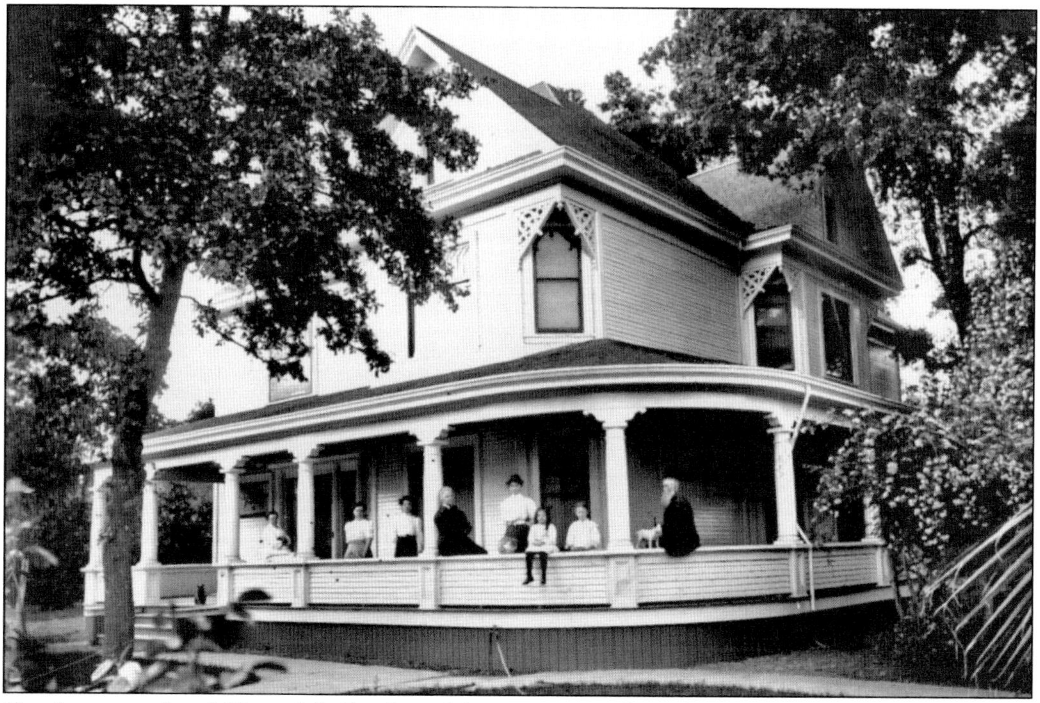

On the east side of Cloverdale Boulevard between Fourth and University Streets, on property currently occupied by the Fred Young Mortuary, once stood the home of prominent Cloverdale citizen William T. Brush, seated on the far right, is pictured with his family around 1906. A&W Root Beer was located on this site in the 1970s.

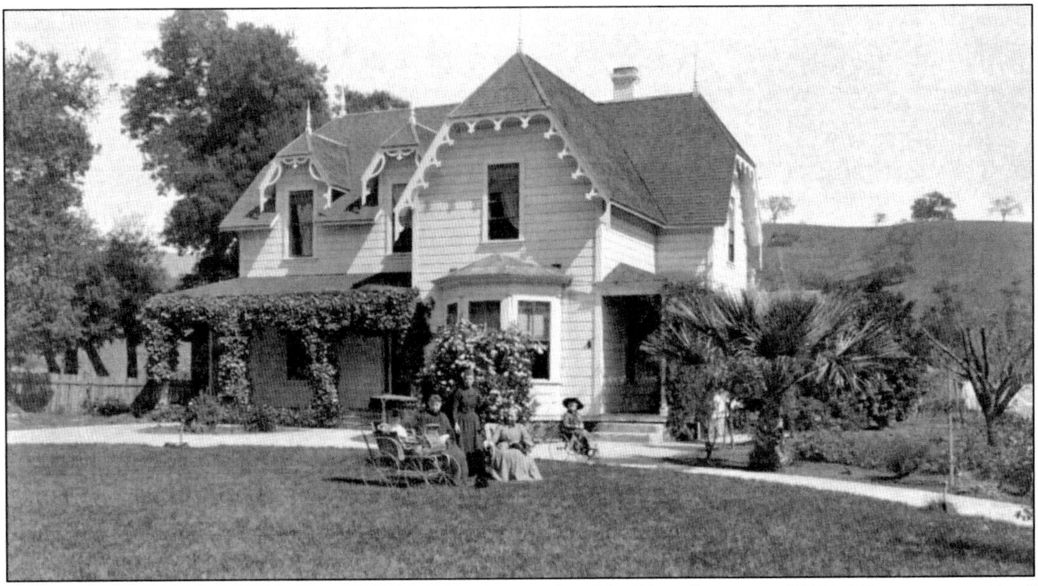

This house, built by David Brush in the 1860s, was the Chalfant home in 1892. The property had a barn, a carriage house, a workshop, and a large orchard. The house was moved in the 1960s to Fourth and Main Streets, and a restaurant currently occupies the site at 504 North Cloverdale Boulevard. Identified are grandmother Susan Chalfant (seated right), Susan's daughter Nellie (seated left) and Susan's daughter Martha Chalfant Porterfield (standing) with her two children, Alice (on the velocipede) and Helen (in the carriage).

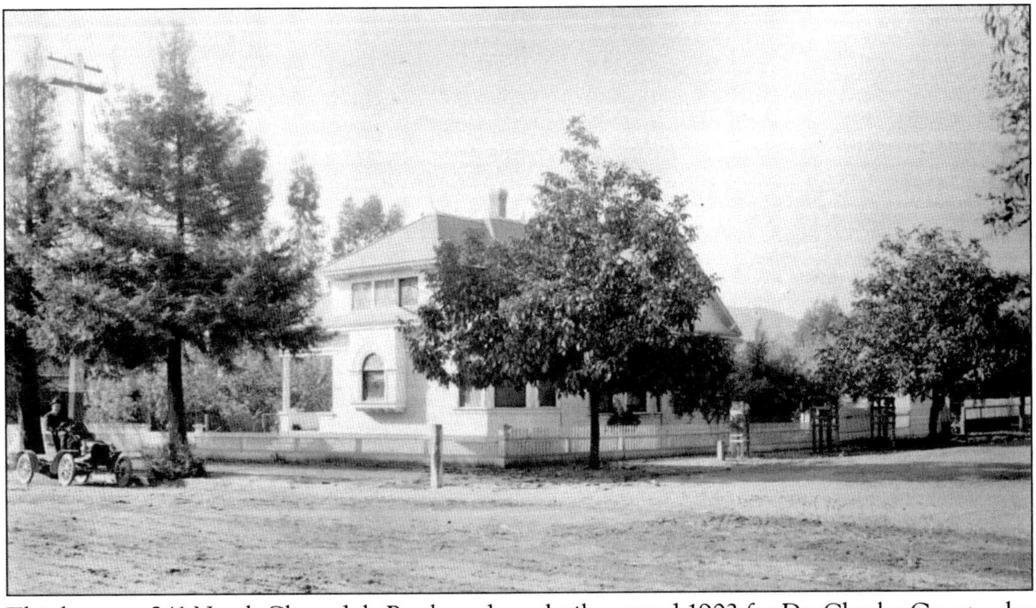

This home at 241 North Cloverdale Boulevard was built around 1903 for Dr. Charles Grant, who owned a local drugstore with partner Fred Reichers. For four decades, the house continued as a residence for Cloverdale's doctors: Dr. William C. Shipley in the 1920s, a Dr. Wheeler in the early 1930s, Dr. Frank Sohler Jr. from the mid-1930s to the 1940s, and Dr. Marlin Greenhalgh up to the 1960s. The house is still owned and occupied by the Greenhalgh family.

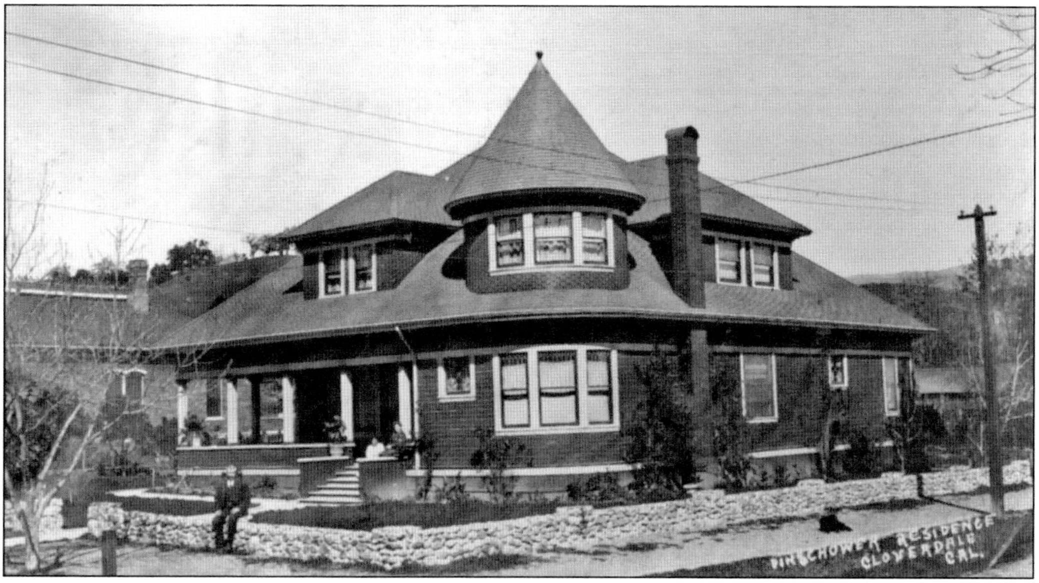

This large Victorian, listed on the National Register of Historic Places, was built at 302 Main Street in 1901 for Simon Pinschower, a wealthy merchant and mining executive. The subsequent owner hired Petaluma architect Brainard Jones to remodel the house and add two additional towers. In the 1920s, it was used by a Dr. Wheeler as a full-service hospital. Today the restored home operates as Vintage Towers Bed and Breakfast.

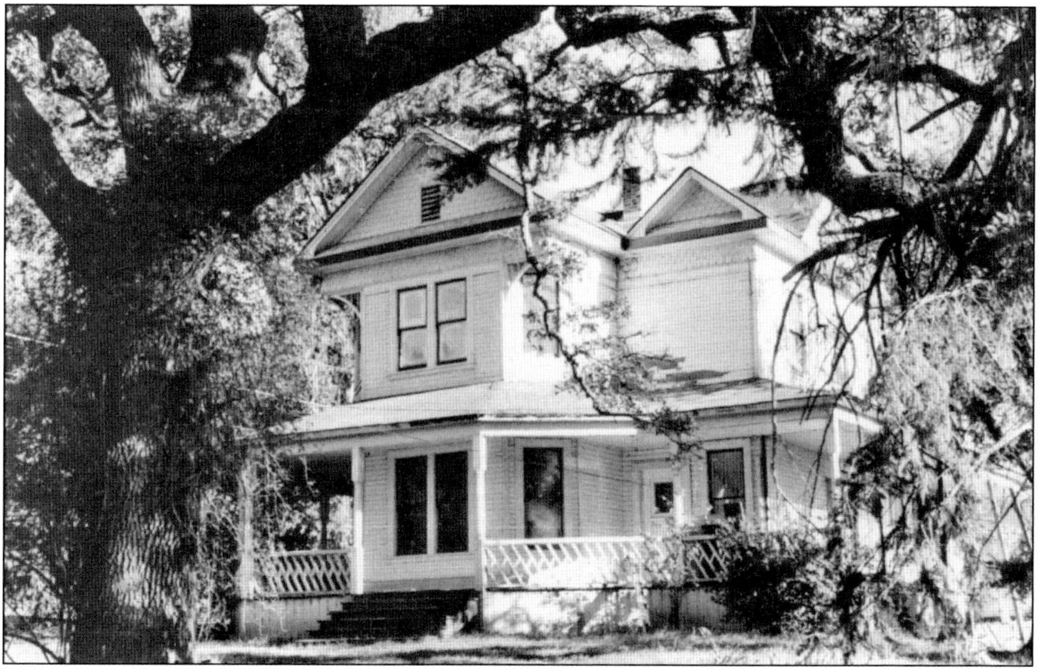

In 1885, Erastus Shelford built a house on property given to him by his father, John Shelford III, who had purchased the land in 1863 as part of the Rancho Musalacon Land Grant. This house at 29550 South River Road was built on the site after a 1905 fire destroyed the original structure. Six generations of Shelfords lived here for more than 120 years. Today this fine Victorian is a charming inn.

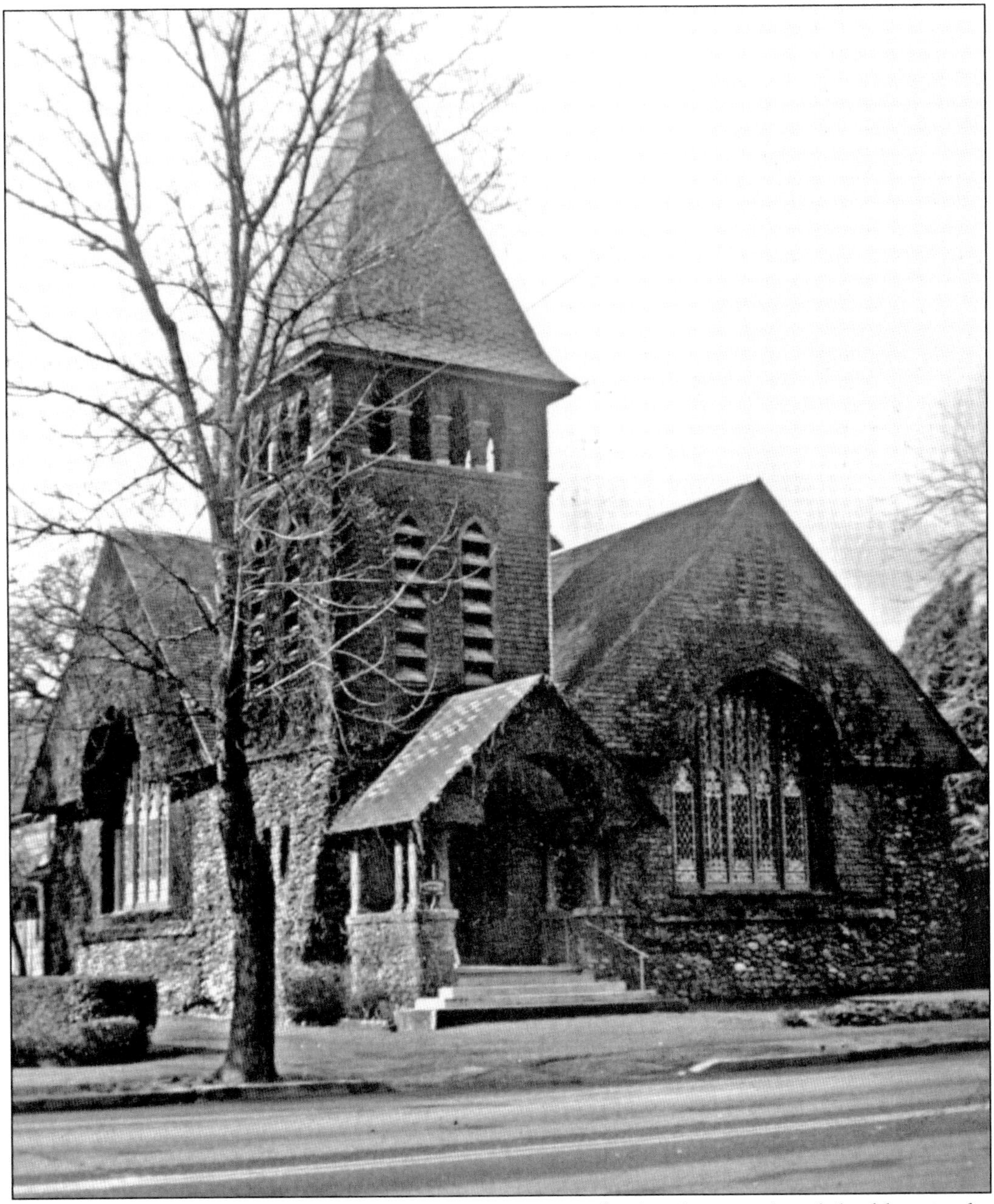

The Congregational Church, pictured here in 1962, was the first known church building in the area. It was built on North West Street in 1869 on land donated by James Kleiser, and the sanctuary was added in 1906 with money donated by Susan Chalfant in memory of her husband, John. The church organ was powered from a Pelton wheel located in the basement and connected to the city water system, and when the local water wagon would fill its tank, the water pressure would be reduced, muting the sound of the organ. The Congregational Church became the United Church of Cloverdale in 1979 when it joined with United Methodist, itself a union of the Southern Methodist branch, organized in 1865, and the northern branch, established in 1871. The United Church, also known as the "Ivy Church," is famous for the brilliant colors of its surrounding foliage each fall.

Cloverdale's first Catholic mass was celebrated in the Cloverdale Hotel in 1866. When the community built old St. Peter's in 1879 at the corner of Main and Broad Streets, there were 20 families—12 Irish and 8 German. Twenty years later, parishioners were almost equally divided between Italian on one hand and Irish and German on the other. The church, pictured here in 1920, was used until the new St. Peter's was built in 1962.

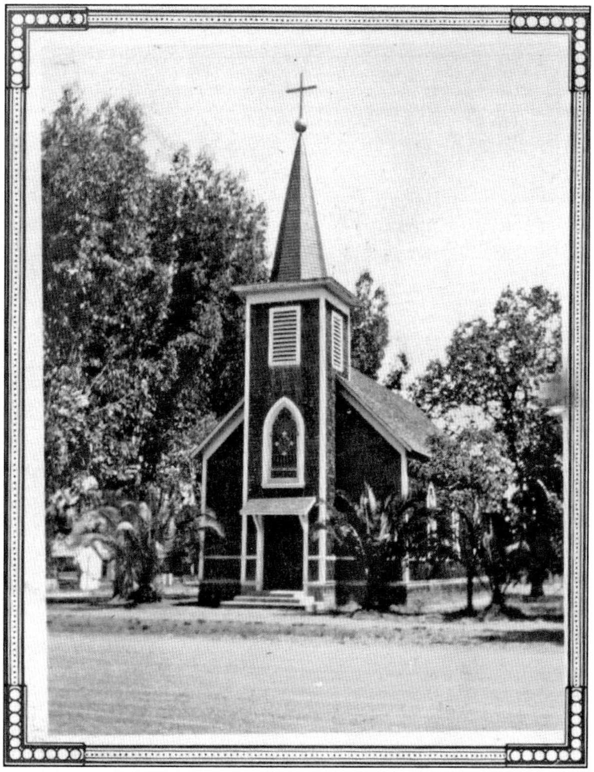

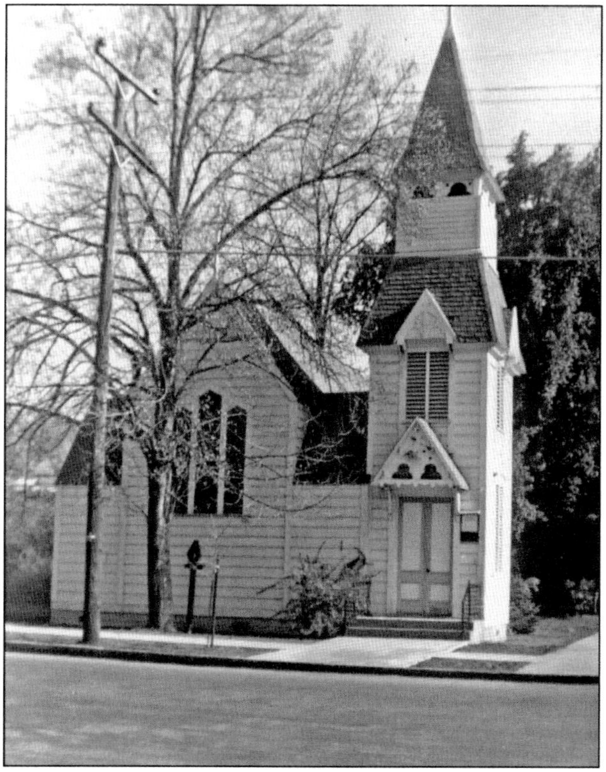

Episcopal services were held in the Union Hall as early as 1885. Fund-raising to build a church began in earnest the following year, with contributions coming in from all quarters, including the Methodists and the Catholics. The Episcopal Church of the Good Shepherd was built of redwood in a delicate Carpenter's Gothic style.

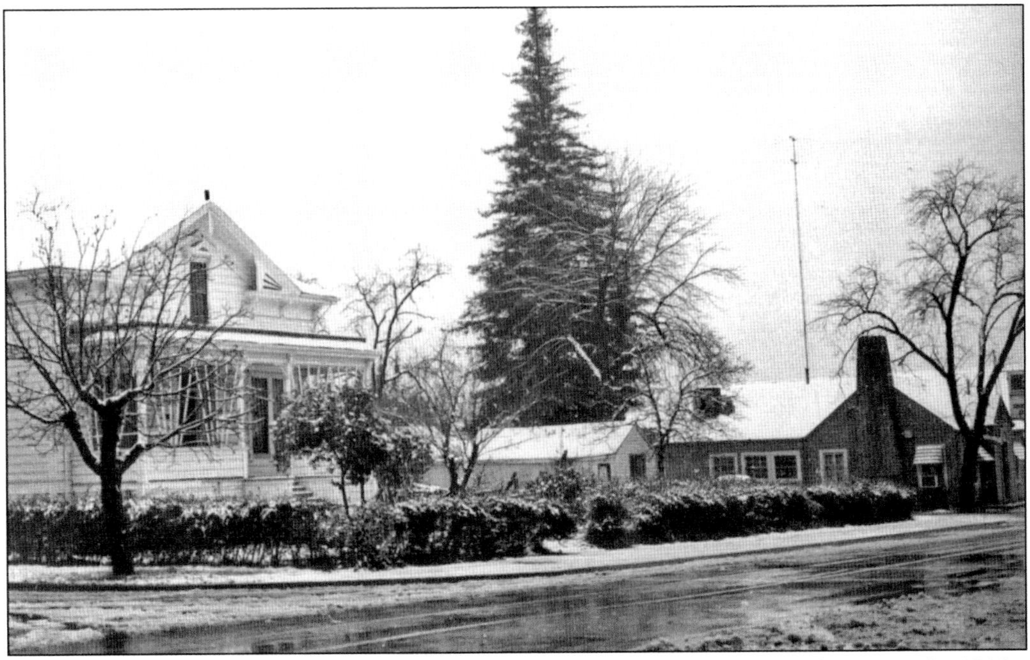

This home on the southeast corner of West and Third Streets underwent a makeover in the 1980s. Developer Tom Dean raised the two-story Victorian 13 feet, transforming it into a colorful creation with copper roofs and twisted brick chimneys. John and Terrie Spenst, who bought the property in 1988, completed the renovation. This 1970s picture shows how the house looked before it became the Copper Towers Health Center.

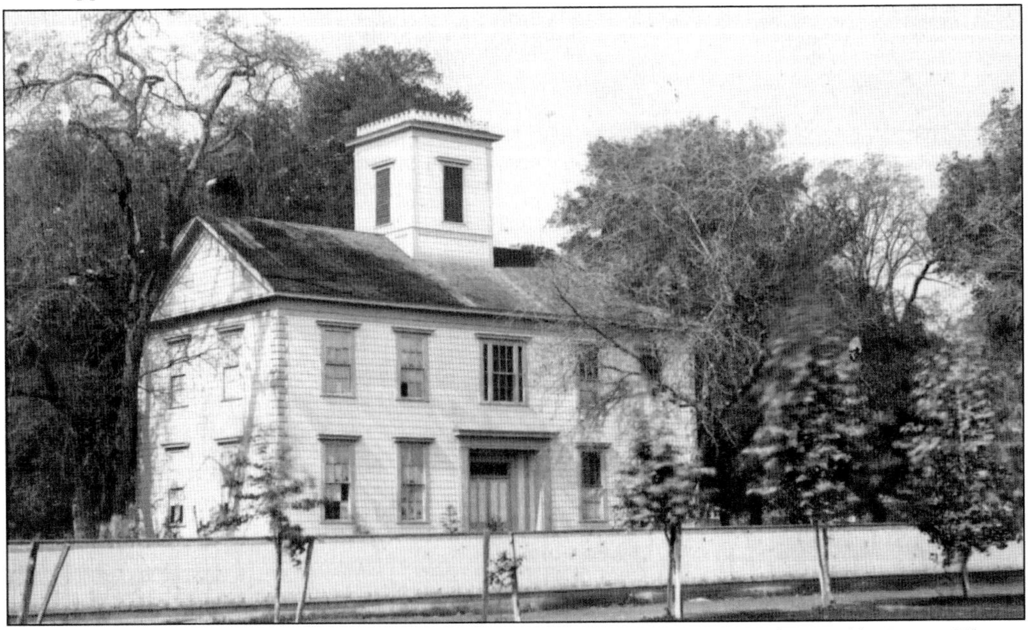

The first school in town was a log cabin with a stone fireplace on property donated by James Kleiser just north of what is now the United Church. In 1860, a new school was built on the site. Four years later, it was enlarged to the two-story wooden building pictured here around 1900. The school served the community until 1917, when it was replaced by a concrete building.

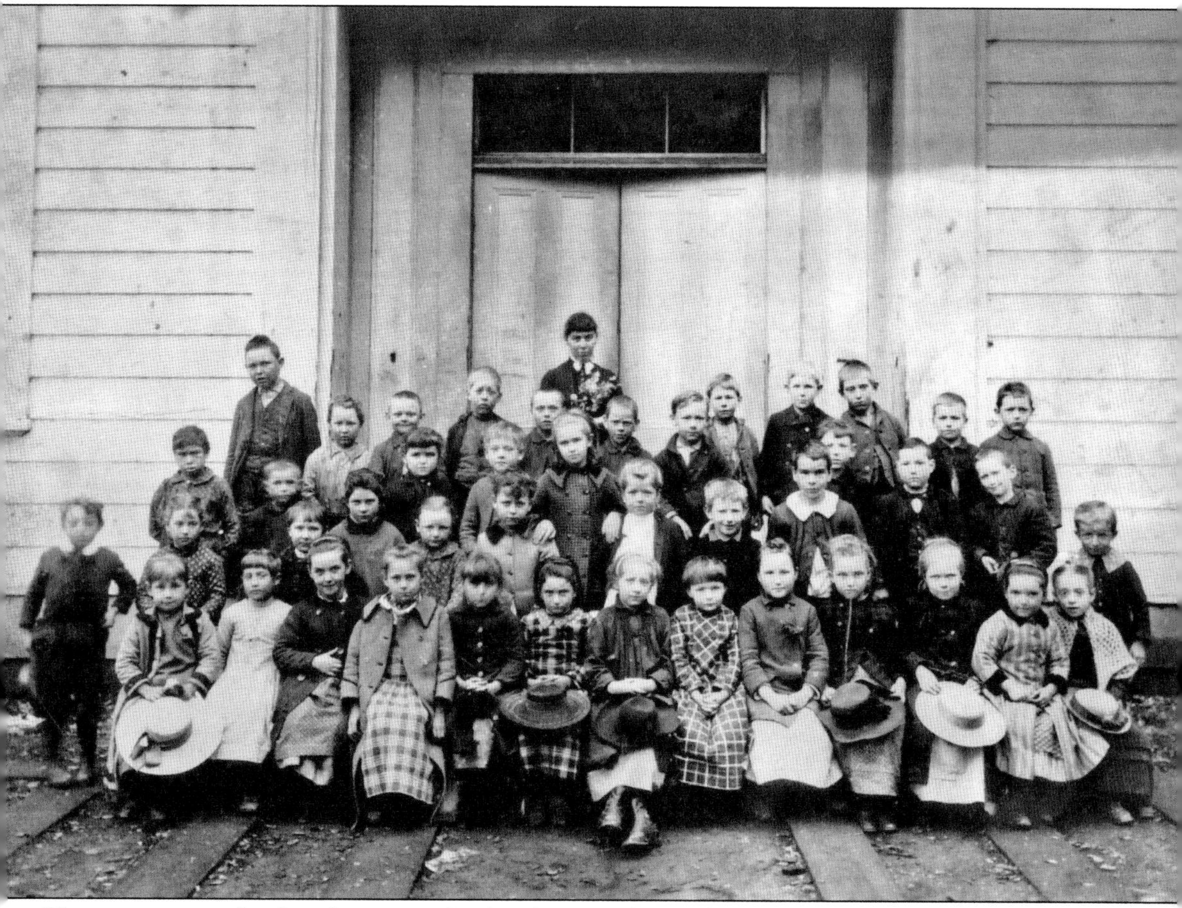

These grammar school students pose for the photographer with their teacher, Bessie Fowler Sink, in front of the Cloverdale School sometime in the late 1800s. Some of the children have surnames that are familiar to Cloverdale residents today: Addie Sink, Agusta and Herman Reger, Helen Yordi, Mary Sedgley, John Menihan, and Nellie Shelford. Pictured from left to right are (first row) Ada Schultz, Emma Ford, Lily Stockwell, Julia Hemsath, Kate Murphy, Josie Vragnasion, Agnes Mason, Nellie Sedgley, Annie Koester, Addie Sink, Wilda Stockwell, Agusta Reger, and Fielding Kinley; (second row) Jimmy Kerr, Helen Yordi, Ruby Dodson, Myrtle Graham, May Caughey, Mary Sedgley, Lucy Sacrey, Jim Finnerty, Harry Marshall, Walter Crigler, and John Menihan; (third row) Frank Hess, Fred Graham, Nellie Shelford, Jim Hayes, Amy McCausland, Cyrus Dodson, and Herman Roger; (fourth row) Fred Brown, unidentified, Chas Nicholas, Russell Beasley, Bernard McKenna, Owen McKenna, Bert Graham, Earl Casey, Justus Elden, Phillip Crigler, and George Frain. Teacher Bessie Fowler Sink is standing in the far back.

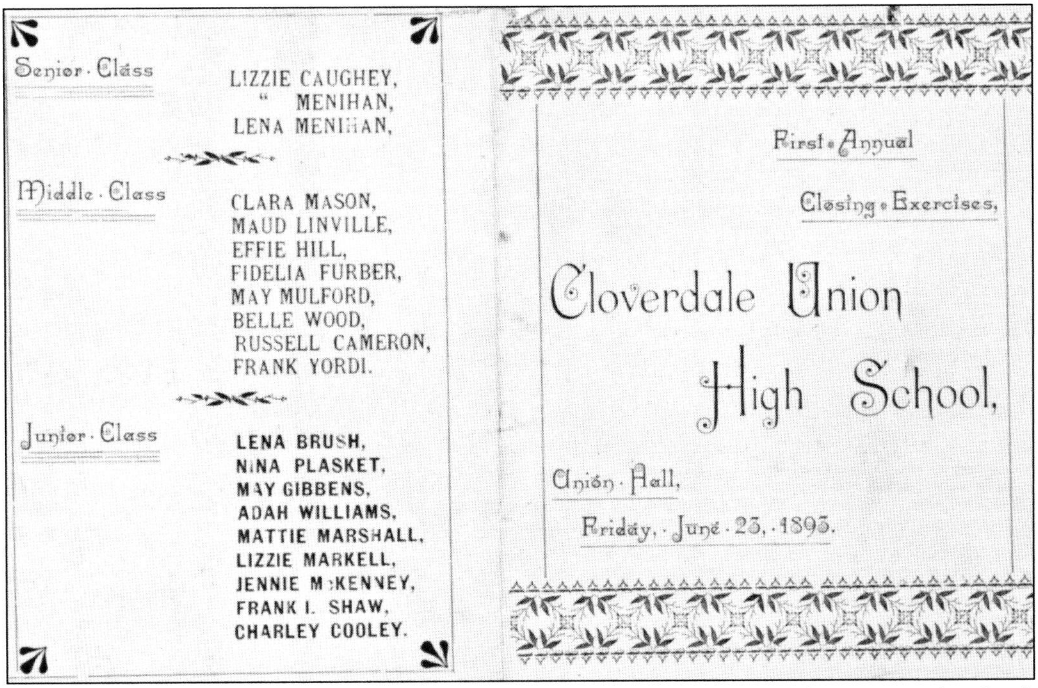

Senior Class

LIZZIE CAUGHEY,
" MENIHAN,
LENA MENIHAN,

Middle Class

CLARA MASON,
MAUD LINVILLE,
EFFIE HILL,
FIDELIA FURBER,
MAY MULFORD,
BELLE WOOD,
RUSSELL CAMERON,
FRANK YORDI.

Junior Class

LENA BRUSH,
NINA PLASKET,
MAY GIBBENS,
ADAH WILLIAMS,
MATTIE MARSHALL,
LIZZIE MARKELL,
JENNIE McKENNEY,
FRANK I. SHAW,
CHARLEY COOLEY.

First Annual

Closing Exercises,

Cloverdale Union

High School,

Union Hall,

Friday, June 23, 1893.

This souvenir program marked the First Annual Closing Exercises of Cloverdale Union High School, held in Union Hall on Friday, June 23, 1893, when E. E. Hollopeter was the principal. Members of the class of 1893 were Jean Smith (salutatorian), Oscar Tyler, Charley Cheeks (valedictorian), Jessie Wood, and Grace Wilcox. Instrumental entertainment was provided by Lizzie and Lena Menihan and Fidelia Furber. The second part of the program consisted of "cunundrums, quotations, declamations and songs."

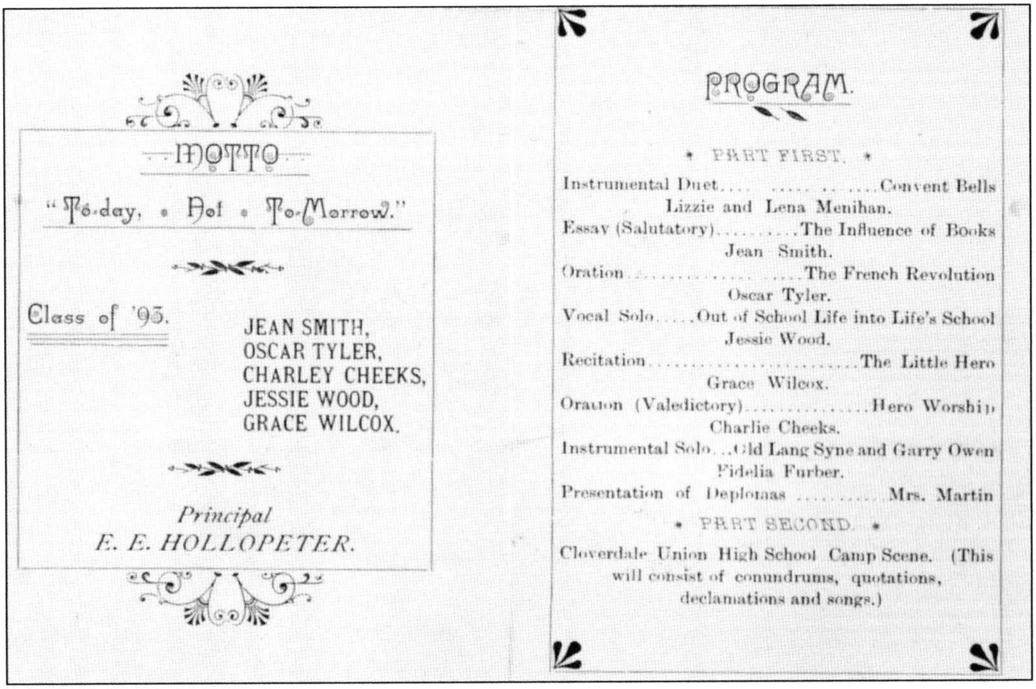

MOTTO

"To-day, Not To-Morrow."

Class of '93.

JEAN SMITH,
OSCAR TYLER,
CHARLEY CHEEKS,
JESSIE WOOD,
GRACE WILCOX.

Principal
E. E. HOLLOPETER.

PROGRAM.

• PART FIRST. •

Instrumental Duet.... .... Convent Bells
Lizzie and Lena Menihan.
Essay (Salutatory).......... The Influence of Books
Jean Smith.
Oration.............. ..... The French Revolution
Oscar Tyler.
Vocal Solo..... Out of School Life into Life's School
Jessie Wood.
Recitation........................ The Little Hero
Grace Wilcox.
Oration (Valedictory)............... Hero Worship
Charlie Cheeks.
Instrumental Solo...Old Lang Syne and Garry Owen
Fidelia Furber.
Presentation of Deplomas .... Mrs. Martin

• PART SECOND. •

Cloverdale Union High School Camp Scene. (This will consist of conundrums, quotations, declamations and songs.)

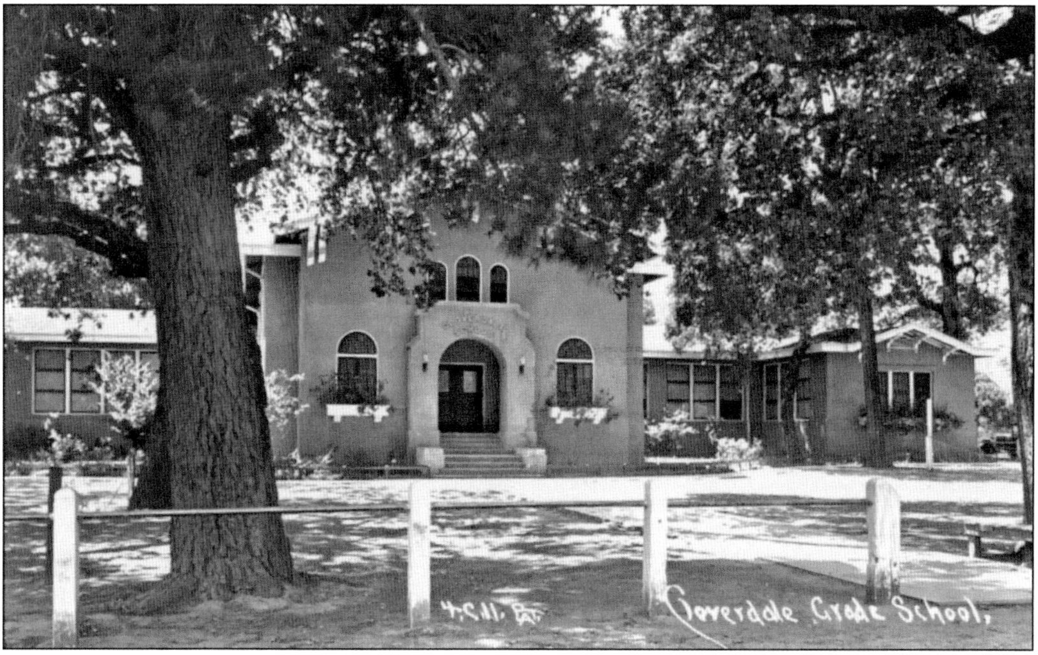

This school, located where Kleiser Park is today, was built in 1917 to replace the two-story wooden building erected in 1864. An imposing gray stucco, it was considered quite modern for its time. Until 1936, both the grammar school and the high school were housed here. In the center and separating the two schools was the gym. Showers and a music room were located across School Street in the "Cottage." Pictured below is the new high school, for grades 9 through 12, built in 1936 on School Street across from the old building. Students in seventh and eighth grades got to start using the coveted "high school" wing of the old school. The well-built stucco structure housing the grammar school was torn down in 1960 but was quite difficult to demolish.

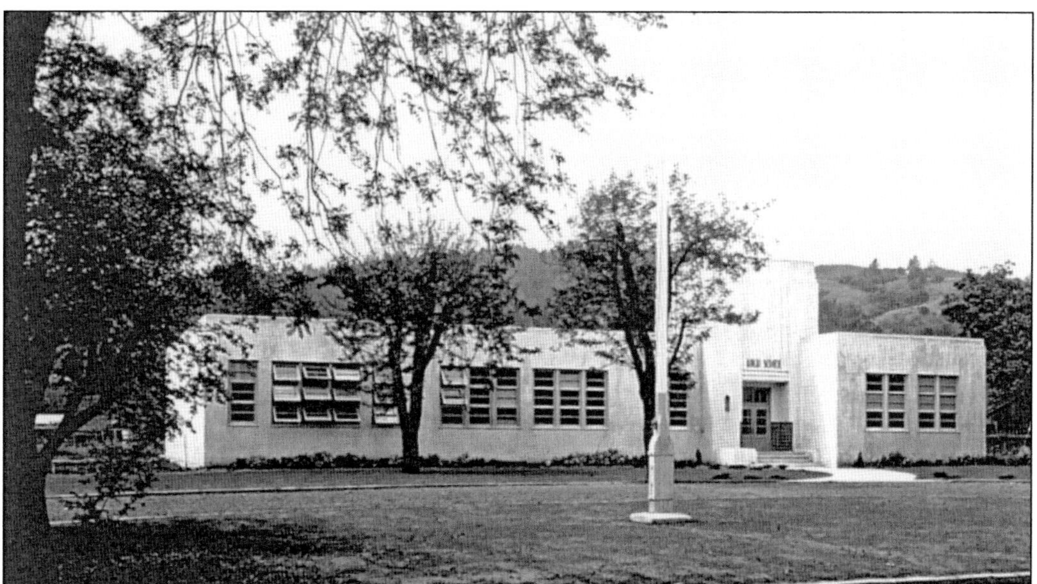

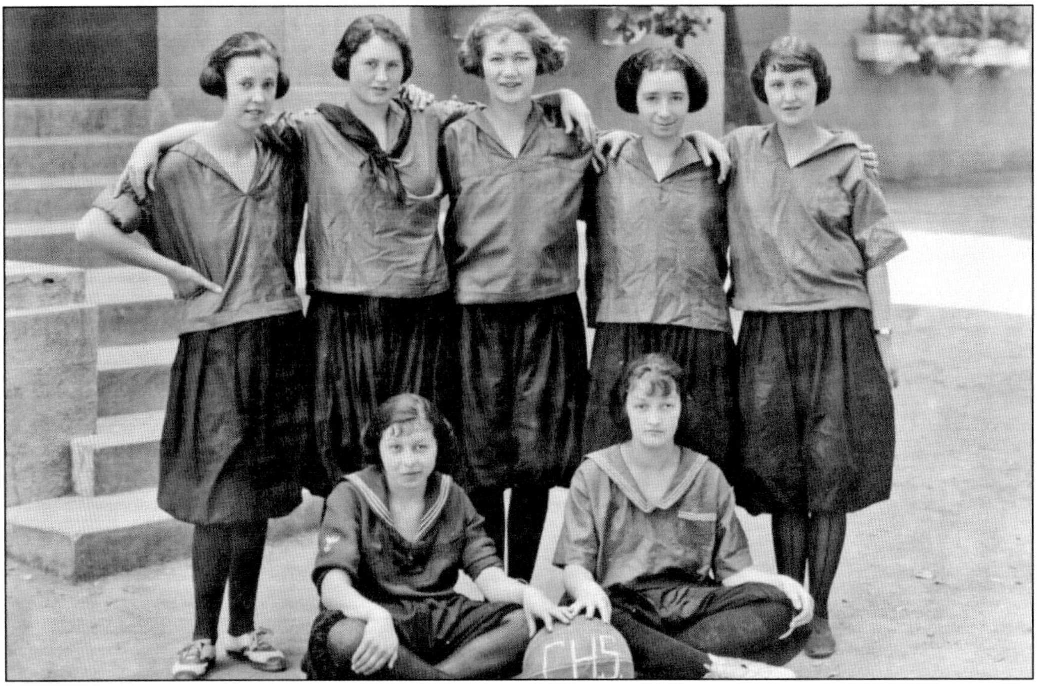

The Cloverdale High School girls' basketball team of 1923 is pictured here. They are identified from left to right as (seated) Anita Sanford and Evelyn Cook; (standing) Jane Leist (captain), Dicy Hurt, Esther Sink, Mary Bassetti, and Isabelle Murray. The girls beat Boonville but lost to both Geyserville and Ukiah that year.

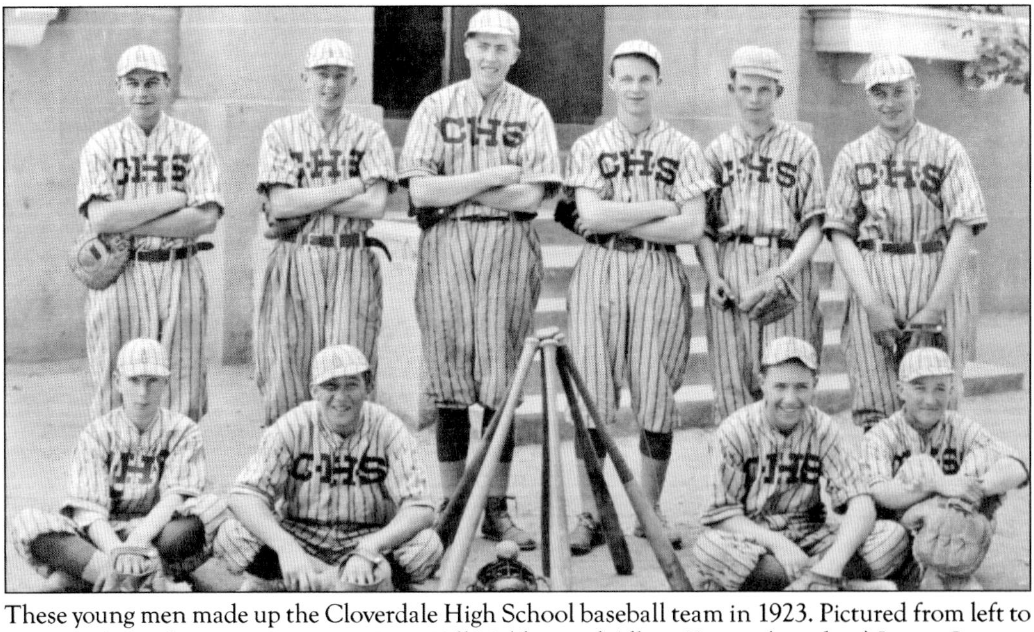

These young men made up the Cloverdale High School baseball team in 1923. Pictured from left to right are (seated) ? McCray, G. W. Hiatt, Yell Nobles, and Albert Foster; (standing) Lewis Osmon, Herbert Porterfield, ? Rutherfield, Warren McChesney, Wash Hiatt (captain), and Robert Mazinni. Although they did not enjoy a winning season, the men did manage to beat Hopland in 10 innings.

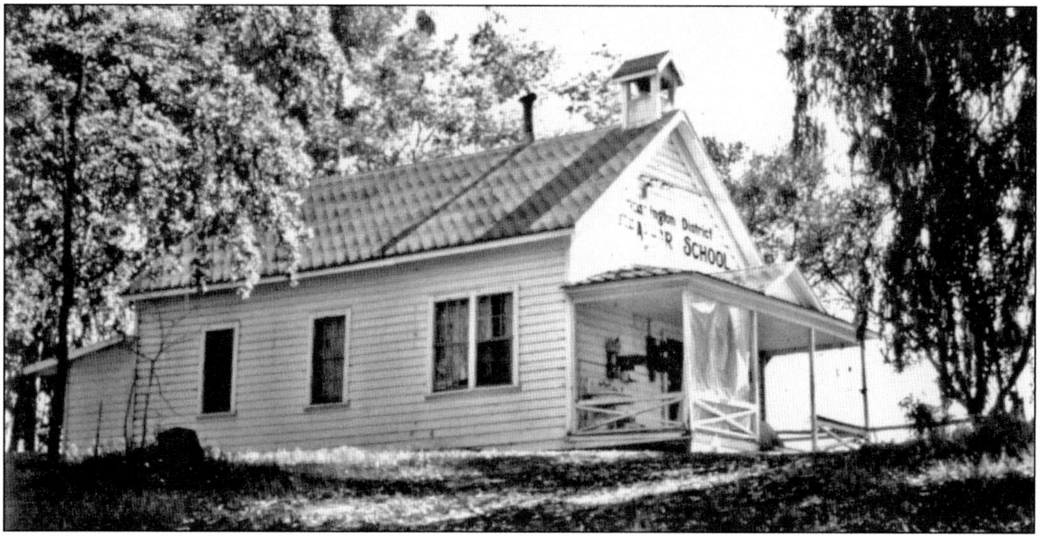

For many years, children residing outside of town received their education in one-room schoolhouses. The Washington District Grammar School on Asti Road (pictured above) was used by winery workers' families from 1872 to 1966. Other one-room schoolhouses included one at Alder Glen and the Icaria school, built in 1885 by French colonists. Others were located on Dutcher Creek Road, at the Mercury mine, on Pine Mountain, and at the junction of Hot Springs Road and Kelly Road.

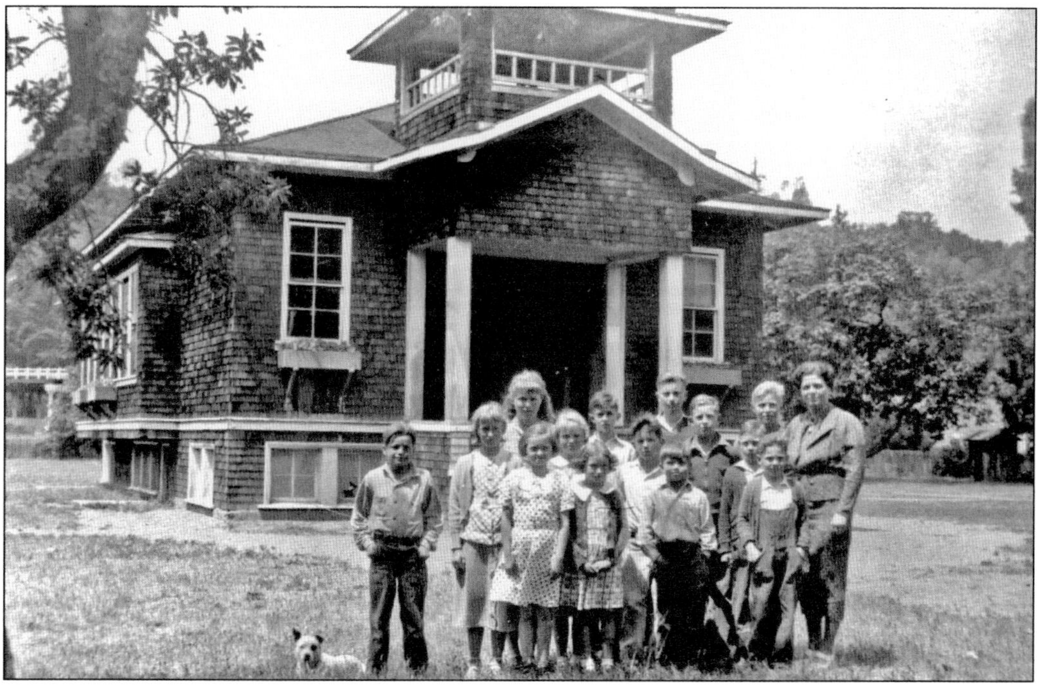

The Preston School, located on McCray Road, was for the children of Preston and those along Geysers Road. These pupils posed in 1937 with their teacher, Mary Imperiale. Among the children identified are Margaret Burgans, Eugene Sambucetti, and Walt Samanski in the first row and Katherine Burgans (Greppi) and Gladys Burgans (Burger) in the second row. The old school has been remodeled and is now a private residence.

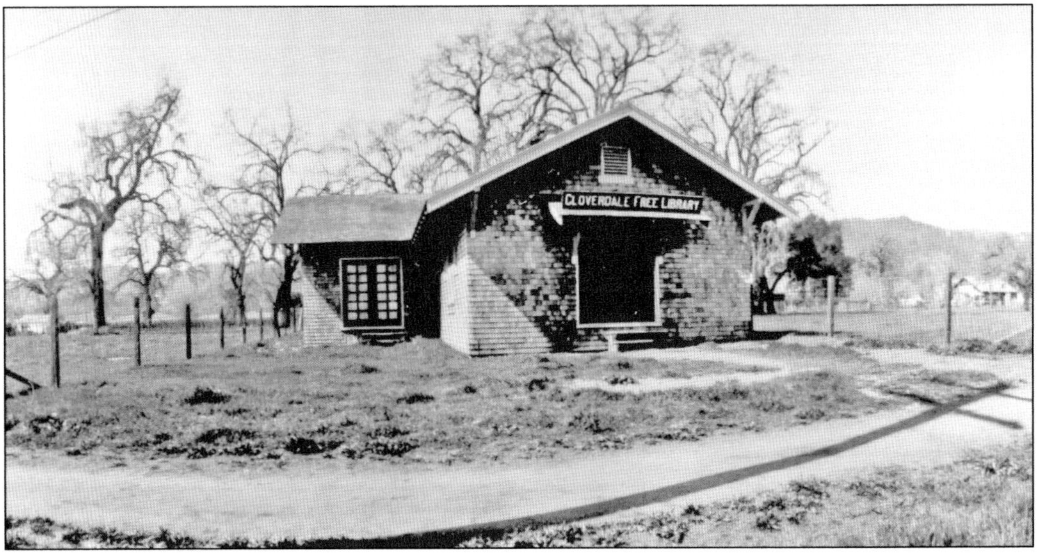

Cloverdale's first library was actually started in 1894 in Library Hall at 231 North West Street. The Cloverdale Free Library, seen here in the early 1920s, was built in 1921 by the Women's Improvement Club on land donated by Ida (Hoadley) Humbert. The building, still standing today to the south of Pick's Drive-In, became a wholesale lumber office in 1979 and currently houses two businesses. (Courtesy Sonoma County Library.)

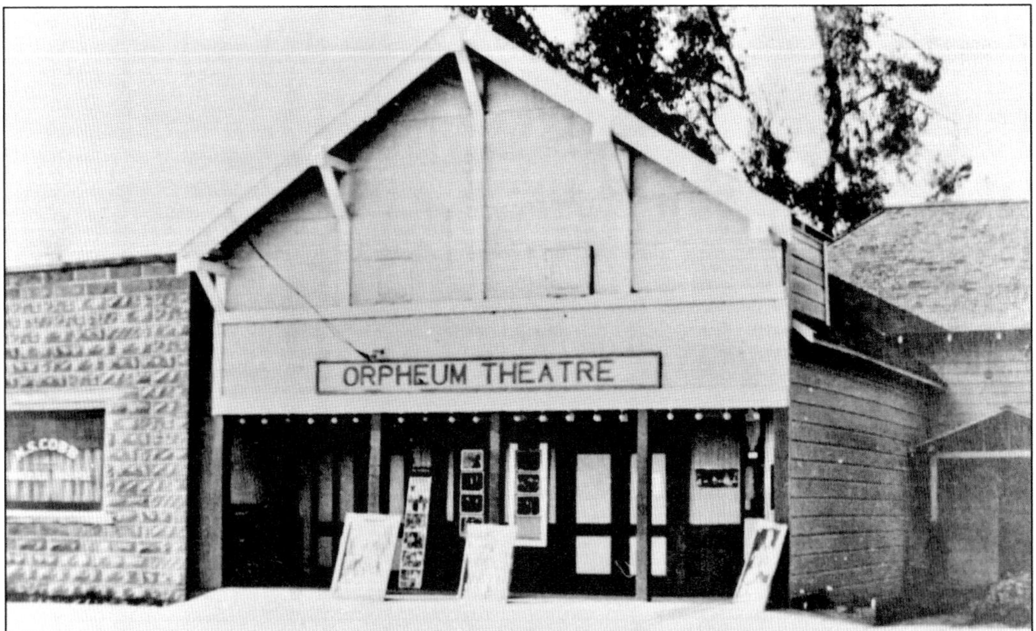

The Orpheum Theatre, located at 233 North West Street and seen here in the 1930s, was operated by a Mr. Perry. It featured stage plays as well as films. Next door was the furniture store and mortuary run by Edna Cobb Gorden. The building was home to the Dunk n Run donut shop in the 1960s and the Kalico Kitchen in the 1970s.

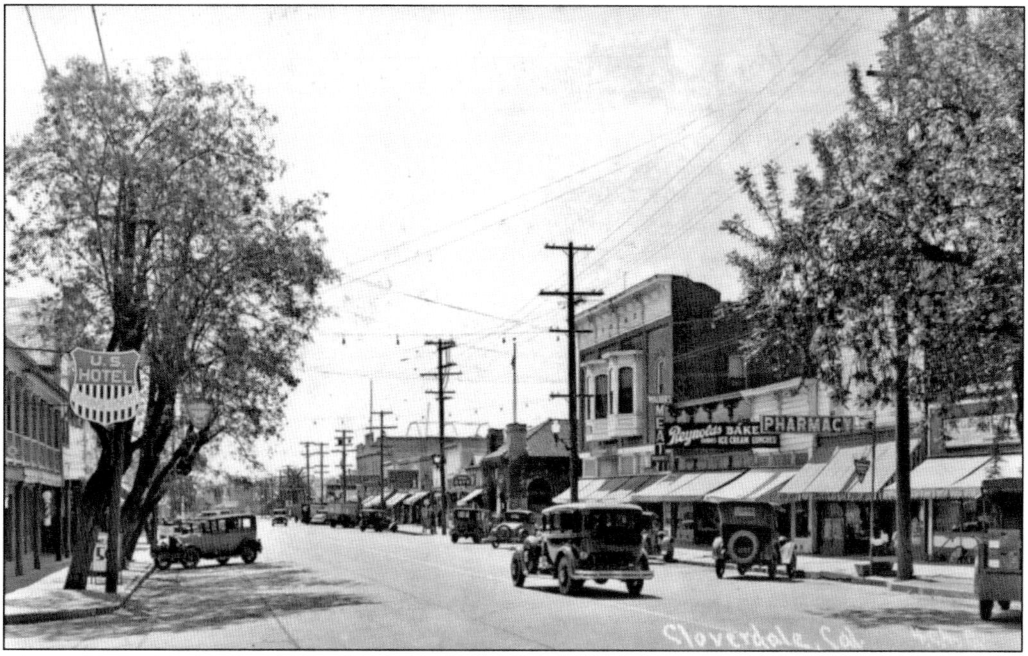

This is how Cloverdale appeared in the 1920s looking south from Second and West Streets. On the east side was the U.S. Hotel. On the west side were a pharmacy, Reynold's Bakery, Walker's Meat Market, the H. G. Grant department store, First National Bank of Cloverdale, the Cloverdale Café (featuring lunch for 35¢), Oldham Drugs, Mitchell's Sandwich Shop, and the Druids Building.

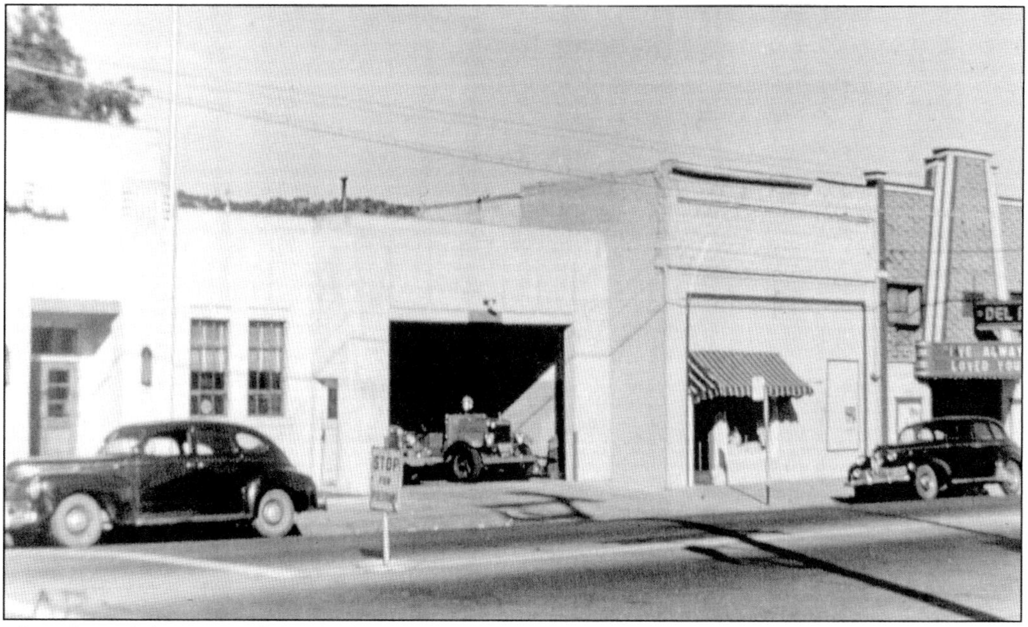

The Cloverdale City Hall (far left), built in the 1930s by New Deal workers as part of the federal government's Works Progress Administration program, is seen here in 1946. South of it, on the northeast corner of Broad Street and Cloverdale Boulevard, is the Del Rio Theater. This building, constructed in 1905 by Dr. M. O. Trask, over the years housed a hardware store, a Ford agency, a bar, and a video arcade before being torn down in 1985.

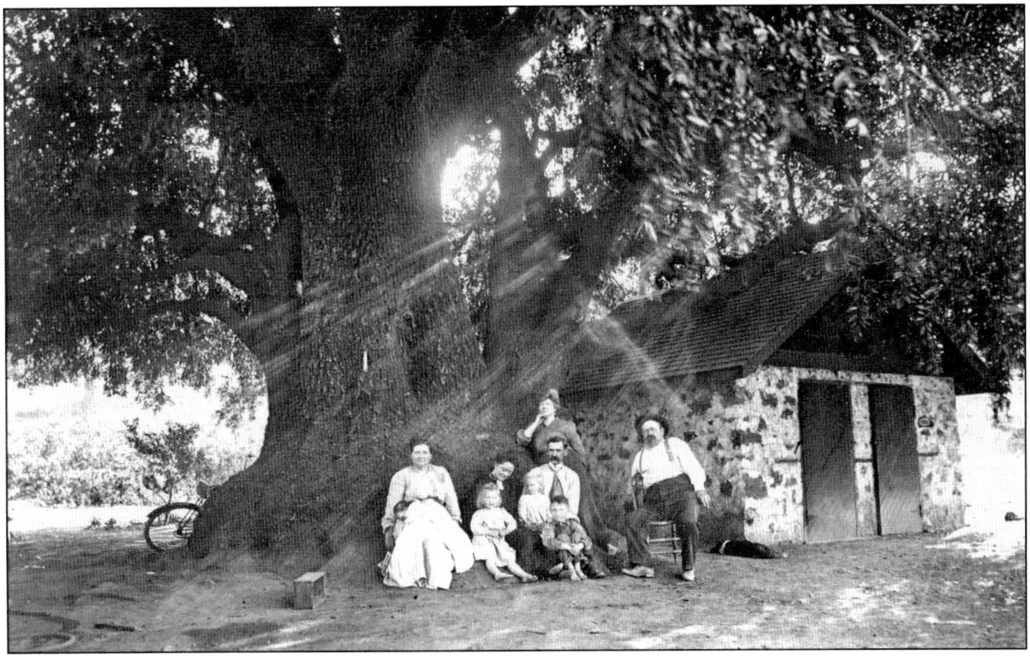

Daniel Sink founded the ranch and started the family with the longest continuous presence in Cloverdale. A forty-niner from New York, Sink arrived in Cloverdale in 1859, establishing his homestead in Oat Valley under the largest laurel tree in Sonoma County. Unidentified members of the Sink family are seen here in the early 1900s resting at its base. The Heritage Laurel—and Daniel Sink's descendants—still live on the ranch today. (Courtesy of Lucille Sink.)

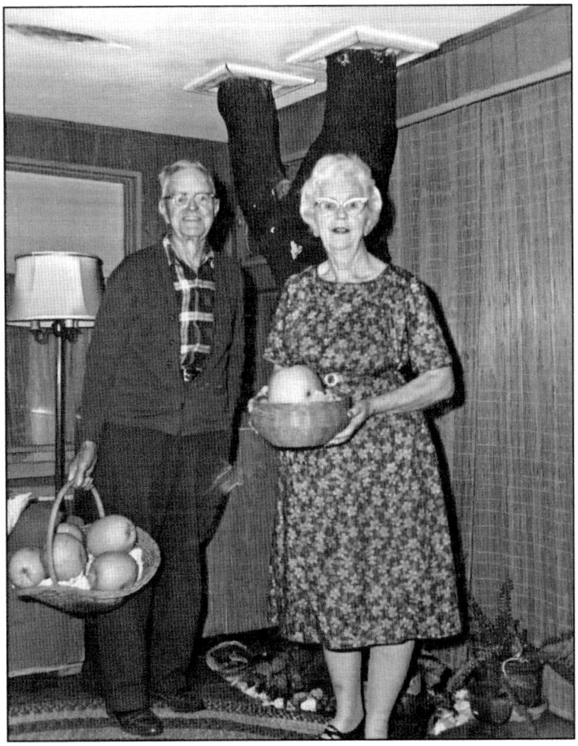

William Brush Wilson and his sister Louise (Wilson) Butler, descendants of pioneer David Brush, pose in the Simonson home at 112 University Street, where the trunk of a tree actually grows through the roof of the house. In 1944, Walter and Mildred Simonson built a residence around an orange tree that had been planted on the Brush property 73 years earlier. This 136-year-old tree is alive and still bears fruit.

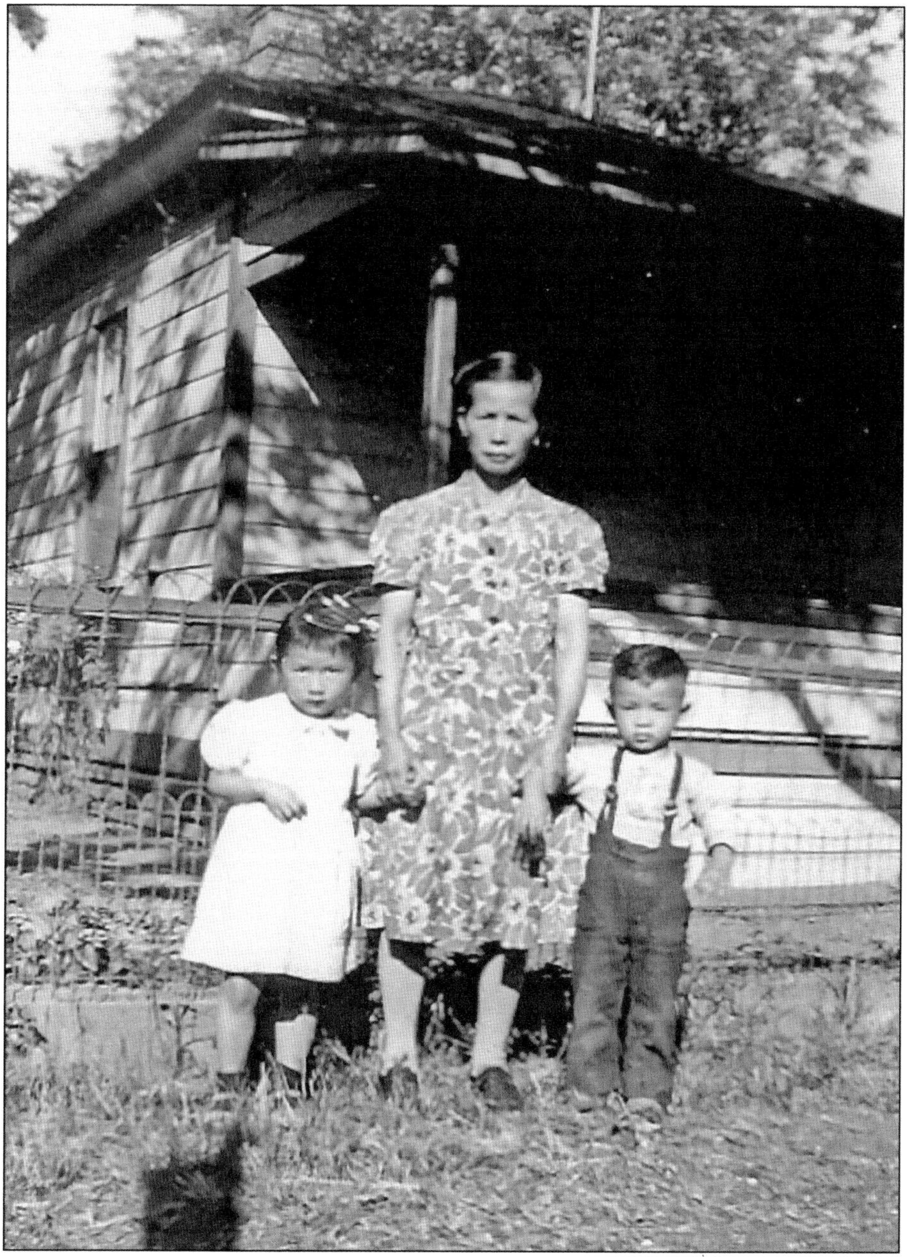

Pictured here are Amy Eng and her children Virginia and Lester. Amy was the wife of Lim Eng, who came to the United States from China as a young man in 1914. In the early years of World War II, when the Italian Swiss Colony was no longer able to import straw-wrapped bottles from Italy, Lim Eng, then working in San Francisco, was asked to create the distinctive bottles needed for ISC's Tipo Chianti. Eng and his son George redesigned the bottle and created the machinery to do so. In 1942, a plant site was located on Lake Street next to the rail line. At its peak, Cloverdale's Tipo bottle business employed 72 people. The Engs were the only Asian family living in Cloverdale at the time. Although they experienced prejudice in the beginning, the hardworking Engs were eventually accepted. In fact, George and his wife, Mildred, became highly respected leaders in Cloverdale. (Courtesy Sonoma County Library.)

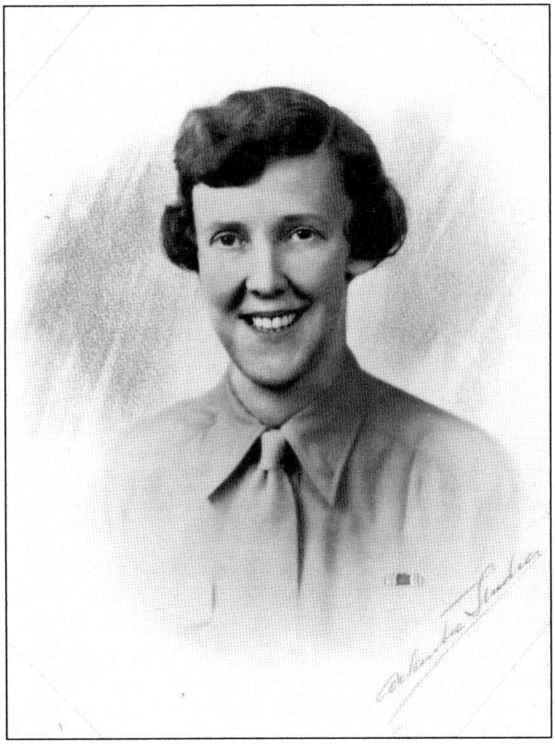

Jane Leist was born to William and Kate Porterfield Leist in 1906. A shy but excellent student, she went on to graduate from the College of the Pacific in Stockton. She returned to Cloverdale and began a teaching career that extended from 1931 until 1962, with a stint in the Women's Army Corps during the war years. Jane Leist was a beloved teacher and was regarded with great respect and affection.

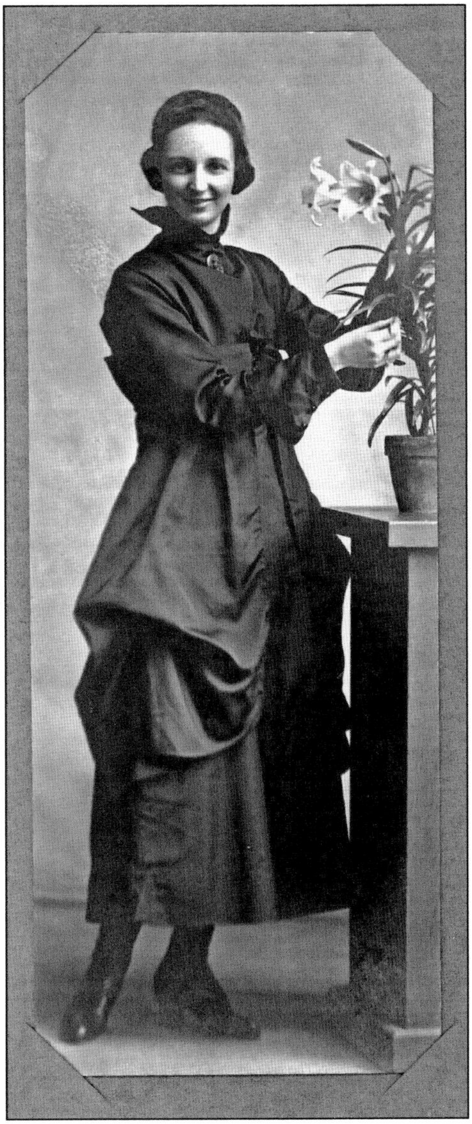

Edna Cobb Gorden, pictured here in 1918, was an accomplished musician and dance instructor. She was also the first woman mortician in California. In the 1940s and 1950s, a building located at 229 North West Street housed her businesses—a furniture store offering bedroom sets, flooring, and other items in the front, and an undertaker's parlor, where she conducted funeral services and performed her duties as a mortician in the back.

The building housing the Clover Cinema, opened in the 1950s as the Blair Theater, was built by Cloverdale contractor David Davini, a key player in Cloverdale's postwar development. Davini built much of the East First Street commercial area, developed the town's first subdivision on the old Haehl property, and built the new pavilion for the 1951 Citrus Fair. (Courtesy Cloverdale Chamber of Commerce.)

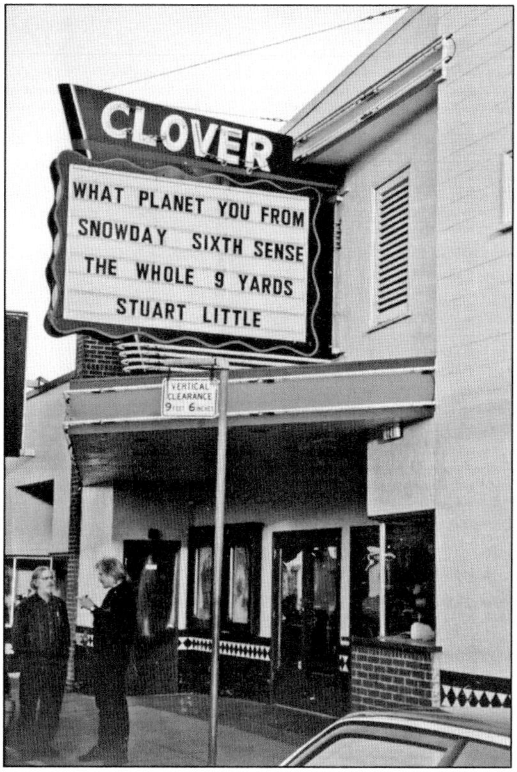

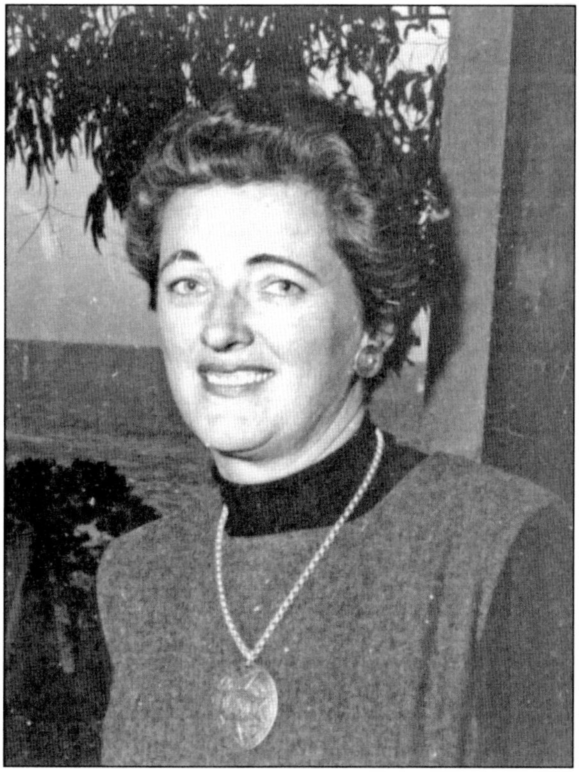

Marie Vadon Hill, seen here in 1966, is a lifelong resident of Cloverdale, a community leader, and author of the history book *Cloverdale Memories*. Her father, Fred Vadon, was the son of pioneers who came from France in 1892 and settled on a ranch south of Cloverdale, where they grew prunes and grapes, and had a winery. Marie's Anderson Valley roots date to 1859, when her mother's grandfather Cass Ingram arrived in California by wagon train. (Courtesy Marie Hill.)

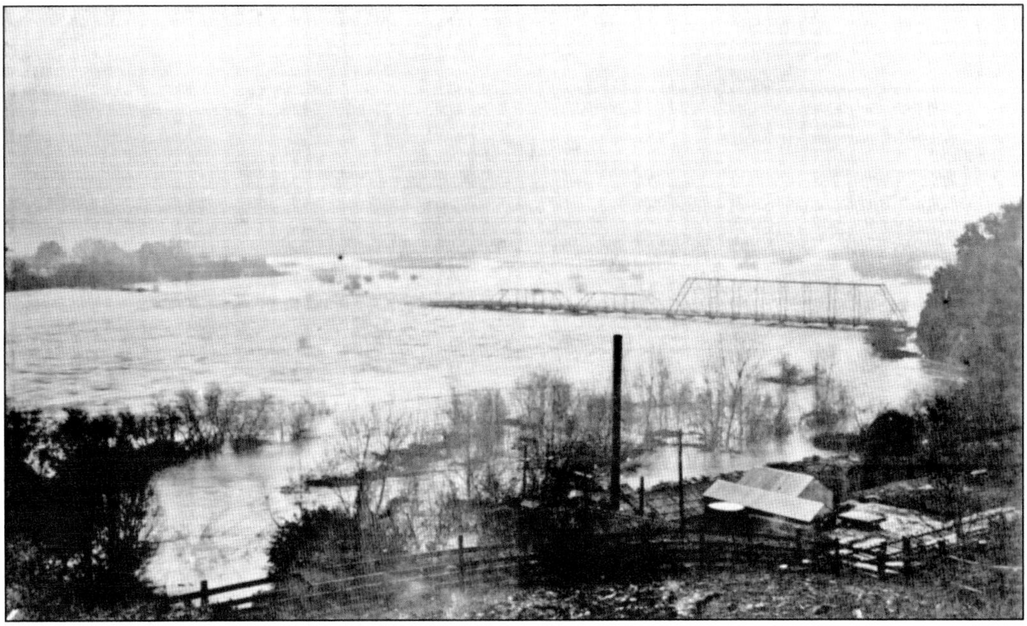

This photograph of the Russian River at flood stage during the winter of 1937–1938 shows the old First Street Bridge partially submerged. This bridge was replaced with a new one 300 feet to the south in 1939, and a levee was built as part of a flood control project in 1940, when Fred Vadon was the director for the district.

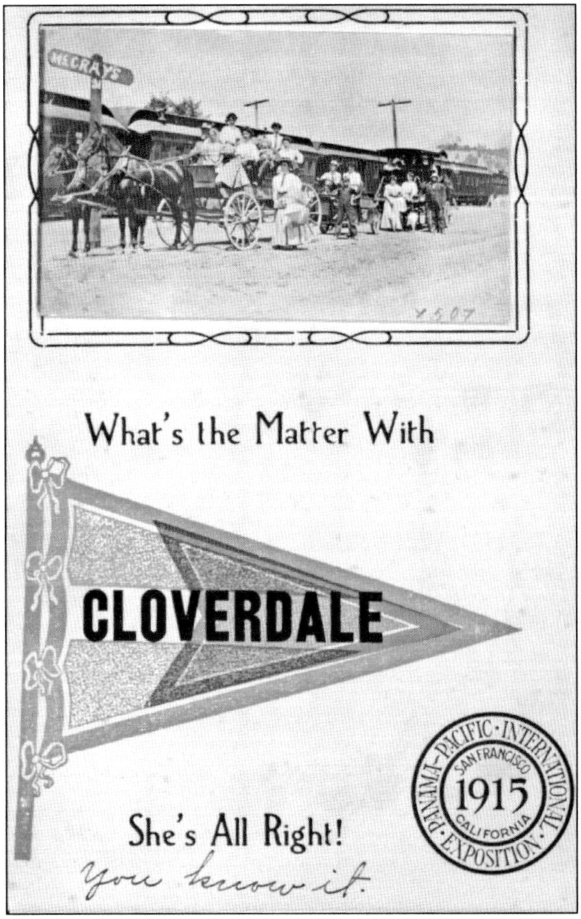

In the early 1900s, many photographers made postcards of their images available to the public. This postcard from 1915 is one example of this popular hobby. It not only pictures a group of vacationers waiting to embark for McCray's resort; it also captures a little of Cloverdale's civic pride. The writer apparently agrees that the town is "All Right!"

Eight

The Changing Face of Cloverdale

In recent years, Cloverdale has had to confront a number of economic, logistical, and social challenges. In the 1980s, the city was dealing with the loss of several major employers. The Italian Swiss Colony winery had closed, and lumber and logging were in decline. Highway 101 still ran through the center of town, where the infamous First Street intersection imposed on travelers what was then the only stoplight between San Francisco and Willits. Completion of the 101 bypass in the mid-1990s successfully eliminated the traffic congestion that had plagued downtown Cloverdale, but it also dealt another blow to the economy. Demographically, Cloverdale was changing as well. Its schools had to address the needs of the growing number of students with limited English proficiency, primarily a result of the growth in the Hispanic population, which increased almost 700 percent between 1980 and 2000.

During this same period, the population, which stood at just under 5,000 in 1990, surged 67 percent to 8,400 by 2007, making Cloverdale Sonoma County's fastest growing community. This growth spurt was fueled partially by the development of the Del Webb Clover Springs retirement community and partially by the growing recognition that the town was an attractive and affordable place to live. In other words, Cloverdale had been "discovered." Undeveloped land and vineyards were transformed into new residential neighborhoods, stretching the city limits more than two miles to the south.

Meanwhile, city fathers were coping with the realities presented by the completion of the freeway bypass—the loss of non-local traffic and the need to revitalize the economy of the downtown core. After more than a year of effort involving citizens and other stakeholders, a "Downtown Specific Plan" was adopted by the city in November 1990. Eighteen years later, the City of Cloverdale is continuing to implement its grand design to refashion itself into a distinctive destination for visitors without losing its original identity as an attractive and friendly hometown for all its residents.

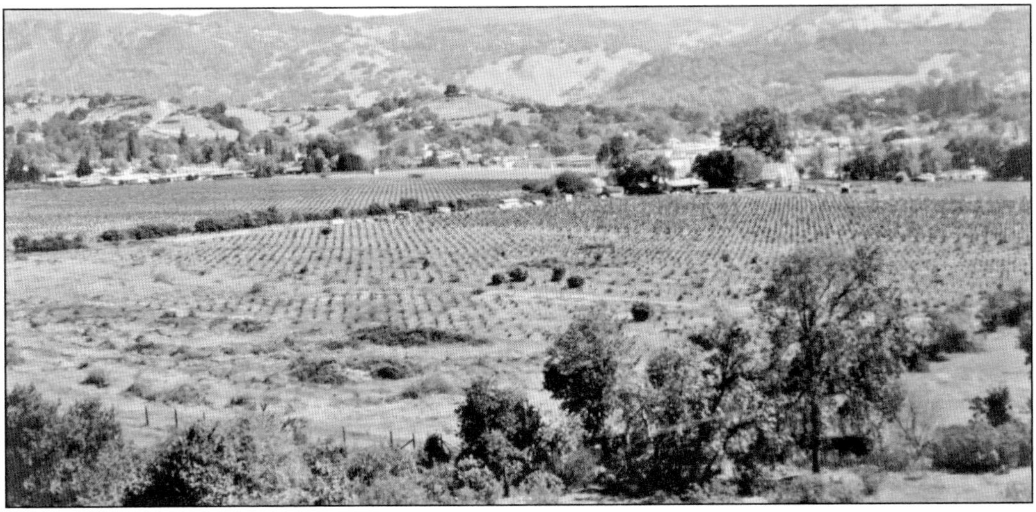

When the above picture was taken in 1980 from a viewpoint off Cherry Creek Road, the site was filled with rows of grapevines growing on Arthur "Buck" Boehm's ranch. A viewer standing at the same spot today would be struck by the change in the landscape, now dominated by the 172 homes of the Cherry Creek Meadows and Vintage Meadows subdivisions. These developments, built between 1990 and 2000, are visible evidence of Cloverdale's growth spurt and of the increasing number of people who were attracted by the city's livable features and hometown atmosphere.

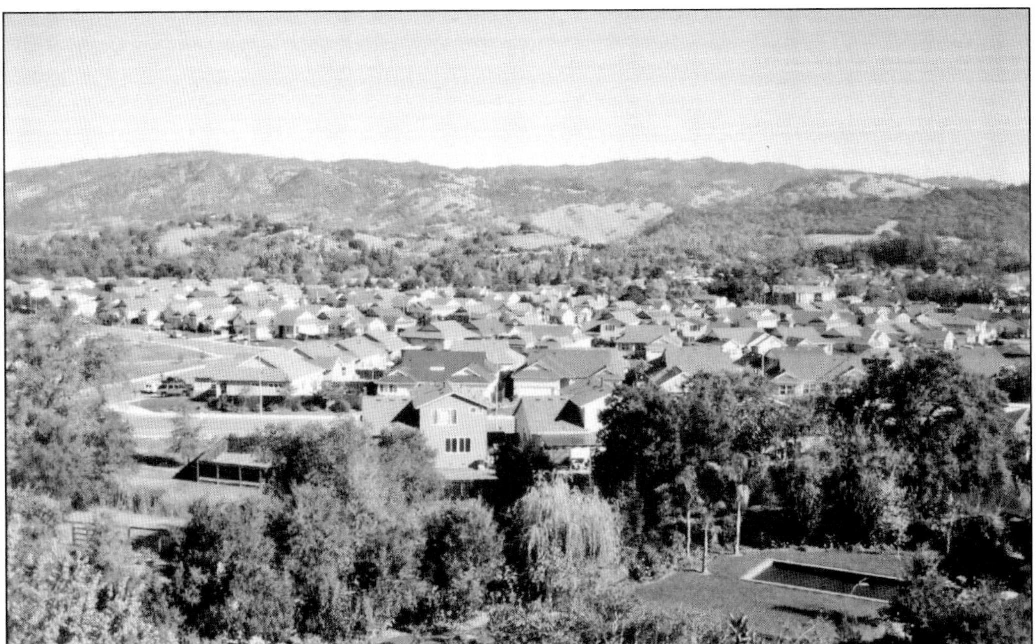

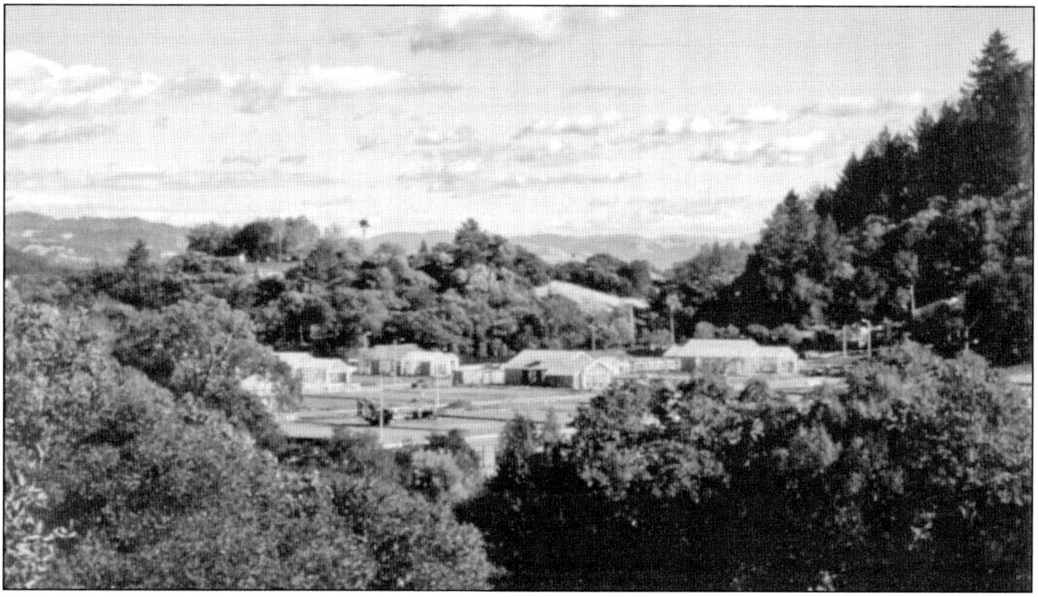

The Del Webb Corporation purchased 175 acres of the former Albertz ranch in south Cloverdale in 1988 to develop Clover Springs, an age-restricted community of 363 homes. Phase I was completed in May 1998 and Phase II in 2002. Phase III was never built. That land was purchased by the City of Cloverdale and the Sonoma County Open Space District, and was declared an open space in 2007. (Courtesy Clover Springs.)

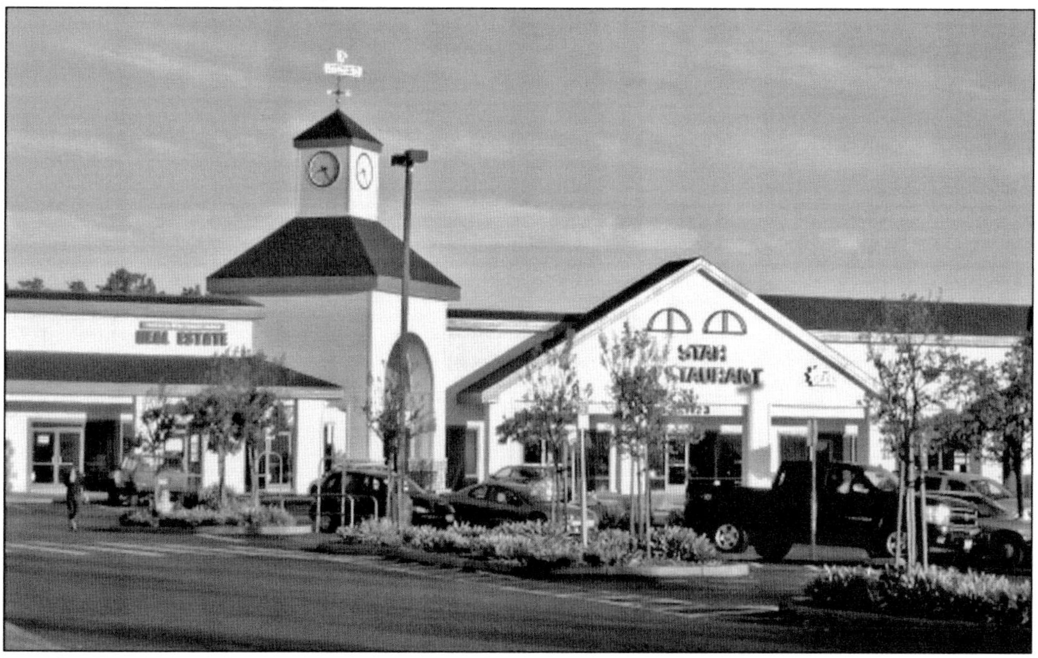

Development of Furber Ranch, the property immediately to the south of Clover Springs, was initiated by Al Furber and sons in the late 1970s. Their first house was completed in 1987 as part of the Rancho de Amigos subdivision, where all the streets bear Furber family names. In 1997, Furber Ranch Plaza was developed. This was followed by the Christopherson's Cottages subdivision on land that once grew zinfandel and petite syrah grapes.

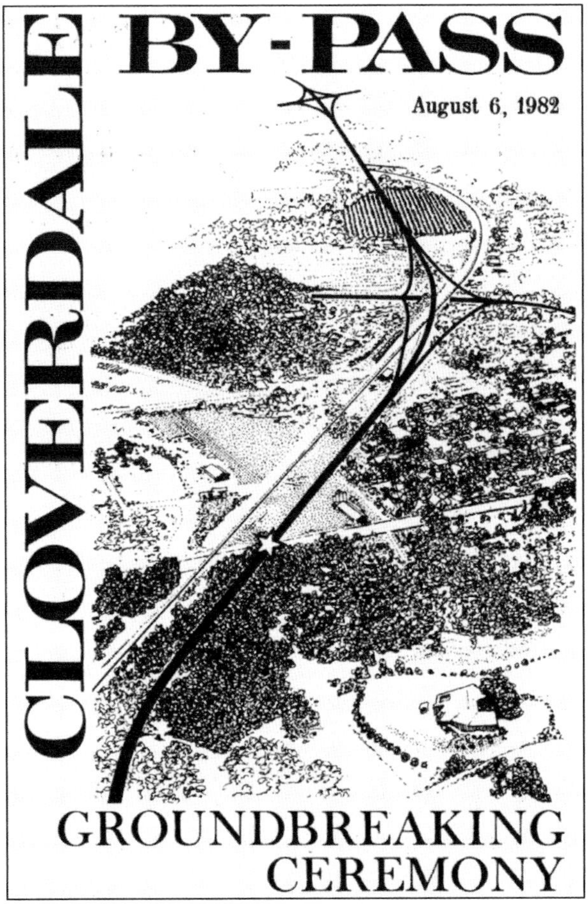

The ground-breaking ceremony held on August 6, 1982, marked the beginning of the long-awaited staged construction of the 4.4-mile highway bypass around Cloverdale. Highway 101 virtually bisected the town, disrupting the community and creating serious safety concerns. In 1989, two separate accidents north of town resulted in the deaths of eight people, spurring a community campaign to keep the long-delayed project on schedule.

Another ground-breaking ceremony was held on October 29, 1992, at the First Street overpass to mark the commencement of the final phase of construction of the bypass. Seen digging the earth beneath the overpass are, from left to right, Dan Hauser, Bev Hansen, Carol Chase, Mayor Tom Sink, general contractor Dean Rasmussen, Jim Teague, and Caltrans representatives Preston Kelly and Burch Bachtold. (Courtesy R. C. Hall Photography.)

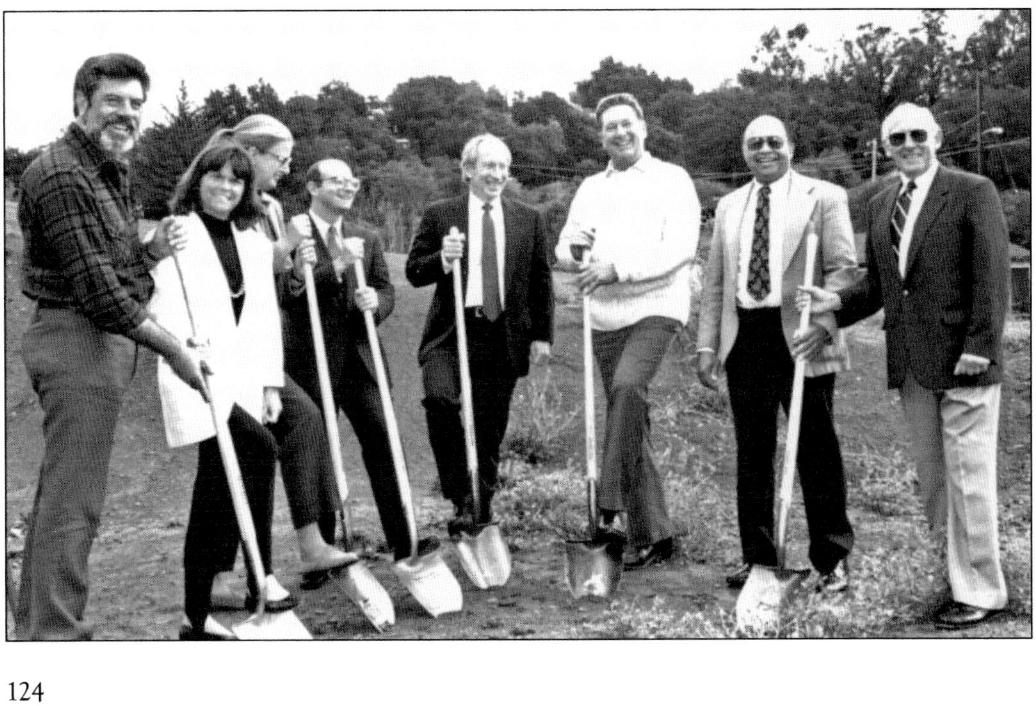

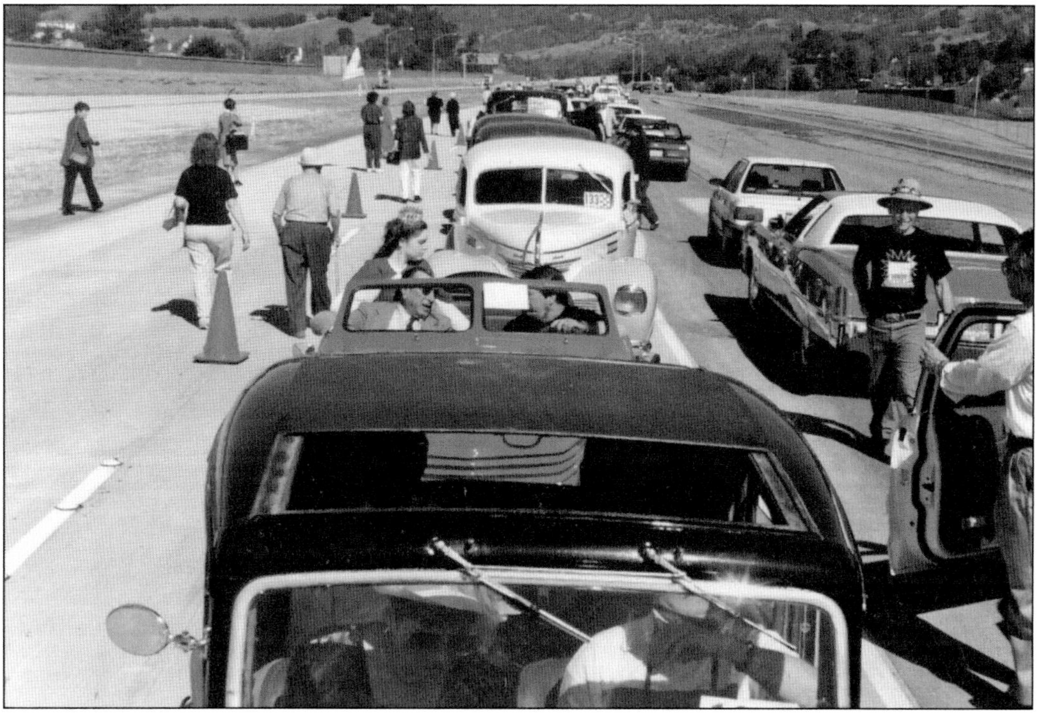

The northbound lanes of the new freeway bypass were finally opened on March 3, 1994, one day after the grand opening ceremony to mark the conclusion of the 45-year project, which had been plagued by a history of starts and stalls. Pedestrians were permitted to walk down the highway as part of the celebration. (Courtesy City of Cloverdale.)

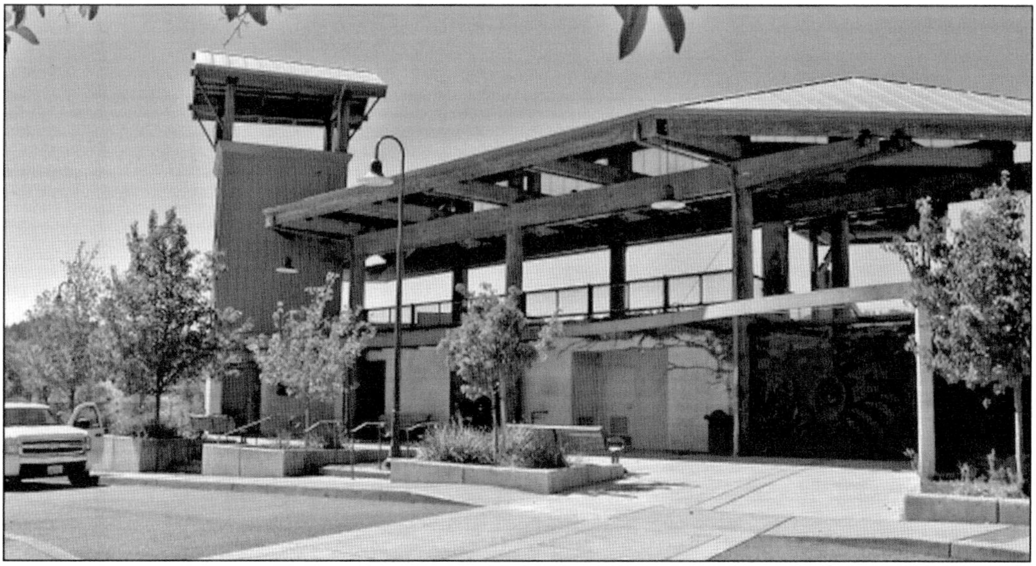

When the new Cloverdale Depot, at the corner of Asti Road and Citrus Fair Drive, was completed in May 1999, the public was invited to attend the dedication ceremony to "show support for the rebirth of the Northwestern Pacific Railway." The transportation center, funded with federal, state, and county money, eventually included a park-and-ride lot, bus loading bays, and office space. To date, folks are still waiting for the trains to arrive.

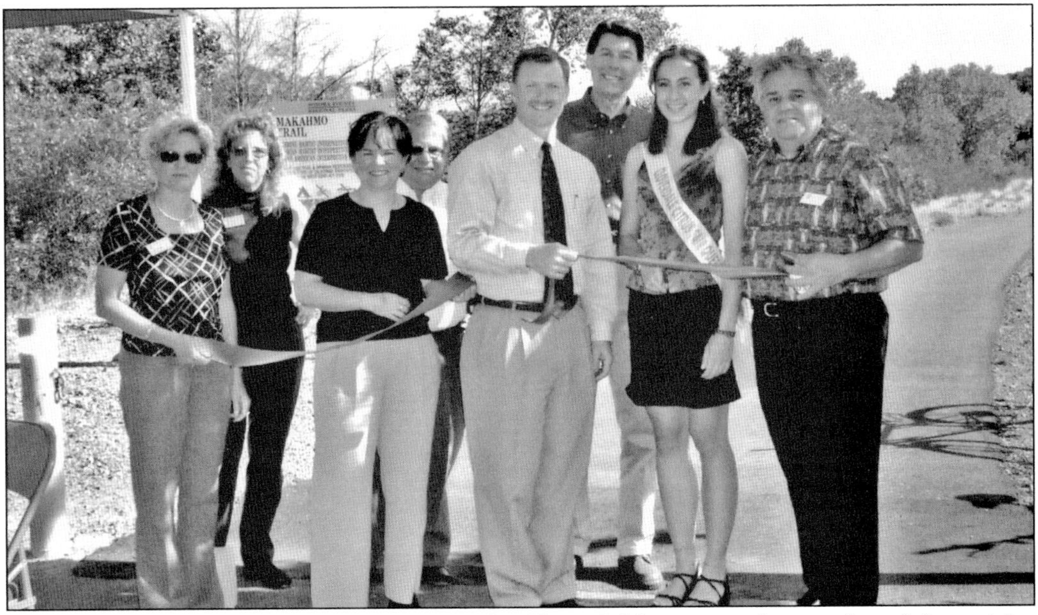

At the June 2004 ribbon-cutting ceremony for Cloverdale's river trail were, from left to right, dignitaries Lorena Fisher, Maddy Hershfeld, and Andrea Mackenzie, along with Doug Laurice from the chamber of commerce, supervisor Paul Kelley, council member Bob Jehn, Citrus Fair Queen Madison Holsinger, and Mayor Gus Wolter. The 1.1-mile River Walk Park was a joint effort of the City of Cloverdale and county agencies. (Courtesy *Cloverdale Reveille*.)

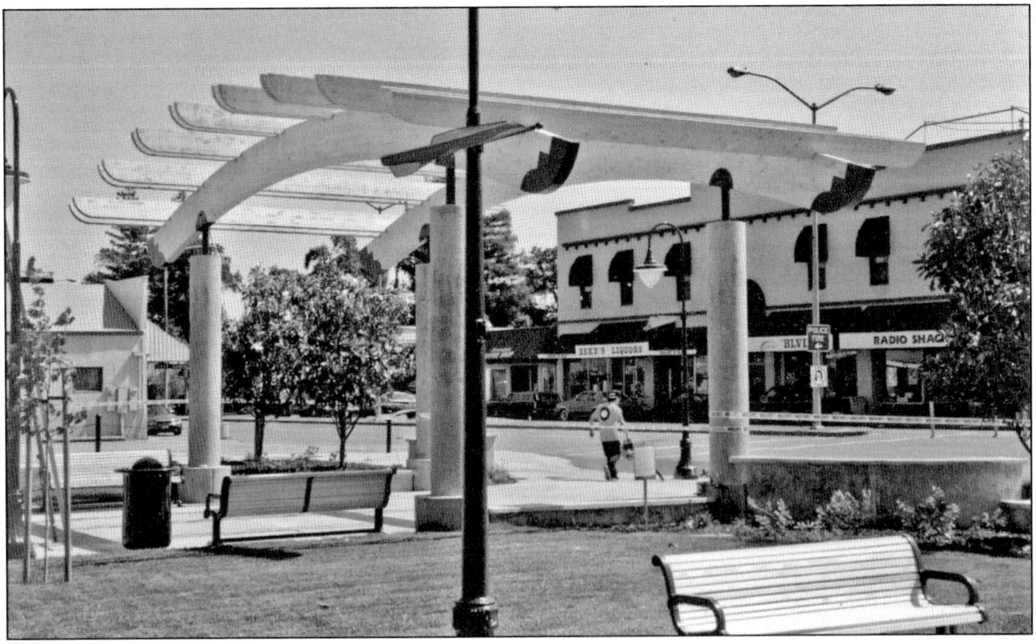

On May 31, 1996, when the newly completed Cloverdale Plaza was dedicated to the community, a plaque was displayed declaring the plaza "the center of the rebirth of our downtown." Its design provided for landscaping, a stage, shade trellises, and historic lighting. The plaza was part of the first phase of Cloverdale's Downtown Improvement Program, most of which was funded with redevelopment agency funds. (Courtesy City of Cloverdale.)

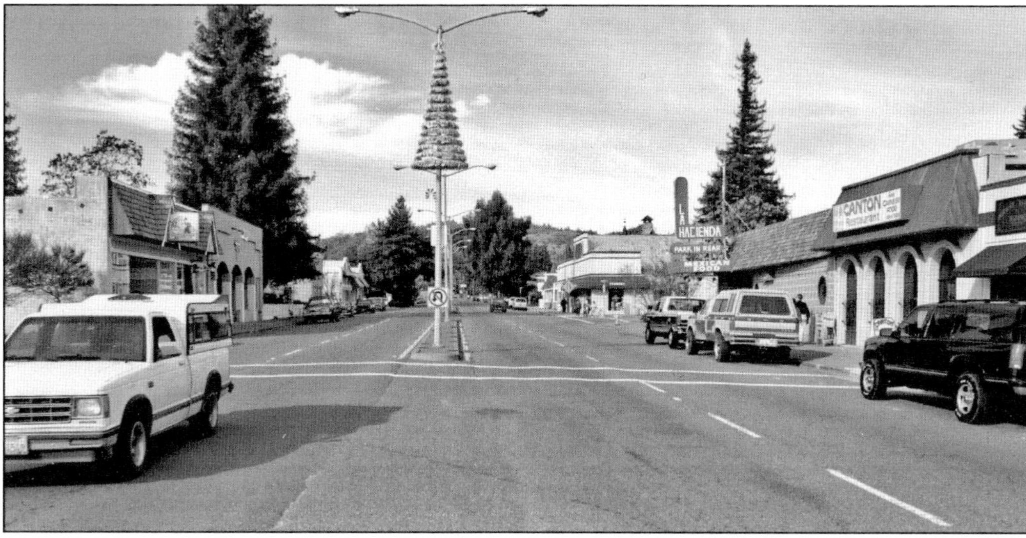

After the completion of the freeway bypass, Cloverdale set about reclaiming the former stretch of Highway 101, seen above before the redesign. What once had been four lanes famous for noisy trucks and snarled traffic was refashioned into a two-lane boulevard with landscaped sidewalks, vintage light posts, welcoming benches, and attractive trellises. Funding for the $4-million project came from redevelopment funds, the Bay Area Transportation for Livable Communities program, a low-interest loan from the State Infrastructure Bank, and other federal and state grants. The reconfiguration of Cloverdale Boulevard to accommodate a pedestrian-friendly environment was one of the most crucial components of the Downtown Specific Plan to revitalize the economy of the downtown business district.

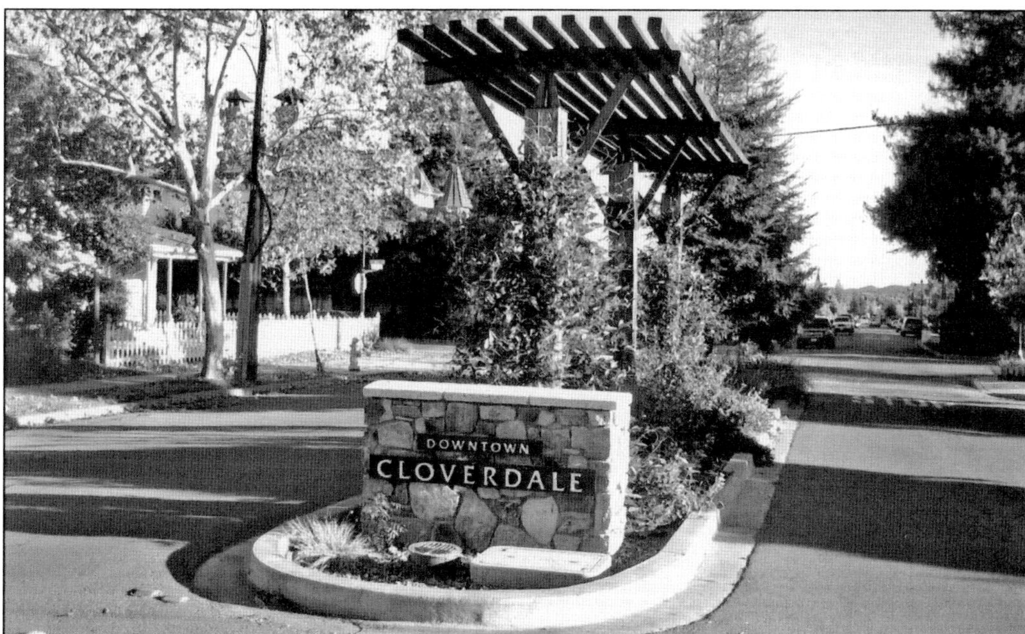